PRAISE FOR
WORKING TO RESTORE

"This book is rooted in optimism. The concrete examples of success stories like the ones found throughout this book show us that it's possible to reverse the course."

—JAY COEN GILBERT, cofounder of B Lab

"As an entrepreneur focused on building a sustainable business model that is achievable and also scalable, I have often turned to Esha Chhabra for her advice and mentorship. She has spent over a decade documenting innovative solutions that inspire and actually create some excitement for the future. She demonstrates how companies can help heal the planet while still prioritizing economic success. With *Working to Restore*, there is finally a place to see examples of how a company's success and their environmental responsibility are not mutually exclusive. *Working to Restore* provides insight into many models on how various companies operate without compromising."

—SHILPA SHAH, cofounder of Cuyana

"As the market paradigm shifts, slowly then suddenly, regenerative businesses—and regenerative mindsets—illuminate pathways to future success. Esha Chhabra's *Working to Restore* introduces next-gen leaders working to reinvent, restore, and regenerate."

—JOHN ELKINGTON, founder and chief pollinator,
Volans, and author of *Green Swans: The Coming
Boom in Regenerative Capitalism*

"In an age of fast-paced, mass consumption and consumer waste, Chhabra's wonderful and diverse stories of human-centered business models and the people who are engaging them around the globe remind us that we don't need to sacrifice our quality of life or feel bad about not having more. We just need to value what we've got and ensure enough for all."

—MELISSA HO, vice president, World Wildlife Fund

"As usual, entrepreneurs are leading the way to transformative approaches to what ails the world. Now, global leaders and corporate executives need to get on board—and they can start by reading *Working to Restore*."

—TOM POST, former managing editor, Forbes Media

"The idea that we can do things differently and enrich each other rather than only ourselves is powerfully animating and the examples in the book genuinely surprising.'

—STEPHAN CHAMBERS, director, Marshall Institute, LSE

"In a world so focused on short-term profit that our very survival often gets short shrift, it's easy to despair: *what choice do we have?* My advice: choose to read this book, to start. Esha Chhabra has traveled the world to share the stories of businesspeople with heart and vision, and after reading *Working to Restore*, it's clear that a regenerative, healing approach to business can preserve jobs, economies, *and* the world. Be excited about the future for once! Covering novel business solutions in health, energy, finance, the environment, and more—from brilliant, creative people, rich and poor, on six continents—Chhabra offers the one solution we need most and can apply anywhere: a better way of thinking. This book offers practical hope, backed by effective actions. Make reading Chhabra's work one of yours."

—BOB HARRIS, author of *The International Bank of Bob: Connecting Our Worlds One $25 Kiva Loan at a Time*

"For years, Patagonia has appreciated Esha Chhabra's excellent reporting on purpose-minded business. Focusing on this sector long before it was a trend or a movement, she is by far most qualified to present this overview of not only how but why entrepreneurs choose to use business to empower humans and heal the earth."

—RYAN GELLERT, CEO, Patagonia

"If capitalism is to be transformed into the engine of inclusive, just, and sustainable prosperity we need, a new generation of purpose-driven companies must lead the way. Chhabra's compelling book tells the stories of some of the best of these game-changing businesses and is guaranteed to inspire."

—MATTHEW BISHOP, author and former business editor of *The Economist*

"We will need new laws, and we will need creative entrepreneurs ready to step up to today's challenges. Esha Chhabra leads the way, highlighting the companies and the people creating a new path and a future we can actually be excited about."

—MAXINE BEDAT, author of *Unraveled: The Life and Death of a Garment*

"Esha Chhabra's work overlaps with an area foundational for Dr. Bronner's practices, i.e., a true shift in business practices to 'constructive capitalism,' now often referred to as a 'regenerative economy' beyond the green- and fair washing in abundance today. *Working to Restore* presents a range of credible companies, older and younger, that dared to challenge the primacy of the financial bottom line and made social and ecological goals part of their DNA, with the aim of helping regenerate natural and societal resources degraded by business as usual."

—GERO LESON, vice president of special operations at Dr. Bronner's and author of *Honor Thy Label*

"Saving our planet always comes down to the same thing: talk less, do more. Business leaders have a responsibility to regenerate Earth and her communities by revolutionizing our economy—and *Working to Restore* tells the stories of exactly that. Thoughtful, probing, solution-oriented, and hopeful, this beautiful book portrays everything we need in this time of planetary crisis to reverse our current downward spiral back up into a more virtuous circle."

—ELIZABETH WHITLOW, executive director, Regenerative Organic Alliance

"We are entering the Regenerative Era. Chhabra provides portraits of innovation, resilience, and commitment to the planet and humankind that can help lead business into this new era."

—DR. ROBERT STRAND, executive director, Center for Responsible Business, University of California–Berkeley

WORKING
TO
RESTORE

Harnessing the Power
of Regenerative Business
to Heal the World

ESHA CHHABRA

BEACON PRESS
BOSTON

BEACON PRESS
Boston, Massachusetts
www.beacon.org

Beacon Press books
are published under the auspices of
the Unitarian Universalist Association of Congregations.

26 25 24 23   8 7 6 5 4 3 2 1

This book is printed on acid-free paper that meets the uncoated paper
ANSI/NISO specifications for permanence as revised in 1992.

Text design and composition by Kim Arney

Library of Congress Cataloguing-in-Publication Data is available for this title.
Hardcover ISBN: 978-08070-0851-5
E-book ISBN: 978-08070-0852-2; audiobook: 978-08070-0834-8

This book is dedicated to those seeking solutions and honest conversations. I'm grateful to those who shared their visions, passions, and know-how of building more equitable businesses. And thankful to those near and dear who remind me each day that betterment is a process, an intentional act, and that no one solution will be perfect for the challenges we face.

In an age of acceleration, nothing can be more exhilarating than going slow. And in an age of distraction, nothing is so luxurious as paying attention. And in an age of constant movement, nothing is so urgent as sitting still.

—PICO IYER, *The Art of Stillness:*
Adventures in Going Nowhere

CONTENTS

THE REGENERATIVE ERA

This is a book about business—how to do business more thoughtfully, consciously, and equitably. In an increasingly divisive political and economic landscape, it's become easy to point out what's wrong in the world. These pages, however, focus on solutions: here's the problem, but here's a potential solution. This book is an exploration of what's possible, a selection of stories from around the world that are held together by a common thread: a regenerative and restorative approach to business, which isn't limited to the environment. These two words, "regenerative" and "restorative," suggest rejuvenation, a reconnection with one's well-being—that pertains to a business's attitude towards people as well. It's an exploration of how business could work if it truly took into account its two major stakeholders—the earth and the people that it draws energy from.

It's not a new idea; rather, it's one that's evolved. When I began my career over a decade ago, I wrote about social enterprise, the concept that business can have a social (or environmental) bottom line. The term "social enterprise" was coming into the everyday lexicon of the business world. People were asking, "Is the sole purpose of business to make money for a select few at the top?" Although there had been talk about the shortcomings of our global capitalist system, these social entrepreneurs were operating rogue—building nimble enterprises and often not well known to the public.

That changed in 2006 when Muhammad Yunus, of Bangladesh, was awarded the Nobel Peace Prize for founding Grameen Bank, a microfinance institution that gave loans to individuals and small businesses that traditional finance deemed unreliable. He then went on to argue for "social business," a term that challenged the mandate for profit maximization. Instead, he argued that business should have earnings and profits, but these needed to be funneled back into the business itself and serve a greater purpose. All of a sudden, media started covering this convergence of philanthropy, business, and finance more closely. Yunus joked that he had been talking about these concepts for decades while building Grameen in the 1970s. But his ideas had been ignored until he won the Nobel Peace Prize.

We humans sometimes need a wake-up call. So many of the injustices and the damage we see in the world today are not recent developments. Remember the Disney movie WALL-E, which came out in 2008 and was some years in the making, about a lonely robot cleaning up mounds of junk, courtesy of our obsessive consumption as a species. That was well over a decade ago. The alarm bells were ringing then; they're still ringing.

As I started writing this book, the subject couldn't have been more relevant: the temperature in Los Angeles was hitting 110°F (43°C). Some areas were surpassing that, hitting 115°F (46°C) in urban spaces, not the desert. The hum of air-conditioning units had become a daily backdrop. Every day it seemed we were breaking records; news articles kept using the term "apocalyptic" to describe the changes around us.

Unfortunately, it was not just happening in my corner of the world. England had seen a heat wave that turned idyllic green pastures into dry, brown rolling hills similar to those here in Southern California. Norwegians were being advised not to barbecue in the 90°F (32°C) weather in their forests, out of fear that some "inexperienced" folks may cause fires. In North Africa, a region familiar with heat, temperatures were surpassing 120°F (49°C)—too hot even for locals to continue to work.

It's hard to ignore the reality that we humans are changing the climate, and we're adding pollution and waste into the earth's system daily. Apparently, only 13 percent of the oceans remain unaffected by our plastic trash.[1] That plastic has now entered our digestive systems—yes, we're excreting plastic.[2] And all this plastic waste for what? Stuff. Stuff that supposedly makes our lives better, easier, and faster. But are we happier?

We have offset the balance. Just as our bodies rely on homeostasis for health, the earth does too. And many would argue that the "stuff" is not making us a happier species; it is just making us out of balance. Surely there must be a greater meaning in life than just acquiring things, accruing debt, and living on a hamster wheel in an endless pursuit to pay the bills?

This may all sound quite bleak, but there are solutions on the horizon. Companies are looking to connect with a younger generation that wants business to have a greater purpose.

Business is a powerhouse that can steer the economy and consumer behavior, and the impact all that has on Mother Earth, in a direction for the better. Business plays a major role in social and environmental problems: businesses employ people, source materials from remote corners of the globe, and move millions of people and tons of cargo around daily. The business community can put us on a different path if we support the type of businesses that prize restoration over growth. The pandemic compounded this reality for us: while working from home had its comforts, it also led to thousands of Americans quitting their jobs, seeking change, thinking about the preciousness of time and what they want to do with their waking hours and healthy days—ultimately, trying to understand their role in this larger web of capitalism.

We have seen the results of business that is fixated on ROI (return on investment) and providing wealth to an elite group, its shareholders. Many people are fed up with this approach. Will it always be necessary to be a global force in order to be profitable? Will it always be necessary to build supply chains that favor only the few at the top to make the business a so-called successful venture? Certainly not.

As I have been reporting on the evolution of this business landscape, I've seen it mature from the simple idea of "buy one, give one"—a model that utilizes philanthropy by giving away free product for every purchase—to a more nuanced examination of business, leading to the rise of the B corporation, the benefit corporation, the purpose-driven economy. This is all part of a new lexicon and is a real challenge to the conventional thinking that business is primarily a profit-seeking enterprise.

But to build a company with a purpose requires more than just writing a progressive mission statement and slapping up some inspirational quotes around the office. Political and corporate leaders say that we can build a more "sustainable" world. Yet they've been trying since 1987, when the term "sustainable development" entered the lexicon in a three-hundred-page document known as the Brundtland Report, published by the United Nations under the title *Our Common Future*. The report talked of building a more sustainable future. It listed the interlocked crises affecting humanity, including water shortages, drought, famine, pesticide runoff, and overdependence on chemicals.

So can we really build a more sustainable world, given that we've been talking about the same issues for the past three decades? Everyone I spoke with for this book was pretty fed up with the word "sustainable." Sustain what? This imbalance?

Instead, these entrepreneurs want to rewrite the rules of business to focus on transparency, simplicity, compassion, and equity. If these values were upheld and put into action every day, we could begin to restore the balance, ecologically and socially.

Let me be clear: there is no ideal solution. Humans create a footprint. It is in our nature to desire, lust, and run after what we do not have. Even many of the companies highlighted in this book acknowledge that they're producing a physical product that has a footprint. But they can do it without the injustices of the modern supply chain, without exploiting populations, without over-extracting resources, without damaging what we need for life itself: the earth.

Using the United Nations Sustainable Development Goals, a framework of seventeen global goals that call attention to the fundamental social and environmental challenges we face, this book looks at business models that address these challenges. Thus, each chapter contains the stories of a few businesses that have structured their enterprises to tackle complex problems like soil health, renewable energy, waste systems, women's rights, and conservation of open spaces and wild-life—-all of which tie back to the concept of restoration and regeneration through business.

These are stories of entrepreneurs who are trying to restore civility, integrity, and transparency to business. Many have been doing this long before it was trendy, long before these notions became buzz-words in the business world. Some of these businesses are classified as B corporations, but those that are not likely exhibit the qualities of the concept. These entrepreneurs admit that their companies are not perfect. They are fusing elements of business that have long been practiced—a focus on quality, self-funding ventures, building slowly, developing community—and doing so in a manner that suits the present and the aspirations of future generations, while being transparent about the challenges along the way.

In a global economy, it's hard to operate in isolation. It's unlikely we'll go back to cottage industries and entirely local economies. Thus, it's vital to look at companies that are working at scale, and across continents. These businesses are proving that we can source coffee from East Africa and have small farmers be a bigger part of the business model; have fashion-forward ethical shoes that are made entirely in one country, using natural materials, and shipped in empty spaces in containers; and take textile waste in factories, cut it up, and turn it into usable fabrics. The models exist if we want to explore them, invest in them, and let them function without obsessing over growth.

The capitalistic world order has deep roots around the globe. Designing this new economy is not an easy or overnight task. In fact, many of the companies discussed in this book have been at it for more than a decade, and progress is slow. The tentacles of dirty money have gone far and wide. The business practices that have led us to this point are entrenched. A quick cleanup will not work. It requires thought, reflection, tenacity, and a certain stubbornness by CEOs and founders to slowly build a new model along with the employees and workers to carry that out.

There's one critical difference to start with, though: these companies are built around a challenge, a larger problem, or an issue.

Hence, the goal is not growth, but to solve a dilemma: How do you create a closed-loop product? How do you make sure that every bit of your supply chain benefits from the business? How do you feed the planet while not pilfering from it in the process?

These entrepreneurs are in the business of restoration, fixing a system that has long been lopsided and is fundamentally broken. No perfect or single solution exists for each of these monumental challenges, but this could be the beginning of a new era of regeneration. Let these stories serve as a brainstorm for what can happen, if business thinks beyond profit.

WHY THESE INDUSTRIES

When planning this book, I opted for a handful of examples across industries to indicate that this is not a movement specific to one industry. Rather, it's happening across the board: entrepreneurs and companies are rethinking how food, fashion, travel, health, finance, and more can be made more regenerative. In fact, we need to make it happen across industries to truly make a dent. Thus, I looked at the breadth of reporting I had done coupled with the UN's Sustainable Development Goals and saw how there were clusters of innovation cropping up in the most fundamental of industries: agriculture, manufacturing, energy, finance—industries that are the backbone of society. Each chapter opens with an explanation of how we've derailed, pointing out the damage or inequities that exist—yet I don't dwell on these. I present stories of businesses that are plucking away at these flaws and challenges.

The hope is that you walk away feeling that change can be made—and it can start with you. The entrepreneurs featured come from all kinds of backgrounds—some have grown up in low-income neighborhoods, others have served in the military and experienced war, and many have spent time failing for years before they found a model that actually worked. Whether one is sitting in a corporate office, at a nonprofit, on a dirt field in the middle of the countryside, or serving others in hospitality, there's a story of change waiting to be told.

Even the industries that have seen an influx of funds, media attention, and resources are facing ethical and environmental crises.

Agriculture, for example, has been seeing a steady transformation by the organic-farming movement over the past three decades. Yet have we paid attention to soil health as much? No. Or have we put as much importance on fiber as we have on our foods? After all, the clothes we wear, the bags we carry—much of this is made with one kind of fiber, cotton.

Cotton consumes Vikrant Giri, a Nepalese immigrant to the US who is the founder of LA-based Gallant International. He's been making custom tote bags for corporate and nonprofit clients out of organic cotton, working directly with farmers in India, for about five years. We connected one evening on a visit to a local organic farm in southern California, looking at how they were transitioning to re-generative farming. As we walked through rows of organic amaranth plants, he told me about his annual visits to farms in India. It was, needless to say, drastically different from California. In the heat of the midday sun, he said, he would take a break and sit in the shade with the farmers to share some tea and snacks. They spoke openly to him about how farming organically had changed their lives: they were making more money and living healthier, their families were happy to see that they were not exposed to chemicals, and they were continuing to grow food crops in between rows of cotton that they could sell in the local market or eat themselves. They had no desire to turn back, he said. And in India, where cotton has for decades been grown from GMO (genetically modified) seeds, using conventional methods, and been plagued with cases of farmer suicides due to the debts they incurred, this was a welcome change. "Can you imagine the damage we do just for a T-shirt or a tote bag?" he said. "And all it takes is for us to pay a few cents or a dollar more, so that we can do things the right way."

Thus, I had to open with soil and agriculture, something so fundamental to human existence, and look at companies across the spectrum: from making fertilizers out of waste to encouraging more organic farming to a global shoe brand that's been knee-deep with farmers in northern Brazil to build an organic cotton community in an area that's seen wild swings in weather. And there are also good examples of farmers close to home—here in California and in the Midwest—who are challenging the well-established narrative of large-scale conventional farming in the US.

Each chapter takes on a theme, or an industry, and explores its various facets to illustrate that this is not a movement restricted to the do-gooders or activist-minded only. Rather, it's happening everywhere, in places we don't even suspect. And if these businesses can prove their success—by simply remaining in business for more than five years, turning a profit, and building a market—then it can be done by others as well. These might be the slightly wonky entrepreneurs who are not afraid of risk, but their models are not limited to their own companies.

The regenerative mindset centers around circles, as a collective, be it on a farm, in a factory, or in a business. While I highlight one specific aspect of each of these businesses—such as their focus on soil health, their innovation in finance, or their alternative take on energy—the way these companies operate, how they choose to do business, what they deem as "usual," is straying away from the norm: there's a conscious effort for all aspects of their work to have an impact. After all, they're driven by change, not profit. So that seeps into the day-to-day ways of operating, their engagement with suppliers, their approach to marketing. It's a comprehensive effort to regenerate the art of doing business, and in the process, regenerate the people and resources that make that business happen.

In the second chapter I explore waste, looking at an eclectic mix of entrepreneurs, from a furniture and boat builder in Amsterdam to a British barefoot-shoe company to a beer brand. Their common thread? Regenerating waste. If we thought waste was restricted to the stuff you throw in your trash or recycling bins, these entrepreneurs are going far and beyond: turning trash from the canals of Amsterdam into sleek boardroom furniture, using algae from excess algae blooms in lakes for the soles of shoes, and giving leftover wedges of bread a new life as beer. There clearly isn't a limit to what can be recycled, and how.

Thus, these are stories of companies that illustrate ingenuity but also some degree of success. They're not so fearful of being different and taking an unconventional path. To regenerate now, we must look beyond what's been done in the past.

Marius Smit, a self-described "plastic fisherman," spends his days in an office that overlooks the Amsterdam canals. He's not fond of meetings and discussions—stated in a framed motto hanging above his desk. He prefers to get to the point. "There's so much talk these days! What I want to see is doing. Even if you don't get it right, do it," he says. It's taken him years to transition from a one-man eco-activist in Amsterdam to running Plastic Whale, a social enterprise that now makes contemporary furniture from canal waste, among other things. But he got started the old-fashioned way—putting up ads around the city, asking if others would join him on a fishing adventure down the canals for trash. Most people thought he had gone bonkers in the beginning, he says, laughing.

It's that gumption, that slightly "I don't care what you think" attitude that's intrigued me about so many of these entrepreneurs. They're smart, savvy, humble, and a bit wild. But that is what business needs today to address the oncoming challenges—not arrogance, but introspection, humility, and a zest for the elusive.

Although much of the emphasis around the word "regenerate" is environmental, that is too limiting. Yes, so much of what is on our horizon is our lasting impact on the planet's flora and fauna, but we also need to regenerate the social aspect of business. Is a simple certification enough to say that a business is actually socially conscious? Probably not.

Giri, for example, goes to visit the farms he sources his cotton from; he then follows it all the way to the cut-and-sew facility, where he knows the owners intimately. They are more friends than business partners, one could say. "They always have a room at my home, if they come to stay," he says. On top of all the existing certifications, it's the personalization of a massive global supply chain that gives Giri satisfaction that he's manufacturing in the most ethical way possible. And he's never quite satisfied, always on the lookout for how he can improve the lives of the workers, their families, and their working conditions.

Getting that intimate with your supply chain is what is truly needed. The individuals who grow our food, make our clothes, and help the global economy run are not merely numbers on an auditing document. They're more. And therefore, certifications are a mere baseline. Konrad Brits, founder of Falcon Coffee, a coffee-trading company, says that the regenerative economy will truly emerge if we see each of these individuals as a powerful economic force: when they succeed, the earth will also succeed.

So I explore in this book companies that truly put people first—be it in the so-called developing world or in an office in the US. How do we create a business mindset that doesn't just dwell on the finances (yes! That's important, no doubt)? But these companies are reflective enough to realize that people make business happen, and those people ought to be respected and looked after for their contribution. There are also those who have been deemed outcasts of society because they're from underserved communities, have had a tumultuous past, or live with chronic illness. Do we just forget about these sections of society? Of course not. Instead, several companies in the book embrace the dignity of every person and help create jobs for all—and in the process prove that these individuals can be productive, efficient members of the company, not just objects of a charity mission. These finer details are part of the regenerative vision—to regenerate the soul, through work that brings an emotional fulfillment as well as a financial one.

Although some of these topics may be obvious—such as food, energy, and fashion, where we have seen a great deal of debate, discussion, and media scrutiny—there are other industries where the vision to build a regenerative economy is not as straightforward. Travel, for one, has no clear answer. You can continue to wear a dress or a pair of shoes, grow your own food, and opt for wind or solar energy to power your life, but "regenerative" transport is tricky, unless you limit yourself to walking, biking, and mass transit. What do you do when you need to go somewhere farther away, not served by mass transit? What if there aren't any trains or buses? What if you don't have an eco-friendly vehicle? Also, do you stay in any hotel? Do you go the Airbnb route? Is it selfish to get on a plane? The mind games are endless here.

The travel industry has a certain degree of waste and energy consumption built into it. And as someone who has spent a good chunk of her life sandwiched into an economy seat on twelve-hour transatlantic flights, I'm well aware of the work that needs to be done (we can start with all that excess plastic packaging of airline snacks!). Despite the horrors of single-use coffee pods in hotel rooms made with subpar coffee, endless plastic cups of water on flights, and the vision of thousands of tourists descending on areas of natural beauty, I have hope that change is coming. Eco-friendly jet fuel is in the works. And hopefully after living through a pandemic, we will all think twice before getting on a plane for a mere one- or two-day work event. In a later chapter, I look less at the energy consumption of travel transportation, and more at how the hospitality industry can actually lead the way at every price point. All it takes, I learned, is for us holiday goers to do a bit of research and take an interest in supporting positive changes.

The travel chapter shares the tales of three different hotels—a boutique hotel near Bournemouth, on the English coast, a slow Norwegian escape in the fjords, and a high-end safari that works tirelessly towards conservation across the African continent—but the source of my inspiration was actually some of the hotel experiences I had back in my home country, India.

In fact, it's these kinds of trips and serendipitous stays that have reminded me there are entrepreneurs everywhere, looking for a different model. More than five years ago, I found myself in Pondicherry, a coastal town in south India famous for its Portuguese influence. I booked a stay at the Villa Shanti, a relatively new hotel with modern amenities along with a strong Indian aesthetic. One night at dinner, the owner, Ségiyane Sylvain Paquiry, came to check up on my meal. We went on to chat for hours about how he had put together this hotel and a nearby property, after having being raised in Pondicherry and wanting to bring a hotel to the mix that celebrated the historic and playful elements of this colorful city. It wasn't just his love for

Indian handicrafts, arts, and painstakingly preserving the old, crumbling architecture that came into play but also his desire to make the hotel an enriching place to work for all his staff.

He explained to me that Pondicherry, being a smaller city in India, had fewer people with a formal training in hospitality. Plus, many of his hotel staff would leave upon reaching marrying age or due to other family-related issues. So he set up a social scheme for them, offering to make loans to them for any major life events or emergencies, and he invested in their training. These are simple things, he told me, but for someone who would otherwise go to a loan shark or be too timid to acknowledge that he doesn't know how to do something, it helped them feel more at home. He didn't think of his hotel as a social enterprise; it was a fun, forward-looking place for travelers to convene every night. Yet Paquiry had honed in, unknowingly, on how a business can regenerate a community. He brought that spirit of a collective to his business, and that's what this book is about—people who run businesses with some thoughtfulness.

If travel is a hard industry in which to pinpoint "right" answers, the world of finance is even trickier. To fund all these businesses, money is needed, yet what we see is that the big banks, especially here in the US, have supported big agriculture, coal and gas, and ammunition sales, among other contentious industries. I first learned about a new breed of financiers, called impact investors, over a decade ago. The term has since gone mainstream, but to find a true impact investor is still a tall task, I hear from entrepreneurs. Thus, finance is perhaps the industry that needs to work most for change, with banks and investors that are able to shift their mindset to one that is actually long term. Even in the era of cause-driven, direct-to-consumer brands and all the rhetoric about companies with a mission, I hear from founders that they struggle with their investors: the pressure is always on to perform—on spreadsheets and scale.

That's why I was intrigued when I stepped into the forest-like enclave where Triodos Bank has its headquarters in the Netherlands. This was a far cry from Silicon Valley. And here was a firm that was inspired by the biodynamic movement, whose philosophy argues that all farming should be holistic, using components found on the farm as much as possible to grow organically. Sound a bit hippie-dippie? Well, Triodos is a bank with more than twenty billion euros' worth of assets under management. Not quite your local co-op.

Triodos is not alone. There are others who are trying to make the pursuit of fundraising more palatable. The Seattle-based investment firm Capria Ventures has been working tirelessly to make capital less US- and Euro-centric. In East Africa, which has seen a surge of entrepreneurial activity, they want to help identify local investors for local startups. Rather than always having to turn to American or European investment firms for capital, they argue that there's enough cash available locally for investment; it's a matter of connecting the dots. This is not merely for convenience—it's also to create a culture of investment across the continent and help train the next generation. This investor jokes about the tendency of those with capital to invest to participate in "parachute investing"—drop in, assay the landscape, and then leave. That's certainly not sustainable.

As I completed this book I saw a shift happening. Ideas of sustainability that were deemed fringe have become more mainstream. When big-box retailers start putting out impact reports and establish goals to become carbon-neutral, it seems the message is spreading and being heard. The COVID-19 pandemic forced companies to look at how they treat their employees and staff. While this may all seem like good news—and some of it is—it has raised concerns about greenwashing and the tendency to join a trend because it is the topic of the moment.

So let's address the G-word: greenwashing. It's definitely an issue. I've seen countless examples of entrepreneurs who love to play up their green impact, who make grandiose statements about their company's reach—frankly, if you're a customer just reading marketing jargon on their website or social media feed, it can be hard to determine what's genuine and what's phony.

Yet what I saw over and over again as I engaged with so many of the CEOs and founders when researching this book is that the ones who are truly looking to redefine business often walk their talk.

They're living simple lives; are approachable and eager to debate and listen; spend time one on one with partners in their supply chains; refrain from seeking the limelight; and are more involved in the intricacies of their business than in marketing lingo.

In fact, most of the leaders of the companies featured are not pursuing this because it's trendy, or because they think the time has come to pay attention to their impact. Their motivation comes from their conception of a business, and that is the driving factor. Call it regenerative, restorative, or any other word you'd like. For them, it's not about a buzzword. It's about facing a deeper dilemma that needs to be addressed. Buzzwords come and go. But the impact that a business makes, either good or bad, is lasting. And thus, that's where they've placed their attention.

It's worth noting that some of these companies may fail in the long run; that's the reality of it. But these entrepreneurs chose to try an alternative, and I believe it's worth examining their work to see what gems can be taken away for the 2.0 version of business.

CHAPTER ONE

SOIL

The Most Fundamental Ingredient

S oil is probably the last thing we think about when we buy stuff. How did the production of this T-shirt, or this shoe, impact soil? How did our coffee impact the soil it grew in? Was the soil improved, or degraded? Healthy soil—not dirt—is crucial to the commodities traded in the global economy: cotton, coffee, tea, rubber, cacao, wheat, oats. So many of the things we consume every day are grown in soil, not manufactured in factories. Soil isn't sexy, but it's what keeps us alive—truly. We come from soil and return to soil. It is at the core of human existence. And soil is facing a bit of a crisis at the moment. If the soil doesn't have nutrients, it doesn't matter what seed we put in it—the seed will struggle to grow.

Soil is crucial to the global economy. Consider furniture, which relies on timber. Consider our shoes, which are often made of leather, a byproduct of the meat industry, which relies on animals that consume grasses. The classic T-shirts we love require bales of cotton to manufacture. Livestock, forestry, and textiles are all connected to soil health. The farming of animals concentrated in one area can have a negative effect on soil quality and lead to overgrazing; land cleared for animal husbandry or for timber extraction affects the flora and fauna of that area; aggressive cotton farming can deplete soils.

Much of the world's soil has been turning to dirt, says David Montgomery, a University of Washington professor of earth and space sciences and the author of *Dirt: The Erosion of Civilizations,*

1

which describes the problems that result from stressed soil. Turns out societies that degraded their soil didn't prosper in the long run.

Montgomery jokingly describes fertile soil as a "marriage of geology and biology." To make such soil, he explains, "the mineral matter of the rocks has to break down. Not in solid El Capitan [of Yosemite] form. But [as] smaller rocks that slowly engage with the organic matter, made of living organisms or the once-living organisms. Those two things marry to create healthy fertile soils. Plants need the mineral elements to build their bodies and grow. They need those micronutrients that ultimately come from rocks. Problem is, though, that rocks break down really slowly."

When that marriage between stone dust and organic matter goes awry—when topsoil is blown off or washed away, leaving only rocks—societies struggle to farm on the resulting weak soil. Rebuilding topsoil isn't out of the question. But it is harder to do if all the nutrients and organic matter are missing. When Montgomery published *Dirt*, in 2007, he was trying to awaken people to the impending reality of soil loss. It seems we are still trying to do that, even though the evidence of the consequences is now starkly in front of us.

According to a UN-backed study released in 2017, one-third of the planet's soil is now depleted. Fertile soil is being lost at an astonishing rate of twenty-four billion tons a year.[1] The stats are not complete, and it could be worse than the information we have indicates. Comprehensive worldwide data for desertification (where fertile land turns into desert) and degradation of soil (the depletion of organic matter in the soil) is difficult to compile. It is held in specific country-level agencies and is missing altogether for big chunks of the planet. To monitor this more closely and develop a strong set of global data, the United Nations Convention to Combat Desertification created a new publication, the *Global Land Outlook*, which is responsible for mapping soil quality around the world.

The Joint Research Centre of the European Commission outlined the reasons behind this phenomenon. In the last two decades, agricultural production has increased, and the amount of irrigated land has doubled, but such intensive farming—often with the addition of chemical-laden fertilizers and pesticides—strips the soil of nutrients.

If the land loses fertility, then farmers abandon it, resulting in desertification. Hence in 2017, the Joint Research Centre cited decreasing productivity on 20 percent of the world's cropland, 16 percent of forestland, 19 percent of grassland, and 27 percent of rangeland.[2]

The importance of soil quality is often overlooked. In farming, the focus is on the crop, not the soil in which the crop lives. Yet, everything that grows in the soil draws nutrients from that soil. The problem is that the soil today, in much of the world, is devoid of nutrients. As a result, some experts argue, the crops that grow in it are as well.

In 2004, Donald Davis and his team of researchers at the University of Texas were already looking at the issue. Their study, published in the December 2004 issue of the *Journal of the American College of Nutrition*, comparing nutritional data recorded in 1950 with corresponding data in 1999, indicated that forty-three different fruits and vegetables had "reliable declines" in their quantities of protein, calcium, phosphorus, iron, vitamin B12, and vitamin C. Another fifteen years have passed since Davis and his team released their study, yet agriculture continues to expand with a focus on volume, not quality.

Agriculture is, in fact, the largest human use of land, according to the United Nations. It covers 38 percent of the world's land surface, excluding Greenland and Antarctica. Since the advent of farm machinery in the 1800s, agricultural use of land has significantly increased.[3]

This situation is happening globally. The UN reports that "degraded lands account for over a fifth of forest and agricultural lands in Latin America and the Caribbean," and agriculture is now the "most significant cause of current land conversion in the tropics, resulting in the loss of biodiversity and ecosystem services."[4]

Compounding the problem is our growing population. With more people comes not only the burden of feeding more mouths but also infrastructure development. Between 2002 and 2010, more than eight million acres of farmland and open spaces were taken over by urban and suburban sprawl.[5]

When open land and farmland go to development, not only do we swap soil for asphalt, but we also lose the soil's ability to harness carbon. Healthy soil, researchers argue, could be a great way to mitigate pollution and greenhouse gases. Robert Jackson, a professor of earth system science at Stanford University, studied this very issue: the carbon cycle of soil. In a study published in 2017, he wrote: "Soil is a major component of the carbon cycle; it contains more carbon than plant biomass and the atmosphere combined. It's a no-risk climate solution with big co-benefits. Fostering soil health protects food security and builds resilience to droughts, floods, and urbanization."

The rapid decline of soil health has led the United Nations to create an annual international day devoted to the issue, World Soil Day, on December 5. On World Soil Day in 2017, the news agency Reuters reported from a forum on soil health in Rome, organized by the Food and Agricultural Organization, with some harrowing information: if current rates of degradation continued, "all of the world's topsoil could be gone within sixty years." Volkert Engelsman, an activist who attended the forum, told the Reuters reporter, "We are losing thirty soccer fields of soil every minute, mostly due to intensive farming."

Even though awareness around soil health has increased, the use of chemicals and pesticides, one of the causes of soil degradation, is not declining. The USDA reported in 2010 that 97 percent of corn-covered acreage in the country needed fertilizers. Compare this to 1964, when it was 85 percent. The USDA research goes on to note that farmers in 1964 were putting 58 pounds of nitrogen on each acre; in 2010, that number was up to 140 pounds—more than double.

The Environmental Protection Agency states that "nutrient pollution is one of America's most widespread, costly, and challenging environmental problems, and is caused by excess nitrogen and phosphorus in the air and water."[6] While nitrogen can bolster the growth of microorganisms and algae, in large quantities it can also become a threat. Unfortunately, nitrogen-heavy fertilizers are contributing to this problem. It's so pervasive that more than 210 million Americans could be drinking water polluted with nitrates.

Such farming practices are putting people and the land at risk. Soil health has taken a hit as a result of three different types of degradation, according to the United Nations: physical, chemical, and biological.[7] Physical refers to erosion, resulting in soil that's too weak to retain any moisture. Chemical refers to loss of nutrients and soil that's become highly acidic. This is related to toxic waste, runoff, and overuse of chemicals and fertilizers. And last, biological degradation results when tilling and overtilling actually change the makeup and structure of the soil, leaving it without nutrients.

The United States, which in recent decades has focused on agribusiness and large-scale farming, is seeing all of these issues come to life. More than 50 percent of America's topsoil has eroded, some experts say.[8] Montgomery explains that a swath of land from Virginia to Georgia in the Southeast is dealing with this now: "The topsoil is gone. So farmers are relying on chemical fertilizers to grow high yields. The key question: How long can you do that for and how nutritious is that food?"

In Iowa, it's a different picture, he says: "They've lost about fifty percent of their topsoil. But what they have left is pretty decent soil, and if the organic matter could be rebuilt, it's salvageable."

Gabe Brown, a farmer and cattle rancher in North Dakota, did just that. In 1997, he decided to wean his farm off synthetic fertilizers and take a more regenerative approach. He had previously tilled and treated the farm according to modern conventional methods, but that wasn't working.

Brown now tours the country, speaking at agricultural meetings and farm gatherings, to encourage other farmers to change their practices. In his talks he starts with some basic facts and figures, relying on science and the evidence to make his point about the loss of soil and soil fertility. In 1960, the depth of topsoil in North Dakota was thirty-four inches; in 2014, it was down to fifteen inches—more than a 50 percent loss. The organic matter in the soil had gone from 8 percent to 3 percent.

Catastrophic weather is not always the cause of flooded farmland, Brown says; his perspective is that the soil cannot absorb the water because it's been overtilled. He shows two images side by side: a slice of soil from his farm and a slice of soil from a neighbor's farm. His soil is dark, rich with carbon, wet, and teeming with worms. The neighbor's looks more like packed terra cotta with little room for water to penetrate and infiltrate deep into the ground to be available during drier periods.

Brown is friendly and relatable to his audience of fellow farmers. "The motto of this great state of North Dakota is 'Strength through the soil.' That's what I'm here to visit with you about today," he says.

Since he's lived this evolution from a conventional rancher and farmer who tilled, fertilized, and relied on monocropping (repeatedly planting the same crop in the same place) to now running a profitable five-thousand-acre regenerative farm, he knows the journey—and the fear—connected with turning to a new practice, especially when a family's well-being and finances depend on the farm's success.

"The current model is all about killing, be it a weed, a pest, a fungus, or diversity," Brown says. "But there is another way—nature's way. I would argue this is the conventional model because it's been around for eons."

Regenerative agriculture treats the farm as a collective ecosystem. It's not just about planting rows of organic fruits and vegetables. It's about cover crops, crop rotation, incorporating animals on the farm (and their poop!), rethinking weed and pest management, and also giving those working on the farm dignified wages. As the term "regenerative" is becoming more and more widely used, one needs to distinguish between regenerative as a farming practice, and the certification for regenerative organic. The latter builds on the existing organic certifications and combined with social certifications (think Fairtrade) values every element of the farm. Let's get beyond yields and a list of chemicals that should not sprayed, to how the farm—and its components, from soil to livestock to worker—can play a role in regeneration.

"Nature," Montgomery similarly says, "takes a long time to make an inch of soil, but we can do it much faster by taking advantage of our ability to bring organic matter in to enhance what nature would take a long time to do."

To better understand what has worked, Montgomery traveled around the world to meet with farmers who were trying to rebuild soil. The solution, he says—"and very doable"—is in decreasing pesticide and chemical use; rotating crops and bringing in a diversity of crops; and using cover crops. This is just what Brown has been doing in North Dakota. Both reached the same conclusion, one from his backyard garden in Washington and the other from his struggling farm in the Dakotas.

David Pimentel, professor of ecology at Cornell, told the *Cornell Chronicle*, the university's newspaper, in 2006: "Soil erosion is second only to population growth as the biggest environmental problem the world faces. Yet, the problem, which is growing ever more critical, is being ignored because who gets excited about dirt?" But agriculture, despite its bucolic imagery and the romantic notion that some people have of it, is a business. So if business practices and values can revive soil quality while maintaining profitability, the gloomy stats outlined earlier could be reversed.

STEPPING ONTO HEALTHIER SOILS

While food may seem like an obvious industry to invest in soil health, what about retail brands in fashion? How can companies help improve soil quality when they're not selling tea, coffee, fruit, or vegetables? They're not sitting in the hills or on the farms. Are they actually affected if soil degradation is taking place somewhere else?

The short answer: Yes, very much so.

Cotton is one of the most commonly used materials in clothing and accessories. It has long been grown with a heavy dose of pesticides, which contributes to poor soil quality. When two French entrepreneurs, Sébastien Kopp and François-Ghislain Morillion, decided to make shoes, they didn't know any of this. Today, they run a multi-million-dollar brand, Veja, which focuses on one thing: making the most ecologically sensitive shoes possible. As they've built the company over the last seventeen years, they've also been helping rebuild the soil on organic cotton farms in Brazil and preserving the Amazon canopy and its carbon-rich soil.

I met Kopp in a swanky hotel in the heart of Paris, just outside the Place Vendôme, where Paris Fashion Week was in full swing. Kopp arrived wearing aged denim and a weathered pair of Vejas. In a crowd of women in body-hugging dresses, overflowing with sequins and jewels, he was definitely the odd man out. But he prefers it that way.

"A few days ago, I was in the Amazon, and now I'm sitting here with you," he said, sipping an espresso. "Amazing that it's all on the same planet and in the same week."

Kopp is less interested in what is fashionable and more interested in getting people to see the connection between what they wear and how it's made. He abhors the word "sustainable." "We don't do 'sustainable,' 'ethical,' 'slow,' or any other words used to describe alternative fashion. We just focus on being transparent and fair," Kopp said.

Transparency and ethics have not been at the core of the global athletic footwear market, which was estimated at a whopping $75 billion in 2015. It's expected to go up another $15 billion by 2023.[9] Kopp and Morillion want to see how much of that market they can either gain or transform with their nontraditional ways.

Children of the '80s and students of global development and political science, the duo spent a few years after college traveling around the world to see corporate social responsibility projects in practice. They were pretty disappointed with the results. "It was a lot of talk, not a lot of transparency, or actual actions on the ground," Kopp says.

In 2003, while doing audits for a French fashion brand at a Chinese factory, they discovered thirty workers crammed into a 270-square-foot room with a single hole to drain the workers' shower and also allow them to relieve themselves. "We realized that globalization had gone wrong," Kopp says.

They returned to Paris and instead opted to work with a small French brand, Alter Eco, focused on fair trade. Alter Eco, then in its early days, was building a business around direct supply chains, a "radical but obvious" concept, Kopp says. The company sold orange juice, chocolate, rice, tea, and coffee, which it was sourcing directly from farmer groups to whom it was paying fair-trade wages. Alter Eco started in 1998 and grew in the 2000s, producing offshoots in the United States and Australia. At the time, the conversation in business was still stuck on philanthropy; even corporate social responsibility (CSR) had yet to make its way into the corporate lexicon.

However, Kopp and Morillion, experienced travelers by now and having seen the backend operations of companies, realized that it was possible to build a business that benefited the growers, not the marketers. "Most people don't realize that most of their money is going to marketing, not to the maker," Kopp says.

Inspired by Alter Eco, the two decided to launch their own project, focused on "deconstructing the sneaker." Sneakers had become popular in the late 1980s and '90s as everyday wear, often with athletes sporting and touting the latest styles. But most of the money generated by big brands was going into marketing budgets, not the supply chain, according to Kopp. "We didn't know much about shoes, but it was something everyone wore; we loved them as teenagers, and we knew that we could get all the pieces required for the shoe in one place: Brazil."

He had traveled frequently to Brazil with Morillion previously, but there was a significant problem: neither one spoke fluent Portuguese. That didn't stop them, though: "We just realized that if we, two twenty-five-year-old idiots from France, who didn't even speak the language fully, could figure out how to build a fair and transparent supply chain, then the big companies could do it, too—if they want to."

Investing approximately $5,500 (€5,000) each, they set out to build the first prototype shoe for Veja (the name means "look" in Portuguese and is meant to suggest "look behind the label"). Today, for the shoe uppers, Veja's styles use different combinations of organic cotton, leather, and a material they call "b-mesh," made out of recycled plastic bottles and leather. Twenty-two styles use only organic cotton. The soles are made of a blend of wild and synthetic rubber, delivering performance and durability.

When Kopp and Morillion started, organic cotton was not as readily available. Even a decade later, Kopp concedes, "we didn't always have enough of it to do all our laces in organic cotton."

In 2004, just a year after having their awakening in the Chinese factory, Kopp and Morillion dove into the effort of building a supply chain for Veja. They visited the Association for Educational and Cultural Development (Associação de Desenvolvimento Educacional e Cultural de Tauá, or ADEC), a cooperative then of about thirty farmers—as of 2022, eighty-eight—producing organic cotton in northeastern Brazil. "These farmers had not been able to sell their organic cotton for six years," Kopp says.

They were practicing agroecology, a more nuanced way of farming that surpasses organic. These farmers were forgoing monocrops (of just cotton) for a variety of staples that helped feed their families as well as the soil. In addition to cotton, they grew corn, sesame, and beans—the bulk of their diet.

"At the time, we didn't know much about agroecology. We learned that it was much more than just organic. And then we met the pope of agroecology, Pedro Jorge," Kopp recalls. Agroecology is what the name suggests: agriculture that has a role in the larger world of ecology. It's a recognition that agriculture doesn't have to happen in isolation but can be a part of the messier natural world. Jorge, one of the brightest minds in agriculture in Brazil, shunned traditional agricultural practices that were aimed at increasing yield. Instead, he became a proponent of farming that's careful not to damage resources while maximizing and using the surplus that nature offers for food production.

Kopp and Morillion followed his direction, sourcing their cotton from ADEC. "We went for fair trade organic cotton because the majority of cotton produced every year in the world comes from intensive monoculture crops," Kopp says. "What do monoculture crops do? Deplete soil quality."

In 2007, they went to the first organic cotton fair in Brazil, where they met Maria Valdenira Rodrigues de Almeida, from a village in the northeast of Brazil, whose father was a farmer. Theirs was a family of limited means, but Rodrigues was a university student. She had imbibed that local knowledge and then decided to specialize in agronomy. At twenty-seven, she was at a university learning about agroecology—just what the Veja founders wanted to practice and support. They asked her to join as an agricultural engineer for the startup after she had completed her studies.

Ten years later, Rodrigues became an asset to the brand, Kopp says. "Most fashion brands don't have an agricultural engineer, but if you're making a product with cotton, it makes complete sense."

Growing cotton in this corner of Brazil is not easy. This is a dry, parched area of the country that had been facing drought-like conditions for six years. Climate change is already being felt, according to Rodrigues: "Farmers have had to sell their animals because they had no food and no water."

All of the organic cotton here is rain-fed, not irrigated. However, in 2015, the drought became so severe that Veja was left without any organic cotton crop. They resorted to using recycled organic cotton that year and since then have expanded their supply chain to include organic cotton from Peru to ensure they have enough supply. That's why it's all the more important, Rodrigues says, to think about how they farm: if water is limited, the soil must be fertile in order for the farmers to continuously reap harvests.

That means letting critters control the land, not pesticides, she explains. "Conventional farming uses chemicals to control pests and diseases; [that] chemical [does] not make selection among beneficial or malevolent pathogens and ends up destroying natural predators and soil fauna. The non-use of chemicals in organic production preserves these natural enemies such as a ladybird."

With Veja's investment in the region, and commitment to buying each harvest, farmers are learning from each other about how to better manage these challenges. "It's been beneficial for them to learn sustainable land management," Rodrigues says. "The exchange of knowledge that happens between farmers of different regions at various meetings is helping spread the message."

From 2004 to 2021, Veja has bought 954,358 kilograms of organic cotton. In 2021 alone, Veja purchased 410,000 kilograms of cotton (about 905,000 pounds of cotton) in advance of the actual harvest, the production of two hundred families. The company and the cooperative have decided to make all their transactions public; consumers can view the contracts between the cotton cooperative and Veja.

Kopp is hoping that by disclosing all the details, including the pricing of their supply chain, consumers will start demanding the same information from bigger players in the footwear industry, creating a domino effect.

Similar to their cotton supply chain, Kopp decided to go an unconventional route with the soles of the shoes as well.

"What is the sole of that shoe?" he says, pointing to a bystander wearing a pair of nondescript sneakers. "It's not rubber. They say it's rubber, but it's synthetic rubber, or plastic."

Kopp wanted rubber sourced from the wilds of the Amazon for their shoes' soles. More than ten years ago, when Kopp and Morillion made their first trip to Brazil for Veja, they established a friendship with the *seringueiros*—rubber tappers—in the Chico Mendes Extractive Reserve (Reservo Extravista Chico Mendes), in Brazil's northwestern state of Acre.

"When we went into the jungle," he recalls, "families thought it was crazy that we would pay them to source wild rubber and help manage the trees so we don't overextract."

Now, seventeen years later, the families have become stewards of the land, protecting it from deforestation. "They tell me they're concerned. It's not like what it used to be when they were children. The forest is drier than before. That climate change is coming. But we see that we have impact on the forest through our work," Kopp explains.

By ten o'clock in the morning in the Amazon rainforest, José Ribamar, a fifty-two-year-old *seringueiro*, has visited all 130 of the rubber trees on his property, situated inside the Chico Mendes Extractive Reserve. Ribamar lives on the land but does not own it. Instead, he likes to refer to himself as a protector of the forest.

He grew up in the Amazon rainforest and was introduced to rubber tapping at the age of eight. The son of a rubber tapper, he accompanied his father on his daily visits to the trees. When he was fourteen, though, his father passed away. As the eldest of his five siblings, he was quickly thrust into the role of breadwinner for the family. He did what he knew: Ribamar continued to harvest and sell the rubber for another twenty years. But then the market for natural rubber disappeared, he says. "There were no buyers."

So he left the trees, instead cultivating vegetables and fruits on the land by a river and selling them at the local market. That is, until he heard about Veja and met Bia Saldanha, Veja's longtime partner in the Amazon. A designer from Rio de Janeiro who had been experimenting with natural rubber in fashion and accessories, she moved to Rio Branco, a city of four hundred thousand that serves as the western gateway to the Amazon. Saldanha cultivated relationships with the local rubber tappers, bringing business and organization to a seemingly forgotten market.

Ribamar is appreciative. "The Veja project is great," he says. "It's a blessing, actually, because it's saving so many young people from a life of working with cattle, one that relies on chemicals and is unhealthy for them."

Driving into the jungle from Rio Branco, one sees these cattle farms that line the roads. They're hard to miss. Cattle ranching is becoming a tempting option, seeming to offer the prospect of raising more money per acre than is possible with rubber tapping. Ribamar disagrees. "By the time you buy the feed for the animals and all the things that you need to care for them, are you really making more money? I don't think so."

Beyond economics, he says, the weather is changing. "It's become hotter and hotter. If you don't finish working by ten in the morning, you feel your skin burn," he says.

That's why he gets up at four o'clock every morning and spends five to six hours tapping the trees under the shade of the canopy. "When we preserve the rubber tree, we preserve several other trees, plants, animals—all the other living things that are connected to it," he says.

The Amazon is perhaps the only place left where rubber trees grow wild. Veja started buying solely CVP, or *cernambi virgem prensado*, rubber—a term used to describe coagulated latex collected from the forest. Before the advent of CVP, rubber tappers had to collect the rubber when it was still liquid, usually on the same day, in order to produce sheets of latex. With CVP, the rubber tappers can return to the rubber trail after the latex has coagulated, typically two or three days later, which frees up more time for them to do other tasks. Plus, the rubber tree should not be tapped too frequently, so this method saves time and is more efficient. Given the rise of synthetic rubber in the last four decades, Kopp explains, many of these rubber tappers had moved on to other ways of making a living, such as raising cattle and logging. But both ways of life meant eliminating trees, not preserving them. This has implications for the soil, because such activities break up years of untilled soil that has been sequestering carbon.

Veja now sources rubber from nearly 1,200 families in the Amazon. In the past fifteen years, they've purchased 1,928 tons of wild rubber. "Business is not just about selling stuff, but also making people who live in these environments protectors of their land," Kopp says.

What's most noticeable is that these businesses, which are so fixated on restoring lands, protecting green spaces, and enriching the soil, are actually profitable, viable businesses. Veja sells more than two million pairs of shoes a year and pulled in $115 million in 2020—without any advertising.

"Most shoe brands are taking 70 percent of the retail price and putting that to marketing, not manufacturing. We decided to invest that extra money in our supply chain," Kopp says.

And they're not telling people to buy more of their shoes. "Consumption is a big problem in society; that goes back to the heart of so many environmental problems," Kopp acknowledges. "We have some people who loved the shoes, but then buy too many of them. I would say a couple pairs are enough. Too much of anything is a problem for the ecosystem."

LIQUID GOLD EXTRACTED FROM WASTE

Amidst the growing interest in organic products, there's actually not enough organic food and organic cotton in the world to meet demand. Just as Veja has to deal with drought, climate-related problems, and shortages of organic cotton for their shoes, the same can be said of food producers in the United States. Shockingly, despite all the chatter about organic food and its virtues, less than 1 percent of American cropland is farmed organically.[10] California has the most in the country with over four hundred thousand acres of certified organic cropland, about half of which is used for fruits and vegetables.[11] But it's not enough. Consumers want more organic food, so much so that the major food brands are now trying to create incentives for farmers to convert their farmland to organic.

Dan Morash, founder and CEO of California Safe Soil (CSS), can help those farmers looking to transition to organic and rebuild soil health. Recovering unsold food from supermarkets in the Sacramento area, Morash's company is producing a liquid fertilizer, called Harvest-to-Harvest.

In California, a state that feeds so much of America with its produce, soil quality is being depleted, much like elsewhere mainly thanks to large-scale industrial farming with its heavy use of nitrogen. Nitrogen fertilizers, particularly synthetic ones, require more water to neutralize the effect of the nitrogen and ensure that the plant doesn't burn. The runoff carries the excess nitrogen into the water systems. According to researchers at the University of California, Davis, the use of synthetic nitrogen fertilizer has increased an average of 25 percent between 1973 and 2005. Less than half the nitrogen that is used is recovered. An estimated 419,000 tons of nitrogen ends up in the state's groundwater each year. A shocking 88 percent of that nitrogen comes from agriculture. Worst of all, it just stays there, polluting the drinking water of nearby communities.

When Morash markets his product to potential users, he struggles to have conversations with farmers about the nuances of nitrogen pollution of the groundwater. "Most of the time, they just want to know the NPK [nitrogen–phosphorus–potassium] count in my fertilizer, and that's that. We don't always get into the specifics."

But the details are important. Because organic nitrogen, that same UC Davis study explains, can help rebuild soil health. "The natural process is that plants exude sugar. Microorganisms feed off that sugar. And the byproduct of those organisms is nitrogen, which is food then for plants. So all we are doing is feeding soil organisms, and expediting that process," Morash says. "But that's a long story to tell the grower when he just wants to know the amount of nitrogen in your fertilizer compared to what he's using."

More nitrogen, however, is not always better, Morash continues. "Most farmers are using too much fertilizer to start with. Some fertilizer is a good thing—then a lot of fertilizer is a great thing, right? No. The excess just ends up in the water. It's actually a waste of money," he says.

CSS still has to educate farmers that its fertilizer can substitute for an existing fertilizer the farmers are already using—it's not an added cost. In fact, Morash argues, if they're using synthetic nitrogen fertilizers, farmers could see cost savings by shifting to something that works just as effectively but with a smaller dose. Harvest-to-Harvest comes in a liquid form, making application easy: it goes into the drip lines, not requiring any additional labor or infrastructure.

Meanwhile, Harvest-to-Harvest is repurposing a product that otherwise would have been wasted. Grocery stores, Morash says, cannot sell or donate as much as five hundred pounds of perishable food every day, which amounts to approximately 10 percent of their produce, deli, and meats selections (few grocery stores make that data public, so exactly how much is wasted is unknown). At the time of this writing, Kroger is the only national grocery chain to make a commitment to go to zero waste by 2025. What's worse is that all these grocery stores pay to have that food waste collected and removed.

That's where Morash's business plan makes sense and solves a genuine problem. The grocery stores pay CSS to recover the unsold perishable food at a discounted rate when compared to other waste collectors. While it's great PR for the supermarket, for Morash, it's the prime ingredient in his fertilizer, which he can then sell to farmers, encouraging organic farming and rebuilding soil health.

Save Mart Supermarkets, a grocery store chain based in Northern California and Northern Nevada, signed on to the program, which is in use at 72 of their 211 stores. It's a win-win for them and CSS. They get their excess or unwanted food disposed of at a lower cost, and they get to tout their sustainability efforts. The recovered food is transported to CSS's facility, which is located on a former Air Force base north of downtown Sacramento.

This line of work is a far cry from Morash's early days in investment banking and finance. A Yale and Dartmouth graduate, he entered finance after business school, interested in the renewable energy sector. He managed massive funds solely focused on energy. Now, he's standing in a hard hat and jeans on a factory floor, watching waste get pumped into a giant digester and smelling the lovely scent of rotting vegetables and meats. "It's a very simple concept as a business. And it makes complete sense. The execution is a bit tricky," he says.

He's interrupted by the sound of the digester taking in the recovered food. Since Americans refuse to eat misshapen fruit and vegetables, heaps of edible but misfit produce make their way down the conveyor belt along with leftover meat, corn husks, bits of fish, and lots of lettuce. "We get a lot of the outer leaves of lettuce that are peeled off to improve presentation," he says. "People are very particular about the produce they buy."

Enzymes are added to the digester, and on the other end, the liquid is sifted for any leftover particles. Then the excess fat is separated from the fertilizer. Everything, however, is put to use, Morash says. The fat is rendered as oil and can be added to animal feed. In fact, they're looking to add a new product to the lineup: pet food ingredients that are made from the same concoction. Within three hours, the waste has gone from being a smelly mess to ready-to-use fertilizer, which they produce 4,500 gallons of each day. The final product is tested to see whether any pathogens, such as problematic bacteria, could be passed from the waste into the new fertilizers. Studies done at UC Davis and published in a peer-reviewed journal indicated that the process eliminated pathogens, such as salmonella, E. coli, and listeria, leaving "minimal risk."[12]

"From a technology perspective, all the machines we use are 'off the shelf.' While we do have patents on the process, it's not rocket science," Morash jokes.

While it may seem simple to turn unwanted food into fertilizer—almost obvious—it took Morash a decade to get the process to work and be the basis of a profitable venture. And this was not his first attempt. Back in 2008, in Florida, he tried out a similar business concept—"Not a good time to be starting a business," he says. "But we also got lumped into clean tech and biofuel, neither of which we are."

The company tanked, but Morash bounced back in 2011. After returning to his home state of New Jersey, he connected with his brother, David, who lives in San Diego. The two decided to give it another go—this time in California, the state that grows most of the country's produce. "It makes much more sense here than it did in Florida," he says.

From 2012 to 2016, they worked with researchers at UC Davis to do trials and field testing. When they were confident in the fertilizer—that it could stack up to what was on the market at a competitive price—they approached a few retailers to see about buying their excess perishables. Smaller, local retailers like Nugget Markets, a family-run company with about a dozen stores in the area, signed on. As did Save Mart.

But there was another surprise: the Golden 1 Center arena, where the Sacramento Kings play basketball, agreed to work with them as well. When the center opened, in 2016, ownership signed on with CSS to have their food prep waste collected. Leftovers also go to local food banks. The arena, which has focused on reducing its waste, Morash says, made it a priority. Given how much wasted food goes into the trash bin after a basketball game, this was a welcome change.

Since there's no shortage of food waste, sourcing this raw material is the easy part of the business, say Morash. "The harder part is financing such a capital-intensive business. It's not an app. It requires machinery, even if it's not a lot of machinery, space, labor. It's infrastructure," he says.

Morash has raised $20 million from thirty investors, most of whom are high-net-worth individuals and family foundations. He's routinely on the phone talking to potential investors. During our chat, he took two calls from an investor who was looking to close a deal. "Some of these investors have found us on the internet. They tend to be patient investors who understand what we're trying to do here in the long run," he said. "It's much easier, and better, than venture capital."

He also had to figure out which farmers can benefit from the product the most. "For wheat, soy, and corn farmers in the Midwest, the per-acre yield is so low, say $500 an acre, that it's hard to ask them to use our fertilizer instead. The economics are less convincing," he admits.

But in California, he's focused on farms growing vegetables and fruits that can benefit from the added boost. For instance, for a berry farmer, it's vital that he's producing as many berries as possible to ensure that the men and women picking fruit are getting the most out of their time and labor. Additionally, if growers can extend their season for a week or two longer, when the crop price is higher, they can make some more money. "That farmer is more likely to pay for [our fertilizer]," says Morash, "because the return is higher with berries than it is with wheat, soy, or corn."

However, to get through to farmers, he has to go through distributors. Knocking on individual farmers' doors doesn't work: farming has become a consolidated business, and many individual growers themselves sometimes don't make the decisions that affect their farms. The distributors sell more than a hundred products: they're one-stop shops. "They have to believe in the product," Morash says. "So it takes time. Plus, they don't market the product for you. That means you still have to educate the community that's going to use it."

At first Morash thought that he could get supermarkets to influence growers to use his fertilizer. But he soon realized that with the tight profit margins in the grocery business, that's a hard ask. Furthermore, supermarkets and growers may have tense relationships. "It was logical, but as we discovered the nature of that relationship, it didn't make sense," he admits.

Most of his customers are organic growers; few are conventional farmers. The farms that use his fertilizer can be as big as ten thousand acres, though a farmer is likely to try out the product in a small area, check the yield, and then expand use to all of the fields. These farms are located up and down California in the Central Valley, Salinas Valley, Ventura County, and Santa Maria areas. Most of the organic growers are opting out of hydrolyzed fish fertilizer, an industry standard, which he says comes from wild caught fish not suitable for food but still critical to the marine ecosystem, and using organic Harvest-to-Harvest fertilizer instead.

Morash's vision is to take this idea to urban hubs across the United States. Rather than trying to build similar facilities himself around the country, he wants to license the technology to others who are keen to replicate it. "There's no reason why more cities in America that are surrounded by farming communities couldn't have a similar setup, and we can start living in a circular economy, instead of a linear one," he says.

CSS is a small but critical cog in the organic wheel. If organic farming is not made easier, more affordable, and accessible to farmers in the US, it's harder to convert existing systems that were designed for large-scale conventional agriculture to more regenerative ones focused on soil health. What's even more compelling is that Morash is helping to improve soil health by solving another problem: finding a use for essentially a waste product.

That's the creativity of Morash and other entrepreneurs like him. They're finding opportunities in the trash, literally, and making it work across industries: from the grocery store looking to offload unusable food to farmers looking for liquid organic fertilizer to pop into their drip systems.

GRAINS THAT REBUILD SOILS

Just seventy miles up the road from California Safe Soil's Sacramento plant, the Lundberg family has a direct connection to the soil. The third and fourth generations of Lundbergs currently tend to clay soils in Richvale, Northern California, where they grow their Lundberg brand rice. All the family members are descendants of Albert and Frances Lundberg, who came to the region in 1937, driven there by the infamous dust storms in the Midwest. If degraded soils drove Albert and Frances westward, now, their grandchildren have built an organic food brand, expanding on their grandparents' unconventional farming practices.

In the 1910s and 1920s, the demand for wheat went up—it wasn't just from Americans but also from those in Europe fighting World War I. As a result, many farmers in the United States tore into the soils of the Midwest with their plows to produce wheat and corn. In the process of this groundbreaking, millions of acres of native grasslands disappeared, as well as the rich soils on which they grew.

In 1929, when the Great Depression hit, the price for wheat dropped. Cartoons from the time humorously question what the price for wheat would be post-1930, but the wheat crisis was far from a joke. Drought hit the Midwest at the same time. The soils, already dried up and overused, were put under even greater stress. In 1937, Albert and Frances Lundberg, who had experienced enough of the drought and the dust storms that followed it on their Nebraska homestead, decided to go west to look for better soils and irrigation.

With their four young sons and the essentials—a Farmall tractor and a Chevy truck—they left Nebraska for the Sacramento Valley in California. The conditions were better, but the soil in Richvale, California, their new home, presented challenges as well. It was heavy clay soil that was really only suited for one crop: rice. They'd have to go from being corn and cattle ranchers to rice farmers.

When Albert started planting rice on their forty acres, he noticed that every year all the farmers around him burned the rice straw—a byproduct of growing rice that is basically the chaff that results when rice is harvested and the plants are winnowed to separate the rice grains from the straw. But burning this organic matter didn't feel right to Albert. So he took a different approach.

Grant Lundberg, a third-generation family member and former CEO of Lundberg Family Farms, describes his grandfather as quite an outlier in his ideas of farming. "He decided to incorporate the rice straw into the soil. What a crazy idea." Maybe crazy for the time and location, but plowing the rice straw back into the soil was a long-held practice around the globe, where more traditional farming methods were practiced than in the United States.

It turned out that Albert was ahead of his time. "It wouldn't be until 1991 that this practice of burning rice straw was formally prohibited," Grant explains. He's referring to the Connelly-Areias-Chandler Rice Straw Burning Reduction Act of 1991, which phased out rice straw burning in the Sacramento Valley in 1992 (after 2001 it was permitted for disease control under extreme circumstances).

Albert and Frances were indeed unconventional: they started farming in partnership with nature. Their neighbors laughed at their efforts to turn straw into soil, Grant recalls. "It was an added step. And why do it if it's more complicated? The neighbors clearly didn't agree with them. My grandparents were certainly the oddity in the community. They had strong convictions."

But repurposing things was in Albert's DNA. In the 1940s, when resources became scarce due to World War II, Albert made a rice dryer out of recycled tin and wood from local sawmills so that the family could ensure that their harvest, free of moisture, would not spoil.

"They were really practical people," says Grant. "They had a midwestern practicality—they saw all that energy in the crop residue and thought, 'We gotta get that back in the soil.' Grandpa Albert had a motto that we repeat to this day: leave the land better than you found it."

That environmentalism manifested into a multigenerational business. Albert and Frances's children—Eldon, Wendell, Harlan, and Homer—all decided to farm together in partnership after a period of farming independently. "That was an important decision that they chose to work together," Grant emphasizes. "Without their partnership, Lundberg Family Farms wouldn't exist."

In 1969, they started getting serious demand from customers. Health-conscious consumers came asking for organic short-grain brown rice. "At that time, rice was not consumed as brown rice. But this new health-conscious consumer wanted to retain the vitamins and minerals in the bran—the whole food," says Grant. "This signaled the start of a natural food movement: healthy soils, healthy food, healthy people."

One particular company, Chico-San, had asked about 150 farmers in the region to grow organic brown rice for them on a commercial scale. No one said yes—that is, until Chico-San met the Lundbergs, who had already cut down on their use of synthetic inputs and were repurposing materials like the rice straw into the soil. In 1969, the Lundbergs tested the idea on seventy-six acres.

That was the beginning of what is modern-day Lundberg Family Farms, a business that grows, mills, stores, produces, and markets its own rice and rice-based products—all under one roof dressed with solar panels. By 2003, they were doing all this production and offsetting 100 percent of it with wind and solar power through on-site generation and renewable energy credits.

In 2007, in response to the increasing discussion of genetically modified produce, the Lundbergs supported the founding of the Non-GMO Project, whose mission is to ensure that consumers know they are getting a GMO-free product. Lundberg Family Farms also has its own nursery where they breed new varieties of rice and improve them for organic production and keep alive heirloom varieties that are no longer grown in California.

Doing all this has not been easy, Grant admits: "It was not a road of gold. For the first twenty years, we had to learn how to effectively grow organic rice. We reached out to experts like Robert Rodale and other specialists in organic farming."

Even then, he recalls, some of their fields had crop failure after crop failure as they experimented with different organic farming practices. "I don't know how we made it through that time. We learned things from each failure. But it was definitely a struggle."

Nothing, however, could shake their commitment to organic farming. So much so that in 1973, Homer Lundberg joined with fifty-three other organic growers in California to establish California Certified Organic Farmers, the certifying body that today oversees the certification of organic food companies and growers.

Growing rice organically is not a straightforward task, explains Bryce Lundberg, a third-generation family member and the company's vice president for agriculture. There is an art to making sure the weeds do not overpower the rice crop. Two types of weeds plague the fields, grass and aquatic weeds. Grass dies when under water, whereas aquatic weeds thrive in water, so the Lundbergs use water rather than chemicals for weed management. They flood their fields with ten to twelve inches of water to suppress grass weeds. As those dissipate, the aquatic weeds come up. To get rid of the aquatics, they then dry up the fields for about thirty days.

Whereas conventional farmers would keep the rice under four to six inches of water throughout the growing season, coupled with spraying weed killers several times, the Lundbergs take part in this rhythmic dance with nature instead. It's harder, takes more time, and can result in lower yields. "You have to read the leaves, literally," says Bryce. "The leaves of the rice plant will tell you if it's ready for the next step or not. When the fourth leaf emerges, we can drain the fields."

This extra step allows growers to avoid the use of chemicals. As a result, Lundberg pays organic growers 50 percent more on average for their crop, ensuring that there's a financial incentive for them to keep going. Although six thousand acres of land are owned directly by Lundberg family members, the company also leases additional acreage, and buys from about forty organic growers. In any given year, about sixteen thousand acres are farmed organically for the company. By operating at such scale, they truly have the ability to impact topsoil.

"It can take nature up to a thousand years to create one inch of topsoil," say Grant. "That one inch is responsible for ninety-five percent of the food that's consumed by humans. Humans can quickly destroy that with chemicals and industrial farming."

Instead of synthetic fertilizers, the Lundbergs rely on composted manure, often from poultry. That seems to be working. Soil-analysis reports indicate that Lundberg fields have, on average, 5 percent organic matter in their soils, suggesting positive soil health. "Typically, you're looking at anywhere from 3 to 6 percent organic matter. So we're at the top of that range," says Anders, a fourth-generation Lundberg.

Adding this nutrient-dense mixture keeps their soils productive. Cover crops such as oats, vetch, and fava beans are also routinely planted to keep the soils fertile through the winter months, and to reduce exposure to the elements. Legumes like vetch and fava beans are particularly good at replenishing nitrogen in the soils and rebuilding organic matter. "Areas that have had recent cover crops do show higher levels of microbial activity," Anders confirms.

Although Anders has three generations of Lundbergs before him to share their farming know-how and wisdom, he admits they still face challenges. For instance, the dense clay soils of Butte County, where the Lundbergs' farm is located, can make cover-crop rotation hard. "But we think the extra effort with oats, vetch, and fava beans is worth it!"

These seasonal frustrations keep cycling back, despite the Lundbergs' decades of experience in dealing with them. Bryce Lundberg explains that he's been reckoning with a sizable weed population the last two years. "The weeds can adapt. They're quite resilient. We have to keep innovating our farming practices."

"You have to be pretty committed with these risks and variability in organic farming," Grant says. "If you're just in it for the money, you're probably not going to stay in that long. You'll go through an event that'll make you question why you're doing it. The things that last are the things that are valuable."

In 2017, it was estimated that only 1 to 2 percent of the rice grown in the United States was farmed organically, most of it in California and Texas. Growing this market, Grant says, is going to drive organic farming forward. "We [the organic sector] have to keep creating demand. I want to see organic ag be 50 percent of the market in the United States. That's a lot of demand we've got to generate! And [to] do that, we've got to make a case for organic."

The case for organics is not just about increasing sales. The Lundbergs' style of farming has helped bring back biodiversity to a region of California that was losing it. With wetlands disappearing due to development and further cultivation of open spaces, shorebirds, ducks, geese, and cranes now visit the rice fields when they're flooded, taking refuge (and meals) in this chemical-free landscape. Every spring, Bryce explains, before they start their tractors to prep the fields for planting, they scour up to thousands of acres for duck nests, recover the eggs, and relocate them to a hatchery. These ducklings are then raised and released back into the wild. Over the last thirty years, Bryce estimates that they've helped release more than thirty thousand ducklings into the wild by working with local conservationists and the California Waterfowl Association.

"It's all connected. These farming practices say yes to soil health, wildlife, biodiversity," says Grant. "We all win when farms convert to organic. Maybe it's not always perfect. But it's a good start and it's certainly good for our health, the soil, and the planet."

Amid the cornfields of Nebraska, where the Lundbergs once resided, another farming family, the Vetters, decided to go a bit awry with their farming techniques. Situated forty miles from a Monsanto unit and a Syngenta plant, two giants in the world of agrochemicals, the Vetters live and work in the heartland of "Big Ag." But their 280-acre farm is anything but that. As regenerative organic farmers, the Vetters have long practiced some "strange" farming techniques: intercropping, rotating their fields, planting rows of conifer trees, and using seaweed and kelp to fertilize their plants.

"The neighbors thought we were crazy," says David Vetter, a third-generation farmer who grew up in the Corn Belt of America. "My dad and grandfather were always the topic of conversation around here."

In the small town of Marquette, which has just three hundred residents, little remained a secret. If the Vetters had weeds in their fields or had decided to grow something aside from the much-beloved corn, the neighbors shared their opinions openly, David recalls. One year, when his father grew amaranth to add diversity to his farm and explore new crops, some in the community mistook it as pigweed, a weed that most Nebraska corn farmers feared.

The Vetters' neighbors in Hamilton County were more accustomed to using pesticides, fertilizers, and insecticides provided by the chemical giants nearby. But Donald Vetter shunned those potions to create his own—made of natural ingredients like fish emulsion and sea kelp. Everyone thought he had lost it, his son jokes. "The neighbors were not thrilled. They didn't know what it was; some even thought it was poison."

But for Donald Vetter, the true poisons were the chemicals, developed in wartime, that were being repackaged to Midwest farmers as a one-fix solution for weeds and pests. An army veteran, Donald returned home from World War II in 1945. The same chemicals that had been used in the war, nitro and 2,4-D, were now being sold to farmers as weedkiller. He would attend training sessions organized by companies such as Dow Chemical, where he was "educated" on how these chemical killers worked and how they would liberate farmers from the arduous work of weeding and keeping their fields pest-free. But it didn't sit well with him. As someone who had studied biology and understood how biodiversity and microorganisms in the soil contribute to a healthy farm, annihilating living things in the fields with these chemicals didn't seem right.

In 1953, Donald went cold turkey on the nitro and 2,4-D, pursuing organic (and later incorporating elements of biodynamic) farming free of these chemicals. A year before his passing in 2015, at the age of ninety-five, he spoke to filmmaker Bonnie Hawthorne about why he pivoted away from synthetic chemicals. In her film *Dreaming of a Vetter World*, he says he was cultivating corn one day on the farm and thinking about what the chemicals were doing to him and the land: "When you're cultivating corn, you have a lot of time to think about other things too. I just felt this approach cannot be right. When you're spraying on the crops, you can smell it, and you're getting it. And then you're also putting that poison on the soil. What were we doing putting poison on [the soil]? And life in the soil is soaking that up. So I made up my mind I was not going to do this anymore."[13]

David Vetter picked up on his dad's approach to farming and love of nature. He jokes, "I was probably the only kid in junior high reading the *Biodynamics* quarterly." He then pivoted from a career in medicine to get a degree in soil science from the University of Nebraska. In 1960, his father sadly had to quit farming. He contracted malaria while serving in the war and had to deal with the effects, which made it hard for him to do the day-to-day activities on the farm. At that time, the Vetters made the difficult choice to lease out the land to a conventional farmer. But in 1975, David Vetter came back to the family farm after completing his studies. He took over the farm and started steering it back on his father's course: organic and regenerative farming.

When asked how he distinguishes dirt from soil, he says, "I learned in a class in college that soil is what you grow crops in. Dirt is what you find under the bed. I think that sums it up nicely."

In Hamilton County, most of the soil around them was treated like dirt, David says, and was occupied by one or two crops, corn or soybeans. When he took over the farm from his dad, he had to reckon with a big headache: invasive weeds, particularly shattercane and sunflowers, from continuous monocropping, or planting one crop repeatedly.

Weeds are hard to find in the perfectly manicured rows of conventional farms in this region. In fact, weed-free fields are the de facto style of farming. But David isn't interested in such a man-made look. His 280-acre farm is sliced up into smaller 12-acre fields. Grasses and legumes are always growing on the farm, albeit in different locations, to enrich the soils. And the cows are rotated through the farm's pastures on a regular basis to help improve pasture quality and soil health, and to capture carbon.

Until 2019, the Vetters kept bees on the farm, but that year they lost their hives to what Vetter suspects was exposure to a neonicotinoid pesticide called PENNCAP-M. This is not just a recent problem. His brother-in-law Charlie Ponec, the resident beekeeper, had been managing the hives for thirty-five years on the Vetters' farm, and they had endured losses year after year. The bees, David explains, harvest pollen from nearby corn fields that are saturated in PENNCAP-M, then they return to their hive and "feed it to the brood." Even after sample testing showed residue of PENNCAP-M on the Vetter hives, local farmers were reluctant to change their ways. The state insect for Nebraska? Ironically, the honeybee.

Roads are often the main dividers between organic fields and non-organic fields in this region. For insects, they're no problem. But it's the same with herbicides and pesticides. Wind can easily traverse a thirty-foot barrier meant to protect an organic field from a sprayed one.

"Borders or barriers are not effective for preventing insect problems," says Vetter. "They also have marginal effectiveness for most pesticides if they are not correctly applied and cannot prevent drift of volatile pesticides or GMO pollen."

For Vetter, that means extensive testing before he can label his products as "organic."

And that's just the beginning of his frustrations with the current farming system. While he acknowledges the utility of the USDA organic guidelines, he sees them as just a "starting point. There's organic in practice and then there's organic on paper," he says. That organic in practice is not easy to achieve overnight. It takes years of learning and adapting to what nature demands, he argues. "I think most people don't do it because it's more work and it takes more thought."

With soil at the heart of his farm, he spends a lot of time thinking about how to continuously improve the health of this spongy base from which he's grown a profitable business. "I don't understand why anyone would spray glyphosate on the ground. It's an antimicrobial. The whole point is to improve microbial activity in the soil!"

What Vetter has learned in his now forty-five years on his farm is that much of the farmland around them is not used to grow crops for food. In fact, only a small percentage of Nebraska's production is actually used for food. The rest is feed for livestock, ethanol production, and for industry use.

"And we're still importing 50 percent of organic feed for US needs for livestock farming," he adds.

Despite the challenge of changing conventional farming practice, and thinking, Vetter has made a dent in trying to convince fellow Nebraska farmers to adopt organic practices. Over a dozen farms in his area now are organic. Some of them supply their grains to Vetter's other business, Grain Place Foods, a processing business that the Vetters started in 1987 because there were few, if any, options to turn their harvests into marketable food-grade grains, and to create a commercial infrastructure for other farmers in the region who opted for organics. These days, Grain Place Foods processes grains such as wheat and barley every day, along with popcorn and soybeans, giving local famers a place to take their organic crops and develop a local ecosystem for organic processing.

On the Vetter farm, these grains are grown amid pastures of perennial grasses, legumes, hazelnut trees, and pigs and cows that forage in these fields. The farm operates on a nine-year crop-rotation cycle. Although they have completed just two cycles so far, the eighteen years of experience behind them now convinces Vetter that the approach is working: "Our corn is just as tall as our neighbors'. And we're not buying anything to put into the soil."

Even as the farm has suffered through dry spells, Vetter says that their soils, saturated with water, have been able to keep the crops going. It's the same in reverse. In 2019, when Nebraska saw some of its wettest months on record, conventional farms had to reckon with extensive flood damage as water ran off the surface of their soils and formed torrents. The Vetters' soil absorbed the extra water, instead of it resulting in runoff.

Their fields' edges are planted to attract native pollinators, with strips of tall prairie grass and wildflowers for the birds and insects to feed on. The Japanese beetle, a pest that first appeared in the United

States in 1916, is widely seen in the Nebraska plains. Chemicals are one way of dealing with them. But instead, the Vetters let it munch on smartweed, a flowering plant in the buckwheat family. "Weeds do the same job [as pesticides], and don't cost anything," Vetter notes.

Organic, and in this case regenerative organic farming, he says, is actually more profitable, since he no longer has to buy insecticides, herbicides, or additional fertilizers for the farm.

Vetter points to data from nearly twenty years of rotational organic farming on his land to make his case: average net returns were $300 an acre using the organic system. He compared this to Hamilton County data on what other farmers were earning: continuous conventional corn production netted $60 an acre; corn and soybean doubled the return, to $150 an acre, but that is still just half of the organic returns. It's the savings in production costs, Vetter says, that account for these differences. Overall, though, organic net returns were either higher than or equivalent to just farming corn or corn and soybeans for sixteen out of eighteen years.

The key now, he says, is getting more farmers to adopt these practices across the Midwest and, more broadly, in the United States. "I'm always encouraging organic farmers to buy more organic produce for their own families as well. Economics is going to drive this forward, not just values."

Vetter likes to remind listeners, "How your food is produced does matter." Because it can be a win for the farmer, the soil, and the consumer—a somewhat holy trinity that may seem elusive but, Vetter assures us, is quite attainable if the vision is there.

CHAPTER TWO

WASTE

Aiming for Circles, Not Straight Lines

B rianne West, a New Zealand–based entrepreneur, runs a personal-care company, Ethique, which has one simple goal: to eliminate unnecessary product packaging, particular the plastic bits. Frustrated by how much packaging she was throwing in the trash bin every day, she developed shampoos, conditioners, creams, scrubs, and moisturizers in bar form.

"It seems crazy to me that we don't require businesses to be responsible for the entire life cycle of their product," says West. "We need to put the onus back on the company profiting from a product, to ensure that the packaging will not end up suffocating our planet."

She's part of a new breed of entrepreneurs looking at waste in a new way. Trash is no longer someone else's problem. Rather, it's the responsibility of the brand selling the product that comes in the packaging—a facet of the regenerative mindset which is forward-thinking and solutions-oriented.

Packaging is a good place to start solving the problem of trash. But it's just one piece of the larger conversation about waste. As consumers, we produce so much waste, much of it beyond what we physically chuck in the trash bin. Think of the water wasted by making clothes, or the toxic chemicals from that process that enter water systems and pollute drinking water. Think of the growing piles of electronic waste: not only cell phones, but also hair dryers, razors, irons, headphones. Few companies are focused on the durability and longevity of their products. Companies want us to buy them again and again; that is the basis of their business model.

With massive consumption comes a huge amount of waste. On average, Americans waste seventy pounds of textiles each year when they discard used clothing.[1] In 2017, the EPA estimated that Americans accounted for almost 17 million tons of textile waste: the bulk of it, 11.15 million tons, was sent to landfills.

And that's just clothes. Waste is hard to lump together in one category. There are so many different types of trash: plastic, clothing, chemicals, electronics, food . . . the list goes on. They do have one commonality: there's a lot of trash, and waste management systems are struggling to keep up with the load.

Let's begin with plastic pollution, the waste that we see and hear about the most. Plastic is ubiquitous in modern life. So how much plastic waste is actually out there?

According to a study published in the *Journal of Science Advances*, in 1950, we produced 2 million metric tons of plastic. In 2015, that number was up to 322 million.[2] By 2017, humans will have manufactured 8.3 billion metric tons of plastic. The waste is so pervasive that scientists have found a plastic bag in the Mariana Trench, the deepest ocean trench in the world, 36,070 feet below the surface of the Pacific Ocean. Even the scenic mountains of the Swiss Alps—areas that can be reached only on foot—have micro-plastics in the soils.

According to Jenna Jambeck, an associate professor in the College of Engineering at the University of Georgia with a specialty in the study of marine debris, an estimated 5.3 million to 14 million tons are added to oceans each year from coastal areas. But that's only the plastic that ends up in the oceans. *National Geographic* magazine estimated that 448 million tons of plastic are produced every year, 40 percent of which is disposable. In 2017, Coca-Cola reported it produced 128 billion bottles of plastic in one year alone.[3] While it's easy to blame the companies generating the waste, one has to bear in mind that there's a massive demand for these products. Globally, according to *The Guardian* newspaper, consumers are buying 20,000 plastic bottles every second.

Why? One word: convenience.

Some people argue that if it's recyclable, it's sustainable. Not true. Some plastic is recyclable. The issue, however, is that most of it is not being recycled: only 14 percent of the plastic packaging consumed in the world is reused every year. Europeans are better at it than Americans: they recycled 30 percent; Americans recycled only 9 percent since 2012.[4]

Think about the lifespan of plastic. Plastics break down into smaller and smaller particles. They become so small that they're no longer visible to the naked eye, but they don't disappear. That's the problem in our oceans today, as researchers discover that tiny fragments of plastics have created a new type of toxic waste for aquatic life and could potentially pose a threat to humans who consume fish. "Full degradation into carbon dioxide, water, and inorganic molecules is called mineralization," explains the National Oceanic and Atmospheric Administration. "Most commonly used plastics do not mineralize (or go away) in the ocean."[5] Instead, you're left with millions of pieces of microplastics that are less than five millimeters (less than a quarter-inch) long.

Given that plastics do not decompose, it's hard to dispose of them. Unlike compost waste or food matter, which will eventually break down, plastics have to be treated and recycled, or just burned. For years, the United States and other industrialized countries sent their plastic waste to China for recycling. However, China banned the import of much of this waste in 2018.

According to the 2018 *Journal of Science Advances* study cited earlier, China has been importing almost half of the global plastic waste since the early 1990s. The United States was sending China nearly four thousand shipping containers of plastic waste to recycle each day. But as China's economy has grown, along with the global waste problem and awareness of the environmental impact of importing all this trash, the country is saying no to everyone's waste and putting the responsibility on the countries producing the waste to find new solutions.

This decision has created some short-term challenges, as dump sites from London to Oregon have become backed up with recyclables that have nowhere to go. But it may also be a wakeup call and finally help give rise to an innovative new economy focused on re-purposing waste.

But the plastic problem is not just water bottles and single-use plas-tics. As Susan Freinkel writes in her book *Plastic: A Toxic Love Story*, plastic built the modern world; it's vital to health care devices, the pharmaceutical industry, construction materials, and infrastructure.

Plastic is not just the transparent material that encases almost everything we buy. It's also what we wear, sleep on, and cuddle up in. Plastics are in the majority of textiles produced today—and these synthetic fibers break apart in our washing machines, enter local wa-ter systems, and clog the oceans with microfibers.

Fashion is a major polluting industry worldwide. And as is the case with plastic bottles, very little of the textiles used in our clothing is actually recycled or repurposed: only 0.1 percent of the old clothing that is collected is turned into new textile fiber.[6] The EPA reports that it costs cities $45 per ton to dispose of discarded clothing.[7]

The scale of the problem can be overwhelming and hard to quan-tify. Outerknown's CEO, Mark Walker, wrote in a recap of the 2018 Copenhagen Fashion Summit, a gathering for slow-fashion advocates, that he was shocked by the immensity of waste we're creating. "There were a lot of statistics thrown around but there is one that I can't get out of my head: 50 million tons of clothes are produced every year and 87 percent of them will end up incinerated or in a landfill. And our industry [output] is expected to double. That math is 87 million tons per year burned or tossed!"[8]

Much of what we cannot use, donate, or resell in the United States is shipped to Latin America or East Africa, where it's sold in local markets. Many American sizes are too big and the styles unsuitable, so these clothes are eventually burned. To build their own textile in-dustries and reduce the import of secondhand clothes, several East African nations have tried to stop the flow of imported used clothing altogether.[9] Whether or not the ban is instituted, the real question is, Is it right for Europe and the United States to just pass their waste on to other countries?

The first step to regaining balance in this fight against waste is to recycle more, but the ultimate goal is simply to buy less stuff that needs to be thrown away. While it may be fashionable for the main brands to promote recycling programs, the root of the problem is the high speed and high volume of clothes produced every "season" in the fashion industry. Brands such as H&M, Zara, and Forever 21 bring new styles into their stores every week, encouraging a rate of consumption that only adds to this environmental disaster. "Over the past two decades, American consumers have accepted, and benefited from, the race to the bottom in fashion," says Elizabeth Cline, author of *Overdressed: The Shockingly High Cost of Cheap Fashion.*[10]

But our waste goes beyond our closets, bedrooms, and bathrooms to our kitchen and dining table. In a world that is experiencing a population explosion, it seems ridiculous to have food waste while others struggle to get enough to simply survive. Yet food waste has become embedded in our systems. It's not just about throwing out the leftovers, or the odd rotten vegetable. Food systems have become so complex, global, and fast-paced that the food industry itself produces an exorbitant amount of waste, sometimes merely to create a better display. Fruits and vegetables with superficial flaws are referred to as "misfits," too wonky and misshapen for the grocery store displays and picky consumers.

Though these problems of waste appear massive, almost impossible to solve, some entrepreneurs have figured out how to build businesses that rein it in. While it's not going to lead to an overnight cleanup of the planet, some business owners are steering away from waste and instead toward a circular economy—a term made popular by Ellen MacArthur, the fastest woman (to date) to circumnavigate the world in a boat. After she completed her incredible journey, she decided to devote her time—and money—to crafting a new economy, built on ingenuity and waste systems. She founded the Ellen MacArthur Foundation, focused on furthering the idea of the circular economy. The circular economy considers the full life cycle of a product, harkening back to West's position: all businesses should be thinking about the end state of their product, and about packaging.

Ray Anderson of Atlanta-based Interface was one of the first pioneers of this movement, repurposing carpet in the 1990s, and challenging the notion that a petroleum-based product should be thrown out at the end of its life. Since about 2010, there's been a new cohort of brands that are merging their environmental ethics with commerce, as entrepreneurs have started businesses that are based on using waste itself. For instance, Suga Yoga Mats, based in Encinitas, California, takes old wetsuits and gives them a new life as yoga mats. Nomadix, an outdoor brand, specializes in producing a multipurpose towel made out of recycled plastics. Bureo, a sunglasses and skateboard company, works with fishing communities in Chile to collect used, torn fishing nets from the ocean and make them into usable products. They're now transitioning to fabrics as well, transforming the same raw material into textiles suitable for the clothing industry while removing them from the ocean, where they damage wildlife. Singtex, of Taiwan, manufactures fabric out of coffee grounds and recycled plastic.

Some of the change is also coming from industry stalwarts: Dell, for instance, is now incorporating a new technology that captures soot and turns it into ink. The Indian company Chakr Innovation developed the technology that collects soot from exhaust fumes and transforms pollution into printable ink. Countless high street fashion brands have incorporated recycled polyester into their inventory. The next step is to figure out how to truly recycle these materials: both chemical and mechanical recycling companies have cropped up from Sweden to the United States working with large fashion companies to determine how long can we keep recycling a fabric and build a more circular model where materials are being reused multiple times.

It's highly unlikely that humans will stop consuming in the near future, so the solution to the problem of waste lies in smart, moderate consumption and a circular economy that reduces waste outputs and helps restore the balance. The mounds of waste discussed here actually intrigue many entrepreneurs, presenting them with a challenge to see how we can shift the way manufacturing in all industries can put this waste to work. It's as if they're regenerating the waste itself—the thing we would typically categorize as "dead," is somehow being given a new life. Here we meet some of those imaginative reusers of waste.

BOATS OF TRASH, LITERALLY

This company likes to stash trash. Hidden behind Plastic Whale's sleek, modern, canal-facing office space is a room filled with bags of plastic waste. Marius Smit, an Amsterdam native in his late forties, quit a corporate career in marketing to collect trash from Amsterdam's canals.

"My wife thought I was crazy. And perhaps, I was. I had a strategy but no business plan; I just wanted to do something positive for the environment," he says, sitting on a chair made out of discarded plastic bottles retrieved from the canals of Amsterdam.

We're sitting at a boardroom table made primarily from waste plastic from the canals. Inspired by the form of a whale, the table is a sleek dark gray color with soft contours and an inset center, reminiscent of a whale's blowhole as it surfaces. The outer gray surface is made of felt produced from recycled PET; the foam center is also repurposed PET and sustainably sourced birchwood, to provide structure. Across each end, a scrap-metal border reads "This table is made from Amsterdam Canal Plastic." The table was manufactured in the Netherlands, only about three hours from Plastic Whale's offices in Amsterdam, by furniture maker Vepa.

"So many people point at the problem of trash in the canals, but I was interested in finding a solution. I wanted to do something about the plastic soup," Smit says. "Stop Talking, Let's Start Doing" is the company's mantra. This message appears in their offices and is also splashed across their marketing literature—which is all, of course, fashioned out of waste and recycled materials.

In 2011, Smit set out on his quest to find a solution to the problem of plastic pollution—at least the plastic pollution problem in his own backyard of Amsterdam. "I remember calling my mom, dad, my mother-in-law, and telling them that this is happening. What was going to come out of it, I had no idea."

But he was tired of sitting in meetings that accomplished nothing. "I thought I was bad at my job for years because I just wasn't interested. We're all stuck in meetings, brainstorms, but there's an enormous gap in thinking and doing." He was gravitating toward the latter—and quickly. "I thought, if I start doing something, like

creating a challenge that moves people to join me, then this movement of people will come into existence."

That's exactly what he did. He set up a challenge: build a boat
out of plastic waste. He named the project Plastic Whale. Though a
self-proclaimed anti-networker, he was inundated with referrals from
a small community of friends and family in Amsterdam. All these
people were willing to provide their legal, design, manufacturing,
and accounting services for free.

"People want to help. That was the big lesson," he says.

In 2011, after traveling around Holland, building a coalition of
supporters for Plastic Whale, he came back to Amsterdam, where his
friends and new colleagues suggested an afternoon of fishing on the
canals—for plastic.

"I thought, if fifty people show up on ten boats, it'll be a hit,"
he says.

They created posters, devised a social media campaign, and invited residents to join them for "Old-Fashioned Amsterdam Plastic
Fishing" on a Sunday afternoon. A total of 450 people showed up.
The following year, it was 1,200 people on 72 boats. Plastic fishing
became bigger than building the boat itself. The plastic they collect
is stored, cleaned, and reused to make more boats and later on, to
make furniture.

One year into the project, Starbucks's Amsterdam office called and
asked if they could join with Plastic Whale to establish plastic fishing
as a workplace activity for their employees. "I was pretty surprised,
but thrilled as well," Smit says.

That pivoted Plastic Whale into a new direction, a profitable one.
Smit began organizing plastic-fishing excursions for companies; he
charged the companies a fee for the service. In return, he got more
plastic from canals, and soon, enough companies were eager to spon-
sor the building of the boats from recycled plastic.

Looking through the glass walls of his new office with its doorstep
on a canal, Smit points to a small fleet of recycled-plastic boats, all
tattooed with various company logos. Today, Plastic Whale has ten
boats made of plastic waste, which are used to collect more plastic

from the canals. Every day he sends staff, volunteers, and even school kids out on the canals to collect plastic waste.

Initially, Smit had set up the organization as a foundation. "I was being introduced to so many people who wanted to offer their services for free to us in the early days that I set up a foundation, instead of a for-profit company," he explains. "That way I could assure people that the funding would go toward building these boats and collecting more waste, not lining anyone's pockets."

Now, Plastic Whale Foundation is coupled with Plastic Whale, a for-profit company. The latter has multiple revenue streams: providing experiences for companies, Smit's speaking engagements, consultancy work, and the latest, a new line of office products.

The whale-inspired table is the star of this new product line, and Smit hopes that companies that signed up for the plastic-fishing sessions will consider shifting their furniture options to this recycled solution. It's pricey, Smit acknowledges. The boardroom table with eight chairs is approximately $22,000, but that price will come down as volume increases.

They launched with approximately fifteen corporate partners. "The idea is that they'll need other furniture for the office, so the first table set is just a starting point. People are asking, 'Can we just have a few chairs, or this and that?' So we're broadening the portfolio of products."

For instance, the company has added products at lower price points, such as a lamp designed to mimic barnacles on whales; it has a recycled PET felt shade in a heptagon frame and uses LED bulbs. "It's something that we can sell directly to consumers in the retail market, and go beyond the corporate market," Smit says.

All of the items can be repurposed at the end of their life. The modular furniture is built in a manner that it can be disassembled to be reused, or it can be turned into raw materials.

The idea for furniture and the chairs, lamps, and acoustic panels all came out of a lunch session at Plastic Whale. The team was growing, the space at their lunch table was shrinking, and Smit realized that he needed better and more office furniture. "But we were not going to go out and buy something brand new. That wouldn't be us. We thought about secondhand, and then one person pointed to the foam board in the corner of the room," he recalls.

Made from recycled PET, the foam serves as the core of their boats. "Couldn't this same foam board be used to make office furniture?" One of their shareholders loved the concept and introduced Smit to Vepa, a company run by six families in Hoogeveen, in the province of Drenthe, that manufactures furniture.

"I didn't know much about them, going in. But they're from eastern Holland, where they don't talk much, but actually do stuff. They're a flat organization and make quick decisions and they care about similar issues as we do. On top of it, they produce everything in Holland, which is rare these days."

In six months Vepa helped develop the first prototype. Traditionally, it takes them about two years to build a new line; but Smit says he pushed the team to work faster. And he's thrilled with the results.

The company Plastic Whale also gives 5 percent of total turnover to the Plastic Whale Foundation, which funds a school program and circular-economy projects overseas such as SweepSmart, in Bangalore, which helps streamline waste collection so that waste pickers can collect up to five tons of plastics in a day.

"By investing in these local systems," Smit says, "we can help communities make products that are relevant to them, not a whale-inspired boardroom table."

Smit doesn't have all the answers, and he's happy to admit that. He didn't know much about plastics, or furniture, or product design a decade ago when he started to put the pieces together for Plastic Whale. But he argues that the best CEOs are the ones willing to take a risk on the unknown.

"In Dutch society, the focus is on knowing the answers: How are you going to pay the loan back? How are you going to meet these targets in a year?" Smit says, laughing. "I didn't know. I just knew that if you start doing, building out a community, you'll build something. There's no ideal world, but you have to move towards it."

Galahad Clark, of Vivobarefoot, is on the same path. "Let's start the process to making closed-loop products, even if the first few iterations are not fully so," he says while seated at the bar of the King's Cross Hotel in London, wearing one of his own designs. Clark and his cousin Asher Clark run Vivobarefoot, a UK-based shoe company that advocates barefoot design and use of alternative materials. Shoes with barefoot design mimic the feel of walking barefoot with little to no cushioning of the soles. Both Clarks come from seven generations of shoemakers, as descendants of the family that started Clarks Shoes, a brand that's ubiquitous in malls across the United States.

Vivobarefoot has been working on developing shoes made out of recycled plastics and algae—yes, the stuff that's been blooming in bodies of water and causing public health crises.

"We're about five years out from making closed-loop shoes," he says. "But the answer is not just to make more stuff out of recycled stuff, but also to get people to buy stuff that connects them back to being human, and to nature."

Galahad Clark's inspiration to pursue sustainability (though he's not a fan of that word, like many innovative entrepreneurs) comes from John Ehrenfeld, the author of *Sustainability by Design: A Subversive Strategy for Transforming Our Consumer Culture*. "[Ehrenfeld] basically argued that if you're going to produce more crap in the world, it has to help you connect to nature, to humanity itself, and/or raise some serious environmental questions," Clark explains.

Kate Fletcher, Clark's "eco guru," introduced him to Ehrenfeld's writings and works. Fletcher, herself a self-described sustainability expert who specializes in slow fashion—an alternative to fast fashion that's focused on making clothes ethically and with more eco-friendly materials—helped mold Vivobarefoot's mission in the early days, Clark says, drawing heavily on Ehrenfeld's philosophy.

The company looks at waste and sustainability in three ways: wear shoes that bring you physically closer to nature through the barefoot design, opt for repairable long-lasting products, and, where possible, use entirely recyclable or natural compostable materials. Clark wants Vivobarefoot to use 90 percent "regenerative" materials across their product offerings. The end goal is to "create shoes with minimal bio-mechanical interference that allow the foot to do its natural thing. And have minimal impact on the environment," the company website reads. Vivobarefoot also has its own "re-commerce" platform, ReVivo, which offers "renewed and refurbished footwear," to minimize waste.

Simply put, Clark says, "Sustainable shoemaking is barefoot shoemaking."

He doesn't mince words. "The $80 billion athletic footwear industry is a global lie," he says. "We were not meant to stuff our feet into shoes. We are making shoes with narrow toe boxes, but just look at the Chinese who bound their children's feet so that by the time they were sixteen, their feet looked like their shoes. It's bonkers, really."

The problem of waste, he argues, comes from endless marketing to consumers, focused on trends and fashion, and a PR machine on overdrive. "The foot's a damn good kit, developed over millions of years," he adds.

Galahad Clark self-funded Vivobarefoot in 2012 with startup funds of $645,000. By 2013, the company was almost bankrupt. "Bad business decisions, clearly," Clark says. "You don't do these things unless you're slightly naive and overconfident." But he had support from his wife and family to continue. The first shoe that Vivobarefoot debuted was an all-in-one offering with interchangeable soles for different surfaces. "It was like a sofa bed. Not a very good sofa or a bed," he jokes.

Vivobarefoot abandoned the "all-in-one" shoe offering and focused on four more traditional categories: off-road, exercise, everyday, and kids. In 2015, they launched the Eco Suede and Eco Canvas lines, made of materials that used 50 percent recycled PET. Each pair of Eco Suede shoes, Clark says, repurposes about seventeen single-use plastic bottles. And in 2018, they widened the use of recycled materials into eco-mesh linings and the uppers of their Primus and Motus designs.

In 2017, Vivobarefoot had started its journey toward a plant-based shoe, partnering with a Mississippi-based company, Algix, that had created a product called Bloom by repurposing overgrown algae. "For decades, it's been about petrochemicals. But there are other materials out there," Clark says.

The green Croc-like shoes were designed for running long distances and being in water. The foam center was made of an algae-based foam instead of petrochemicals. The algae acts much like a polymer, Clark explains, making the shoes flexible and comfortable. While this was the first plant-based shoe for the company, they've since incorporated algae-bloom foam into other designs, and Algix has been able to share the foam, called Bloom, with other footwear manufacturers.

Eliminating or reusing plastics has become a new challenge for the fashion industry as a whole, not just in footwear. However, to change an industry, a business-to-business model is critical: the designing of items and the manufacturing of goods all has to be done with the intention of reducing waste and exploring more eco-friendly alternatives before the products hit the market. That's how these solutions can be scaled. Relying on recycling systems and municipal infrastructure to repurpose waste is good, but not the answer. While it's nice to see some brands take the lead on using innovative materials and recycled content, how do you move a colossal global industry, like fashion, to adopt these materials?

Go to the manufacturing source.

Patricia Ermecheo, a transplant to Oregon from Miami, lives in a tiny house about thirty minutes outside of Portland, in the Tualatin Valley. She runs Osomtex, a company that recycles textile waste into yarn that's suitable for apparel and footwear.

Ermecheo has been in the business of recycling trash for the past decade. Before launching Osomtex in 2016, she sold unwanted clothing, the leftovers of donated clothing available at Goodwill stores and charity shops, to buyers in Guatemala. She would ship up to four containers a week, each weighing about forty thousand pounds.

"There was a true need for affordable clothing in these countries, and so much clothing in the United States is thrown into landfills. So, we thought it was a good way to repurpose perfectly good clothes," Ermecheo says.

Fast-fashion brands encourage customers to bring back their used clothes to the stores in order to get a discount on new purchases, and customers think that they're doing something positive. Yet the reality is that very little of that clothing is actually being recycled into new garments. What's worse is that a coupon incentive is encouraging people to buy even more clothing.

Ermecheo learned that if someone like her didn't try to repurpose those unwanted clothes, they'd end up in a landfill. "Many people think that if you're donating clothes to a charity shop, then they'll be reused. But there's too much, and not all of it sells. The vast majority actually ends up in landfills. Also, many Americans wear extra-large sizes that don't resonate in developing markets," she says.

Unable to put all the secondhand clothes to use, Ermecheo began thinking about how to break down this clothing and turn it into yarn, ready to be spun into a new garment. That could create more systemic change in the industry.

Ermecheo partnered with some scientists at North Carolina State University to conduct research on the strength of this recycled yarn. Two years of research at NCSU and visiting manufacturers and fashion experts resulted in a new technology that provided a solution, and Ermecheo founded another company, called Novafiber, to employ the new process. She set up a factory in Guatemala, working with her existing contacts. Novafiber breaks down fabrics and upcycles them without the use of chemicals, dyes, or water. "That's really important," she says, "because the dyes and excessive water usage in the fashion industry is just as bad and we didn't want to add to the problem."

Ermecheo took the solution to the marketplace with a simple offering: socks. It was a low-cost, affordable product with just a couple of sizing options, making it a good pilot. The response was positive. They sold more than two thousand socks in a month, and she began thinking about how to scale the model.

"To get the industry to truly change, we have to work with the big brands, and convince them to go circular," she explains. "So I focused on B2B [business to business]." Rather than creating her own line of products, she invested her time in working with established brands that could transform the industry virtually overnight. Though the change didn't happen that quickly, she did find a receptive audience with one of the world's largest sports brands, Nike. For the past two years, Ermecheo has been working with Nike to drive innovation in its sustainable supply chain, and to perfect this upcycled yarn for its products.

In the meantime, she has received recognition from other eco-friendly brands. For instance, in 2018, Stella McCartney, a women's fashion brand focused on sustainability, featured the socks at Fashion Week in Paris. Each guest at the Stella McCartney show was given a custom-made Osom Brand pair of socks in a 100 percent compostable bag.

"It's definitely still the beginning, but we're starting to see more brands take action, and have a hunger for solutions and change," she says.

Ermecheo's focus is on using postconsumer waste, clothes that have already been worn. This is, perhaps, the greatest challenge in recycling clothing because most clothing today is made of a blend of fabrics and fibers. "That makes it hard when you're trying to break it down and reweave into a new thread. These materials have their own properties and cannot be separated so easily when they're woven together," she explains.

Anders Bengs, the Finnish cofounder of Helsinki-based Pure Waste Textiles, knows this firsthand. In 2006 Bengs started a company called Costo with Hannes Bengs and Lauri Köngäs, an accessories label that refashioned waste textiles into hats. The concept was a hit, and as Costo's popularity surged in the Nordic region, Bengs, like Ermecheo, began to think bigger: How do we revolutionize the industry as a whole?

Bengs partnered with a fellow Finn, Jukka Pesola, and an Italian, Maela Mandelli, to start Pure Waste Textiles in 2013. Having seen the amount of fabric wasted on the cutting table in factories, Bengs and his cofounders homed in on textile waste in the manufacturing process, or preconsumer waste. In particular, they started working with cotton, a material that, Bengs says, "takes a hell of a lot of resources to grow and seems like a crime to waste."

In 2016, they built a factory with their Indian partner, Raj Agrawal, in a small village outside of Coimbatore, India. Situated in the heart of the Indian textile industry, they had easy access to the cuttings from the factory floors. "India is a powerhouse when it comes to knitwear, and as a result, they have a lot of the waste as well. About 15 percent of material is wasted in the manufacturing process," he estimates.

With 100 workers, primarily women, the factory gathers all the cotton clippings from nearby factories and sorts them by color, then mechanically breaks them down to individual fibers.

Like Ermecheo, Bengs is focused on repurposing the material in the "cleanest" way possible. "We don't use dyes or chemicals in the process, and the consumption of water is almost zero," he says. The factory runs on 90 percent wind power, with solar panels on the way to make up the last 10 percent.

To make it easy for companies to work with them, Pure Waste Textiles offers finished products, such as T-shirts, sweatshirts, pants, and bags that can be customized with company logos, slogans, and designs. "We do that because we're working with a relatively new type of material, the recycled cotton blends, which some factories may not be as familiar with, or [know] how to work with properly," he explains. It's easier for them to own the whole supply chain, from waste to a finished product. "We don't have investors, shareholders, or any outside voices telling us what to do," Bengs says, "so we've been able to grow this slowly based on our knowledge and values."

The three founders started with $3,500 (€2,500) in 2013. By 2019, they had an annual turnover of $5 million. With some grants from the Finnish government, they've also invested in research and development. Their latest foray is in learning how to better recycle post-consumer textile waste. They're currently testing potential solutions with local universities and research institutes in Finland.

"We'll definitely be able to do it. It just takes a lot of infrastructure, which is what's lacking right now in the industry. So, we need to invest in the machinery and infrastructure to be able to repurpose all kinds of textile waste," Bengs says.

Despite their need for investment capital, they are not interested in receiving capital from institutional investors. "We like our freedom," says Bengs. "It's let us get to where we are today and build a business that's not about making money but about changing the world."

THE WASTE STREAM ITSELF

To reduce the waste stream, using existing materials is important—first, because some of these items are made of polymers and synthetic materials that do not decompose; second, because of the chemical dyes that manufacturers use to color fabrics in specific shades of millennial pink or sky blue. Dyeing fabrics for both industrial and consumer use eats up precious resources, especially water, and leaves behind toxins.

Not just the dyes can be problematic but also the finishes on these clothes that make them soft, water-resistant, and sweat-friendly. All textiles have some pretty dirty secrets, the textile chemist Matthias Foessel tells me.

Dressed in a denim jacket by Nudie Jeans, a Swedish brand that uses organic cotton and promotes heritage-inspired selvedge denim that has not been prewashed, Foessel wears his views these days. But that was not the case nearly three decades ago when he started his career in textiles.

With a master's degree in textile chemistry from Coburg University in Bavaria, Germany, Foessel was prepared for a lifelong career in textile manufacturing. His first job after completing post-grad was at Ciba Specialty Chemicals, a company that operated in more than eighty countries and in almost every industry where a textile would be used: from car seats to baby clothes to shoes to home linens. In 2009, Ciba became a part of BASF, a German chemical company that is one of the largest chemical companies in the world.

After Ciba he went on to work for Huntsman, an American chemical company headquartered in Texas. It was at Huntsman, in 2008, that Foessel started thinking about alternatives to the thousands of chemicals used in the manufacturing process.

"I had to spend time learning about the industry, and its mistakes, before I could wake up to the reality," Foessel admits. "I needed that time to understand that we can do it better. At this point, I had traveled all over the world, been to countless mills. I could have just sailed into an executive position at a chemical company and lived a very cushiony life. But I saw the effect that all this consumerism was having on the planet. And I couldn't turn away from that. So I quit."

Foessel partnered with friends to start a new era in textile chemicals. It was the beginning of Beyond Surface Technologies, or BST. Using their own funds, they set out to create alternatives to some of the commonly used chemicals in the industry. It took them four years to create their first product—and even that happened by accident.

"Everyone thought we were nuts to start a chemical company that was going to be bio-based, and that, too, in Switzerland," Foessel jokes. "We were mad and stupid. That's the truth."

Luckily, they didn't care what everyone thought. Instead, Foessel, with the addition of Mike Rushforth, a Scotsman with a PhD in chemistry, set out to find a replacement for durable water repellent—DWR, as it is routinely called—one of the most commonly used chemical coatings on outdoor apparel. The job of DWR is to keep you dry when it's wet outside. It does this with the use of chemicals. DWR, until recently, was made with a long-chain (C8) fluorocarbon, but the byproducts of this chemical are toxic and, when mixed with water, can easily end up in the environment.

"After three years of working on different chemistries for DWR, we dropped water on a sample and it absorbed [the water], instead of repelling it," Foessel says. Instead of creating a bio-based alternative to DWR, BST developed the exact opposite, a substance that causes wicking. "Thankfully, we didn't give up. We just kept going with it," Foessel continues, laughing.

Though they didn't find the solution to DWR, in 2015 they did create their first product, bioWick. Outdoor and athletic wear needs to have effective wicking properties, so that when a person sweats, the fabric picks up the liquid and disperses it quickly throughout the material, allowing it to evaporate.

The BST team, based in Basel, did not have the travel budget to market their product to clients. So they reached out to Adidas, a significant name in sports, and conveniently headquartered just a few hours away in Herzogenaurach, near Nuremberg, Bavaria. That year Adidas did a trial run of the bioWick finish on the jerseys for the German World Cup football (soccer) team. If the professionals didn't notice the difference between the bio-based and the chemical-based finishes, BST had a winner.

"We knew we had to create a product that wasn't just about being bio, or natural—it had to perform. And this was the test," Foessel says.

The feedback from Adidas was positive. BST's bio-Wick performed on par with the synthetic concoction. Three years in, BST had a client. Adidas adopted the product for its global football collection in 2015.

"Our solution is 99 percent bio-based. While it's not 100 percent, because we have less than 1 percent of synthetics, it's a serious upgrade from the industry standard, which can be as low as 0 percent [bio-based]," Foessel says.

The chemical waste and carbon footprint from bioWick, as a result, is one-ninth that of conventional DWR. In a life-cycle analysis, BST's vegetable-oil-based bioWick was put up against the traditional petroleum-based wicking concoction; bioWick came in at 2.4 versus 23.4 for the latter (in the units used to measure carbon footprint).

BST aims to make a dent in petroleum usage by the industry: the textile industry uses ninety-eight million tons of nonrenewable resources, including oil, every year.[11] Textile production pollutes water systems; 20 percent of industrial water pollution is attributable to the dyeing and treatment of textiles.[12] BST can tackle both by going bio: the water has fewer, if any, pollutants, and the finishes themselves are largely biodegradable and petroleum-free.

With Adidas on board, BST had established that they can compete with existing industry players and work in big volumes. That goes back to BST's team, which consisted of industry veterans with established networks, and a recognition that to succeed, the product had to be on par with or better than the options currently on the market.

Since 2015, BST has developed some more bio-based alternatives. DWR is still only partially bio-based, Foessel says. "It's better, about 53 percent bio-based, but we're still working on it."

He acknowledges that four bio-based alternatives are a good start but nothing compared to the dozens at his previous job. Although BST is only twelve years old, Foessel expects that product development will go faster than it did during the first three years. "I sure hope that it doesn't take us three years to develop a single product," he says. "But we're learning quickly, and I think we'll be able to iterate faster going forward."

While their emphasis thus far has been on developing bio-based coatings for synthetic and conventional fibers, even materials like organic cotton can be coated in synthetic chemicals for their finishing, which Foessel is keen to highlight: "It doesn't stop at the fiber. And the industry needs to appreciate that. It goes further, and it gets complex."

In addition to Adidas, BST's client base includes some mainstream brands such as Levi's and Tommy Hilfiger, and BST's bio-based products have been used on one hundred million pieces of clothing (annualized) thus far. Surprisingly, approximately 10 percent of that total comes from Tchibo, a German coffee company that also has a chain of cafés throughout the country, for which BST produces merchandise periodically. "What I love about working with them is that it shows that this is not an upscale solution. They're a very mass-market brand. If they can do it, why are you not doing it?" Foessel asks of other brands.

Cost-wise, he notes, bioWick is comparable to industry standards. "After having spent two decades in mills and dye houses," he says, "I knew that I had to make a product that would be just as good and as inexpensive as what the market was using. So there are absolutely no excuses not to convert over."

THROWING A PARTY WITH WASTE

While we've discussed mostly waste in the fashion world, the problem extends into so many other industries, including something we consume even more frequently: food. Given the resources required to grow our food, it's a sad reality that Americans waste 150,000 tons of food every day. It's not just an American problem; as food has become cheaper and more abundant, it has become a global problem. According to the UN Food and Agriculture Organization, one-third of the food produced in the world (for humans) is wasted each year. That adds up to 1.3 billion tons.[13] Yet, just as with footwear and apparel, there's an opportunity to look at this waste with new eyes. That's what one UK company did.

"The alternative to food waste is delicious. It's beer," says Rob Wilson at Toast Ale. "We're not interested in preaching or being righteous. We just focus on making—and yes, it's made from surplus fresh bread that would have been chucked in a bin."

In 2016, Wilson was honeymooning his way through Africa, visiting social entrepreneurs in about a dozen countries across the continent. "It wasn't the average honeymoon, that's for sure," he jokes over a cup of English breakfast tea at London's Kings Cross railway station.

But Wilson had always been interested in how business could be a force for change. He cataloged the stories of the people and entrepreneurs he met into a book self-published in 2012, *On the Up: Inspirational Stories of Social Entrepreneurs Transforming Africa.* Although the focus of the book was not food waste, or beer, writing it cemented Wilson's desire to create a career in which he could work for some larger purpose. When he returned to the United Kingdom, he went knocking on the door of Ashoka, a nonprofit that helps social entrepreneurs around the world scale their ideas.

"I thought they might want to use the book in some capacity," he says.

Instead, he ended up with a job as entrepreneur in residence at Ashoka. Shortly thereafter, when the CEO left, Wilson rose to that position and served as the organization's director for nearly five years. But inside he was eager to dive in and build a business, not just support other entrepreneurs.

Fortuitously, he met Tristram Stuart, a UK-based Ashoka fellow who had been working as a food-waste activist for the previous fifteen years. Stuart had recently tasted a delicious beer in Brussels called Babylone, named after the first-discovered recipe for beer, which dated back four thousand years to the days of Babylon. One of the primary ingredients in the ancient recipe was bread. In fact, bread was used to make beer up until about 1800. Bread provided the starch that would break down into sugars and then ferment into alcohol. "Eventually," Wilson explains, "it became cheaper and easier to just use 100 percent barley or grain directly. But bread historically used to be a key part of the beer recipe."

Surplus bread was easy for Stuart and Wilson to source, given that the United Kingdom has an obsession with sandwiches. From sit-down restaurants to grocery stores to even drugstores such as Boots, take-away sandwiches are always available.

But the hidden reality of all those sandwiches is that there's wasted bread, particularly the end pieces that are too crusty for the perfect sandwich in a British to-go box. According to Toast Ale, 44 percent of bread produced in the United Kingdom is wasted, half of it at home and half of it by retailers and manufacturers. Stuart knew this wasted bread could be a valuable input for a beer business. He went about building a team to create a social enterprise from this idea and invited Wilson to lead it as "chief toaster," or CEO. The duo turned to one of the sandwich manufacturers responsible for mass-producing these easy meals.

Adelie Foods produces three million products in a week. In one of their factories, located in Middlesborough, just sixty miles from the brewery in Yorkshire that Toast Ale was using as a source, on the production line is an employee whose sole responsibility is to pluck off the end pieces of a bread loaf and toss them into a bin.

"Think about that. We're not even talking about day-old bread. This is stuff that just doesn't fit the parameters of what's a sellable sandwich. Yet it's fresh bread," says Wilson. "I mean, this is just ridiculous."

Luckily, nearby is Wold Top Yorkshire Brewery, a family-run operation started by farmers who are as concerned about the flora and fauna on their fields as they are about their brew. Wilson and Stuart put Adelie and the brewery together. "It was an easy case of connecting the dots. And we happened to find one of the most eco-friendly breweries in the same region."

To make Toast Ale's beer, Wold Top Yorkshire Brewery takes the bread from Adelie Foods and substitutes it for one-third of the malted barley in their recipe. The result has been award-winning: at the International Beer Challenge in 2017, Toast Ale's IPA won the Silver Tasting Award in its category.

Even though it's an appreciated recipe, Wilson is not interested in keeping it under wraps. Rather, the company's recipes are accessible to anyone at their website.[14] "The point is to replicate this around the world to eliminate bread waste. So why would we keep it a secret?" In fact, the recipe has been downloaded more than fifty thousand times, Wilson says. "We cannot be everywhere, and we certainly don't want to be shipping our beer from the United Kingdom around the world. That wouldn't work well, given the environmental footprint [of transportation]. So, the solution to scale is to help others do something similar in their respective countries and connect brewers to bakeries."

Toast Ale is just as concerned with other inputs needed to produce their product. For instance, the brewery in Yorkshire relies on two wind turbines to generate power. The barley comes from the surrounding fields and the water comes from a borehole on the brewery property. The hops are repurposed as mulch in the garden. And the spent grains—basically leftover malt, which is the largest-volume by-product of an average brewery—are used by a local farmer as food for his cows. The only other output from the brewing process, water, is filtered through reed beds back into the farmland.

Within two years, Toast Ale had gone from a concept to a reality in supermarkets across the United Kingdom, and major retailers such as Tesco and Waitrose were stocking Toast Ale. In 2017, the company decided to make a foray into the American market—bearing in mind that Americans produce the most food waste in the world. Toast Ale launched in New York City, but instead of selling the beer produced in the Yorkshire brewery, they partnered with Captain Lawrence Brewing Co., a microbrewery in Hudson Valley, north of New York City, to produce a local line. The bread was sourced from a local bakery in New York City.

Toast Ale has expanded into six markets: the United Kingdom, the United States, South Africa, Brazil, Ireland, and Iceland. Ultimately, they want to build a platform and a franchise model, called ToastX, that will help more local entrepreneurs replicate their success.

"We're trying to show that there's some serious gaps in the way we operate today. We ought to be thinking about how we use resources better. We are passionate about driving forward the growing circular-economy movement and proving that exceptional products can be born from what was previously discarded as waste," Wilson says.

The company's profits, after paying its staff of twenty and operating costs, go to a nonprofit, Feedback, which focuses on reducing food waste. Plus, Wilson likes to point out, they've "saved" over 2.5 million slices of bread, which if stacked up they estimate would be three times the height of Mt. Everest—no small feat.

"The bottom line is that to change the world, you have to throw a better party than those destroying it," Wilson says. "Beer brings a whole new crowd on board that would have perhaps previously turned their back on social enterprise, calling it a world of 'do-gooders.'"

Cheers to that.

Waste is not someone else's headache. It's an opportunity to transform: from boats to beer. Even in the most challenging of industries, where change has been slow, some entrepreneurs are questioning the way things were done to make way for more cyclical models of business.

CHAPTER THREE

SUPPLY CHAINS

Valuing the Source

So far most of the examples have been about bringing about environmental change—looking after the soil, repurposing waste, transforming industries to be more aware of their imprint on the planet. That's all well and good. But building a regenerative business model is about more than reducing one's environmental footprint: we need some tweaks in how we do business with other humans. The next two chapters are devoted to that—one looks at how our supply chains can be more people-friendly and the other, at how workplaces can break down hierarchies.

At the end of the day, people are vital in a business's long-term success. If people don't feel looked after, heard, or included, what's their incentive to strive for a company's mission?

One way to ensure that people are being looked after is the B Corp certification, which was started in 2006 and is designed to embed a company's ethical values into its structure and operations. B Lab, the organization offering the certification, looks closely at how a company treats its people and at inclusivity—there are approximately 150 questions that businesses are assessed on to achieve certification. And each year, B Lab runs an Inclusive Economy Challenge: How can your company become more inclusive and thus promote an inclusive economy?

But what, actually, does "inclusivity" mean? Inclusivity, diversity, and respect for employees have become a growing concern—and have acquired new buzzword status. The B Corporation certification defines an inclusive economy as one that "creates opportunity for all people of all backgrounds and experiences to live with dignity, to support themselves and their families, and to help their communities thrive."

Much of the dialogue in the United States has been about workplace culture, work-life balance, and profit sharing. But it's not enough to just focus on the people who work at corporate headquarters. There are the millions of people who allow supply chains to run seamlessly, and many of them are farmers. Much of the world's food is still grown on small farms, not giant monolithic industrial swaths of land.

That's why the businesses in this chapter are looking at inclusivity in their supply chains. Not because suppliers are targets of charity, but because inclusivity builds more resilient supply chains, which in turn support business, which then allows producer groups to flourish and buyers to receive higher-quality products.

Fundamentally, farmers are not just suppliers. They hold very key roles as stewards of the land (if we want to invest in our open spaces, forests, and biodiversity); as promoters of peace (without access to markets, crime and black market operations become more tempting); and as purveyors of indigenous knowledge—which can be as powerful and useful as modern technology.

If one adopts the philosophy that trade-not-aid can develop communities and reduce economic differences, then current supply chain structures do not go far enough. Yes, more companies are adopting sustainability and fair-trade standards, but are they giving members of their supply chain a seat at the board table or equity in the company? The development community has long suffered from a "savior" complex: wealthier individuals donate their time and service to improve the lives of the impoverished. Could business be making the same mistake?

The inequality between the buyers and the producers is evident. Despite globalization, which was initially thought of as an equalizing force that would bring opportunity to all, inequity persists. One World Bank report states that "global wealth grew 66 percent from 1995 to 2014 . . . but inequality was substantial, as wealth per capita in high-income Organization for Economic Cooperation and

Development (OECD) countries was fifty-two times greater than in low-income countries."[1]

Taking into account this growing inequity, the United Nations has set forth the ambitious goal of eradicating poverty by 2030. To inch closer to that goal, or even come somewhere near it, the people making what we wear and eat must be given a bigger chunk of the profits. Much like how we think about profit sharing in companies here in the US, supply chains have to be a bigger part of the equation.

For companies sourcing agricultural products, increasing inclusivity presents a real opportunity. According to the 2017 report of the UN's Food and Agriculture Organization, *The State of Food and Agriculture 2017*, there are five hundred million smallholder farmers in the world, constituting 85 percent of the total population of farmers. They own on average less than two hectares (five acres) each. However, they lack resources. The report states: "They do not have the same technical capacities or access to resources, such as new technologies. This steep international market competition would ultimately lead to the exclusion of smallholder farmers."

Investing in smallholder farmers is vital for two reasons. First, despite wealthier nations' love for industrialized farming, smallholder farmers still feed much of the world. Second, they have the ability to reverse some of the damage caused by climate change. But to prevent further ecological and environmental damage, these farmers need resources and know-how to revitalize depleted soils and preserve wild habitats. If they're strapped for cash, they're less likely to think about long-term gains, and more likely to resort to short-term measures.

Bad roads, weak air-travel links, limited technology, and little working capital have kept smallholder farmers from improving their farming practices and increasing their annual earnings. Yet, as the report goes on to say, "a major force behind inclusive rural transformation will be the increasing demand coming from urban food markets, which consume up to 70 percent of the food supply even in countries with large rural populations."

This demand creates an opportunity for companies to tackle growth in a slow, steady, healthy manner by forming alliances with the farmers in their supply chains. Rather than concentrating all the profits at headquarters, they can share these earnings with the people on the front lines and have a positive social and environmental upstream impact.

Barb Stegemann, who has worked with farmers in Afghanistan, says it boils down to one word: dignity. "Everyone deserves dignity and fair wages for a day's work. If we would give that to someone in our company offices, why would we not treat someone halfway around the world like that?"

Dignity—the B Corp definition of an inclusive economy includes this word: "An inclusive economy is one that creates opportunity for all people of all backgrounds and experiences to live with dignity, to support themselves and their families, and to make a contribution to their communities."[2]

Falcon Coffees, Cafédirect, The 7 Virtues, and Loving Earth, the four companies discussed in this chapter, are businesses that are rethinking their supply chains. The first two are coffee-based businesses; The 7 Virtues produces scents; and Loving Earth is a socially responsible confection company.

The coffee industry is an ideal case study on inclusion. According to the 2018 Coffee Barometer report co-produced by the Dutch aid organization Hivos, coffee production has been growing by more than 20 percent since 2010. And the bulk of that coffee is produced by smallholder farmers: twenty to twenty-five million smallholder farmers produce 70 percent of the world's coffee.[3]

But there's a huge problem. Sjoerd Panhuysen, the report's coauthor, writes: "The coffee harvest . . . depends on millions of farmworkers, an important but invisible group of stakeholders. They remain largely voiceless in the discussions about a sustainable coffee sector."

Obviously, being voiceless prevents being included. These farmers are vital and will only become more important as coffee consumption continues to increase: experts estimate that by 2050, the coffee sector will need three hundred million sacks of coffee annually—at least double, if not triple, the current production.[4] The challenge will be to meet this demand without causing more environmental damage and while promoting fair pricing for the commodity.

Falcon Coffees, a coffee trading company based in the UK, argues for a collaborative supply chain, where the producer receives a fair share of the profits and is treated as an asset and an investment, not merely a supplier. Cafédirect gives producers a share of the business and representation on the board; 5 percent of the company is owned by the farmers who grow and harvest tea and coffee for the company around the world. Konrad Brits, the founder of Falcon Coffees, says, "This needs to move beyond feel-good stories of buying from coffee farmers, to treating everyone in the supply chain in the same fair manner. It's not about rich buyers helping poor farmers. It's about rebuilding an agricultural supply chain with prices based on the value that the individual, or provider, brings." And in coffee, poverty is front and center, Brits says. "Decisions are made [by farmers] based on daily survival, not the long-term health of societies or ecosystems. Yet, these farmers occupy vast tracts of arable land, in and around tropical rainforests, drawing water from rivers, streams, and aquifers. Thus, influencing the management of these global resources is defined by how we buy, what we pay, and how we sell."

Commodity prices, he says, often operate at an artificially low price. Coffee pricing needs to go beyond just the standard cost of the commodity to determine the "true cost" of growing coffee. That more accurate price would include externalities such as the cost of soil and water pollution, as well as insurance and social security for farmers.

Despite the demand for coffee increasing year after year, world coffee export prices have actually dropped by two-thirds in real terms since the 1980s, according to Panhuysen's report.[5] Consequently, through the intricacies of coffee pricing, the real earnings of a coffee farmer have been halved over the last four decades. It's become such an issue with youth in coffee-growing regions, such as East Africa, that they now equate coffee with poverty, not opportunity. If the youth leave farms for the cities, that will have negative environmental and social impacts.

The farmers who are growing more coffee to meet global demand are doing it at the expense of biodiversity. New coffee crop lands in Vietnam, Indonesia, Ethiopia, and Peru are created by deforestation.

According to the Hivos report, "Forests are converted into lightly shaded or full-sun coffee production systems with few or no trees. The annual increase [in acreage] is likely to be well over 100,000 hectares [247,000 acres]."[6]

That's why supply chains need to be more than just a transactional equation. For five years, Charlie Habegger worked as a green coffee buyer for Blue Bottle Coffee, a popular third-wave coffee brand that started in the San Francisco Bay area but now buys more than forty tons of green coffee a year for its stores around the world and its online business. Habegger echoes Brits's concerns regarding the status of farmers who supply the raw product: "We have to decommoditize coffee and develop a more nuanced real price that reflects all the social and environmental factors that go into producing coffee."

Even with all this foreboding news of the coffee industry, there is hope that things can be turned around by looking at the supply chain as a long-term investment and partner on the path to sustainability. Brits, for example, has addressed four critical issues through his trading model: increasing transparency in the multilayered coffee industry; getting farmers the tools they need to grow beans with more regenerative farming practices; paying them more for a better quality of coffee; and last, finding sources of capital for coffee growers who may be otherwise deemed a risky investment.

Concern with suppliers and their communities is not confined to the coffee sector. The 7 Virtues, a fragrance company, works with agricultural communities that have been deemed too risky to do business with because of political instability. The 7 Virtues uses their business as a catalyst for peace; instead of waiting for stability before making an investment, the company is attempting to flip the equation by asking the question, "Can business dollars bring stability, jobs, and alternative income sources to violent communities?"

Loving Earth, a confections company, focuses on weaving indigenous populations into its workforce. As development has spread, indigenous groups have retreated farther and farther away from the expanding urban environment. But with limited economic opportunities, how do they keep their way of life and, with it, their knowledge of the natural world alive?

Given the different industries that these businesses operate in, the leaders of each company must think about the social and environmental issues that affect their farmers and suppliers. But the underlying thread is the same: going beyond a transactional relationship to one of partnership.

THE NEW MIDDLEMEN

Konrad Brits is a coffee trader. He's a middleman. Most businesses these days are interested in eliminating middlemen because they're seen as excess, the fat that adds dollars to the final price, and a possible source of corruption. However, Brits is a trader who is obsessed with traceability and transparency, and most of his energy is focused on the collective whole. In Brits's case, that's smallholder coffee farmers. "Coffee is just the vehicle," he says. "But it's about people. It's always been about people. We just have to decommoditize the product to reveal the people behind it. If we want to have these supply chains in the future, we need to take care of the people who make them happen."

A native of South Africa who grew up during the days of apartheid, Brits is very conscious of inequities in society. At seventeen he was conscripted in the South African military as an infantry officer and was posted to Northern Namibia on the Angola border. This was 1987. Angolans were fighting a civil war that had been going on for the previous decade and would continue until 2002. "I realized things were not right. The system was broken. Yet, I had been apathetic until then. I had not taken action. I felt like a pariah," he says.

After returning from the war, Brits delved into coffee. "I quickly saw that this was a product that was sourced from poor countries but sold to rich ones. Yet the farmers were not fully benefiting from this exchange."

From his base in South Africa, Brits worked as a coffee broker and trader, importing coffees from around the world into his home country. His work eventually homed in on four countries: Zimbabwe, Angola, Congo, and Zambia. But in the early 1990s, when he began his career, he didn't know that it would meet with failure before seeing success.

After trying to run a successful export business in these countries and failing each time due to local politics and global market forces that changed the dynamics in each scenario, Brits was feeling deflated. "Here I was contemplating building a business that was also oriented toward social impact, yet I was being destroyed by corrupt politics, poor infrastructure, and the economics of a global market that was just interested in money."

In 2007, Brits read Paul Collier's *The Bottom Billion: Why the Poorest Countries Are Failing and What Can Be Done About It*, a book that explains why some countries struggle to develop economically. The book eventually became a must-read in the development community. Collier argues that certain countries face "poverty traps," which keep their people locked in the so-called bottom billion. The reasons for these traps include bad governance (either in conflict or just post-conflict status); being landlocked with poor neighbors (lack of access to shipping limits exports); and control of the nation's mineral wealth by an elite minority (nations are prevented from diversifying their economies, feeding conflict and exacerbating the poverty trap). All of the four countries that Brits had been working in had one or more of these traits.

Brits realized that many coffee-growing countries near the equator have these characteristics. Most of these countries—Nicaragua, Congo, Rwanda, Kenya, Colombia—had dealt with violent periods, fractured societies, and periods of poor governance. When he started comparing World Bank data that ranks countries based on wealth, to the roster of coffee-growing countries, the challenge became even more evident: twenty-one of the thirty poorest countries in the world grow and export coffee.

"Think about how business works. If you're coming from a background where you don't have access to education or credit, and are residing in a broken system, it makes for a very predatory and one-sided relationship. So how do we create a working relationship that's more equitable?" Brits asks.

Armed with this knowledge, and the experience gained in several failed past attempts, Brits launched Falcon Coffees in 2008. He didn't just want to treat his employees well; he wanted to treat the entire coffee supply chain with equal and fair practices. He coined a term to describe his vision: "the collaborative supply chain."

The model relies on working in partnership with a variety of entities to come up with a more equitable supply chain. Falcon brings together impact investors, NGOs, producer groups, and roasters. While it may seem counterintuitive to involve more players to streamline a supply chain, Brits's intentions with each party are clear: they have to contribute to the long-term health and vitality of the farms—and the farmers.

While certifications help, Brits argues that they don't go far enough. They're good PR and easily convey a positive message to consumers, but they're not the best way to ensure traceability and equity in a supply chain. In 2015, only about 15 percent of the coffee supply was certified by one of the five main organizations: Fairtrade Labeling Organization, Organic, Rainforest Alliance, UTZ Certified, and 4C Association.[7]

"There's still a lot of box-ticking and greenwashing going on in the world," Brits says. Falcon wanted to challenge that system, and Brits found a few early adopters. During his days in South Africa, Brits had worked with some clients who were a part of that group. Taylors of Harrogate, a Yorkshire-based tea and coffee brand, for instance, has been sourcing coffee from Brits for over twenty years. They had a team of auditors who visited each supplier, he says; they were scrutinizing the process before it became fashionable to do so.

In the past decade, Brits has put his approach of a collaborative supply chain into action. Today, Falcon works with more than five hundred coffee roasters and sources from many countries: over 70 percent of its coffee comes from Nicaragua, Ethiopia, Peru, Uganda, Rwanda, and Honduras, and it is actively expanding activities in other countries, like Colombia and the Democratic Republic of the Congo.

"To not build ethical sourcing into the DNA of your business is delayed commercial suicide," he says. "Consumers are going to demand it more and more. And as technologies become more elaborate, transparency is going to be the only way to go forward. It's also the only way to actually address environmental challenges."

Brits argues that poverty prevents sustainable practices: because farmers do not have the money, knowledge, and connectivity to markets, they're less inclined or able to invest in the health of their crop and the soil in which it grows. "We need our farmers to be commercially viable business partners who view farming coffee as a means to improve the quality of their lives, not impoverished beneficiaries of unsustainable handouts, dependent on our welfare. Therefore, working toward sustainability is not about social justice or taking the moral high ground; it is about investing in the economics of coffee because it makes good business sense," he says.

Falcon's sister company in Rwanda, the Rwanda Trading Company (RTC), brings the collaborative supply chain to life using new communications technology. Since 2009, RTC has relied on texting and mobile phones to build a traceable supply chain and work directly with thirty thousand farmers on agronomy training. By using mobile phones to track deliveries from farmers digitally, each bag of coffee can be traced back to the farmer and the lot of land it would have been grown on. As a result, RTC can provide details to a roaster about the transaction, the amount paid to the farmer, and the farming practices used.

Matt Smith splits his time between being a director of RTC and managing Falcon's East Africa supply chain. He explains the process: each processing station, where beans are washed, is associated with anywhere from seven hundred to three thousand farmers. Washing stations can be quite far for farmers to reach, so RTC has set up collection points at nearer locations. Here, using SMS (short message texting) or an Android app, RTC agents enter the individual ID of the farmer, the amount of coffee collected, and how much is paid. This information is sent to headquarters and added to the database. Farmers are asked to keep their receipts, and at the end of the year, RTC offers bonuses, if possible. The cash tends to come at times when farmers are cash-strapped and that, Brits adds, creates loyalty and a sense of community.

Simultaneously, farmers participate in agronomy training for two years, consisting of twenty classes. The training educates them on farming practices such as mulching, water management, and soil health.

"The value of this training is not isolated to coffee," Smith says. "[RTC helps] farmers grow the yield of their fruit and vegetables as well, thereby improving their food security. But for farmers who think that a coffee tree can be neglected for nine months of the year and then give them a great return during harvest—we're trying to change that behavior."

The agronomy training is incentivized: farmers earn a gold, silver, or bronze rating based on their success in adopting the new practices. This merit system allows for such rural communities, many with high rates of illiteracy, to easily understand how they're performing and who to turn to for advice within their own communities. RTC received a grant of $2.5 million from the Mastercard Foundation Fund for Rural Prosperity to expand their operations in Rwanda and replicate the system in Uganda.

In Rwanda, the model is working, Smith says: farmers' yields have increased by 149 percent since they started the program in 2013. That translates to an 86 percent rise in their income from growing coffee. Falcon and RTC have embedded another incentive in the business to promote environmental stewardship, alleviate poverty, and raise farmers' profits: they reward their coffee growers for producing a high-quality crop. Once the coffee is sold to the roaster, the farmer may receive a second payment, Smith says. After the final selling price of that coffee is determined, RTC sees if a premium was paid by the buyer. If so, the producer receives 50 percent of the premium.

This is a step in solving the biggest problem in the coffee industry: there are far too many players who eat away at profit margins while adding no immediate value to the quality of the coffee or to the farmer as the first link in the supply chain. RTC saw this firsthand when they began working in Bukavu, in the Democratic Republic of the Congo. "We were shocked by how poorly the supply chains operated there," Smith says.

RTC tackled the problem by streamlining the process: farmers in the region were invited to join cooperatives that would then send the coffee to a miller. From the mill, the coffee would be ready for export. As a result, they consolidated many steps into three.

Last, RTC instituted the second-payment approach, incentivizing farmers to grow a better quality coffee. As a result, Smith says, between 2013 and 2014, household income for the 4,200 farmers affected by the change in business practices increased threefold.

The process creates incentives for both the farmers and the exporter. RTC creates a mutually beneficial supply chain. A similar model has been implemented in new locations, such as Peru—one of the largest coffee-producing countries in the world (particularly for Arabica coffee)—and Uganda, located in Falcon's specialty: East Africa. At the other end of the supply chain, Falcon's client list is a mix of mass-market brands and third-wave roasters, all seeking traceable beans. The company has supplied Stumptown Coffee Roasters, Blue Bottle, Starbucks, and Allegro Whole Foods, to name a few.

"This is the only way that our supply chains will survive—if we start investing in the people as much as we do the end product," Brits says.

But to do so, Falcon had to figure out a missing component: financing. Producer groups need working capital to purchase coffee at harvest, yet local banks have tight rules on collateral and are risk-averse. So Brits identified finance partners who would be willing to take on that risk, assuring them that the supply chain would not suffer due to a lack of capital. One such source of finance was a Swiss asset manager, responsAbility, which focuses on investments in emerging markets. They came on board in 2013, and as of 2018 they had provided $15 million in flexible loans to coffee-farming supply chains through Falcon Coffees. These flexible loans, backed up by sales contracts, make it possible to work in communities where capital is limited, Brits says. "By always paying on time, we also create trust, ensuring [farmers] that we'll be buying their coffee for the long term. We do our part, if they do theirs."

Brits sums up the Falcon model as consisting of four core components: First, every part of the supply chain is profitable, not just to one trader or the buyer. Second, the costs are understood clearly. Third, the full value of the product is determined. Fourth, profits are shared equitably, based on the value each party creates in the supply chain.

Habegger, the green coffee buyer with Blue Bottle Coffee, has seen Falcon and RTC evolve as companies in the last decade. He started buying their Rwanda coffee in 2007.

"Middlemen are integral for a company like us who focus on high-quality and micro-lot coffees. We cannot manage so many supply chains ourselves. That's why our relationship with RTC and Falcon is essential," he acknowledges.

Habegger says that Falcon and RTC are standouts. Since 2010 their growth has been exceptional. That's because they have the financing in order, which is essential. It's not sexy, not something that people generally talk about, but it makes the whole process [work]."

Blue Bottle pays a premium price for their coffees. That premium, combined with the premiums paid by many of Falcon's and RTC's other clients, has been able to pay for the salary of an agronomist in Rwanda. The agronomist "helps the coffee farmers improve quality, increase yield, and production value. It was my initiative, but it wouldn't be possible without RTC and Falcon's support. It's a great example of what it takes for buyers to be on the right side of coffee, instead of the wrong side."

The additional investment from Blue Bottle creates a win-win scenario: Blue Bottle gets a better coffee, the supply chain is supported with smart agricultural practices, and farmers produce the best quality product possible. "We are a growing company, so we will definitely need more coffee," he adds.

Christy Thorns, the buyer for Allegro Coffee Company, has been in the industry for more than two decades, purchasing for the Colorado-based brand, which was later acquired by Whole Foods. Thorns started buying from Falcon around 2008, she recalls, and has stuck with them since, making Falcon one of their biggest suppliers. "It's hard to find people in business who are not motivated by profit. And the coffee supply chain needs a lot of support and help. Few suppliers at the time were doing what Falcon was," she says.

Thorns receives spreadsheets from Falcon that show the details of the supply chain: costs and pricing are clearly laid out. "And there's the trust factor," Thorns says. "Konrad's a decent human, and that shows."

Despite the accolades they've received for creating transparency in a difficult supply chain, Smith and Brits are not done yet. They want to apply this model of traceability to other agricultural products and commodities.

The British coffee brand Cafédirect is a more mass-market brand than Blue Bottle; it is sold in grocery stores across the UK. Their model offers another alternative to inclusivity: giving farmers a stake in the business and a voice on the board. The world of coffee, chocolate, and tea has countless brands that are trying to do the "right" thing by investing in certifications, sourcing as closely to the source as possible, and thinking about the long-term impact on their supply chain. Fundamentally, there is no one answer—just a multitude of solutions all aiming for a similar endpoint: making global capitalism a bit more equitable.

I first came across Cafédirect through their tea. Traveling in Kenya, I met Sylvia Ng'engo, the Africa program director for Producers Direct, an independent nonprofit that runs Cafédirect's agricultural programming on the African continent.

"It's the most unique governance structure I've seen in tea and coffee," she says. Representing over six hundred thousand farmers in Africa and South America, Producers Direct is a standalone producer-owned and -managed charity. Cafédirect's shareholders are the public, the farmers themselves, and socially conscious investors. The private entity in the UK works alongside the standalone charity to carry out its vision.

Cafédirect's origins go back to the fair-trade movement. In 1991, a group of organizations—Oxfam, Traidcraft, Equal Exchange, and Twin Trading—joined forces to create Cafédirect, a fair-trade coffee company. Each organization brought something unique to the table: Oxfam had a network of shops and campaigning prowess to bring fair-trade issues to the public; Twin Trading managed the coffee supply chain; Traidcraft was already importing coffee and tea into the United Kingdom; and Equal Exchange is one of the oldest fair-trade companies in the United States.

As a result, Cafédirect brought the first fair-trade coffee into the UK market. The company's intention from day one was to marry commerce with social impact, something that John Steel, CEO of Cafédirect, wants to take further. "There's a lot of smoke and mirrors in the industry. I would like to encourage people to publish real pricing, all the way back to the farms," he says. But this kind of transparency can be tricky, disclosing a roaster's profit margins.

For Cafédirect, the organizational structure of the company has been an important way to respect the thousands of smallholder farmers that enable their business to exist. Despite being the most crucial ingredient in getting quality coffee to the market, these smallholder farmers are not typically involved in the organizational structures of the companies they supply. Cafédirect enables farmers to have a piece of the pie. Cafédirect Private Limited, the cooperative of growers, owns about 5 percent of the shares of the UK company, Cafédirect. "Though a minority shareholder, it's a step up from many companies where engagement with farmers ends in the supply chain," Steel says.

"Our purpose is not to make the owners or founders rich, or sell the brand to some other global player," he says. "We were set up to really help the farmers."

Since the farmers are also on the board, cooperative representatives routinely attend investor meetings, which the company has posted online for transparency. In fact, the producers are on the boards of both the for-profit company and the separate nonprofit entity, Producers Direct.

Sold widely in grocery stores like Sainsbury's, Waitrose, and Tesco in the United Kingdom, as well as online, Cafédirect is not a third-wave roaster. They want to bring an ethical coffee product to the general public at a competitive price to show that this model can work at scale. Despite the company going through some tough times financially, with sales dropping and debt rising, Steel has been able to steer it back toward profitability and even offer small dividends to shareholders.

Cafédirect presents a new way to think about structuring a business that's dependent on its supply chain: 60 percent of the shares are owned by individuals who purchased those shares through an equity crowdfunding campaign, 5 percent are owned by the producers, and the remainder by impact investors such as Oikocredit, which has the largest block of shares held by a single entity, 20 percent.

In 2009, Cafédirect set up Producers Direct, a completely independent charity led by farmers, for farmers. Producers Direct is not a part of the coffee brand, as would be the case with a traditional corporate social responsibility program. Instead, the majority of Producers Direct board members are smallholder producer representatives, and program delivery is led primarily by inspiring farmer leaders within the farming communities where Producers Direct works.

Steel explains: "We set up Producers Direct to be independent and standalone. Its articles of association and governance are such that we are totally strategically aligned. Philosophically, we did it this way to have the greatest engagement, ownership, and ultimately, impact with our producers."

Producers Direct, while classified as a nonprofit, works more like a social enterprise. With an annual budget of $500,000, Ng'engo tells me, their goal is to fortify and support these supply chains in coffee and tea. That translates into farming workshops and helping farmers diversify their crops, to increase soil health and to have a variety of income streams.

"We had some farmers who were plucking tea prematurely simply to make money. The more tea they plucked, the more they could make. But it was not ready to be harvested," she explains.

To stop this, they encouraged farmers to think beyond tea and coffee. In Uganda, where banana wine is a common drink, the nonprofit is helping farmers sell this local concoction. Elsewhere, it's honey. To have a variety of income streams without having to rely just on foreign buyers, she says, is better for the farm: it relieves some of the pressure from one product and ensures that the farmer will be earning throughout the year, not just during the harvest season of one crop.

In 2018, Cafédirect became the United Kingdom's first coffee company to be B Corp–certified. While certainly not perfect, as Steel freely admits, the model presents another lens on equity in the supply chain: Can inclusivity mean literally giving farmers a seat at the table? Even if it's a symbolic first step, it's an invite that could have a lasting effect and provoke change down the road. It also shows that the regenerative approach to business is not a standard formula; what works for one may not for another. But the mindset and end goals are the same: a search for truth, equity, and a respect for humanity.

SCENTS OF WAR

At fifty, Barb Stegemann is a force of nature—and not fearful of big challenges. She chose to create a supply chain out of Afghanistan (prior to the Taliban's return). It was a risky move, but she was determined to change the trajectory of a few farmers through her business. "We were running a social enterprise, building a clean beauty brand, and being mission-driven before these terms even became a thing," she says.

It's true. Stegemann started The 7 Virtues, a Canadian perfume company that sources its ingredients from conflict-ridden communities of the world in 2010, self-published a book on leading a purpose-driven life, then landed a deal on Canada's *Dragon's Den* TV show (similar to the TV program *Shark Tank*), sold more than one hundred thousand bottles of perfume, and got her brand on the shelves of Sephora stores in the United States and Canada.

Brett Wilson, one of the "dragons" on *Dragon's Den*, immediately offered her $75,000 for 15 percent equity in her company, and soon became her mentor and business advisor. He jokingly says, "Barb has been talking since she came out of the womb. When I meet with her, I have to hit myself with a heavy dose of caffeine beforehand and plan for a nap afterwards."

He decided to back Stegemann because of her company's unique mission and ability to marry profit with purpose—something that is rarely seen on *Dragon's Den*, where the focus is on sales and returns for investors, not social or environmental impact.

Stegemann's The 7 Virtues was born out of dire circumstances. Trevor Greene, a friend from Stegemann's college days, had been serving in the Canadian military in Kandahar, Afghanistan, when he was attacked by the Taliban. Greene and his colleagues had traveled to a small village on the fringes of the Pakistan border. They were meeting with village leaders—a routine task to develop a better understanding of what they could provide to local families. Trying to foster friendship, the men had rested their weapons in front of them and Greene even removed his helmet. Out of nowhere, a man snuck up from behind and struck Greene in the head with an ax, severely damaging his skull. Gunfire broke out. Greene was rushed back to base camp for emergency medical treatment.

When Greene returned to Canada, Stegemann was deeply disturbed by what had happened to her friend. He had a severe brain injury and would never walk again; it was a miracle that he had survived the attack at all.

"I knew I wanted to do something to help keep his vision alive and help the people of Afghanistan. I realized, as did Trevor, that jobs were the answer. Here was a country where the women were beaten, treated horribly, and married off for money. Because people need work, and enough [money] to take care of their families," she explains.

That's why so many farmers there have turned to growing poppies for opium; it's lucrative, adding up to $3 billion a year to the country's economy.[8] "But it also brought in gun culture, addiction, the Taliban, and so many negative forces," Stegemann says.

Unfortunately, the economics outweigh all these risks. In 2008, a UN report indicated that Afghanistan produced 90 percent of the world's opium, and the bulk of it could be found on the black market.[9] When Stegemann became familiar with the issue in 2007, 193,000 hectares (477,000 acres) had been cultivated with opium poppies. Ten years later, in 2017, it had increased to 328,000 hectares (811,000 acres).[10]

Afghanistan is the leading poppy producer globally, and it also has the highest addiction rate in the world. Afghanistan's opium crop was valued at $4.1 billion to $6.6 billion in 2017; that's about a quarter of the country's GDP (estimates range from 20 to 32 percent).[11] Despite efforts by the government to give farmers seeds for wheat and urea for fertilizer, farmers are sticking to poppy because it fetches more per acre.

But there is hope in the midst of all this conflict. Stegemann discovered Abdullah Arsala, a farmer and distiller who was turning roses and orange blossoms into essential oils in Jalalabad. He explained that farmers turn to poppies because they're guaranteed pay every year during the harvest. In contrast, new rose bushes need three years before they can be harvested, and for orange blossoms, it's five years before a newly planted tree can provide enough blossoms. Poppy sap, however, can be harvested every year.

Indeed, poppies are easier to farm, and in purely financial terms are a smart business investment. The UN survey found that Afghan farmers earned a combined $1.4 billion directly from growing poppies. That's 30 percent of the value of the legal Afghan agricultural sector. However, the report goes on to say that the opiate economy engulfs local villagers as well as the farmers, and it invites violence and trouble.[12]

The lack of a diversified economy has created a culture of violence, Stegemann says. "[Greene] was attacked by an impoverished young man who was paid off to attack a soldier. Some people are so poor and hungry, they are desperate."

Outside Arsala's distillery is a sign that reads "No Weapons Beyond This Point." His plea for peace was not heard, though. Warlords burned his house, some of his orchards, and killed family members of the farmers who work with him. Yet instead of being devastated and giving up, he wrote to Stegemann, saying that he would rebuild. What troubled him the most were the lives lost.

In 2009, Stegemann, a single mother with limited savings, decided to buy a liter of Arsala's rose oil. It cost $5,000. The oil then had to make the dangerous journey from Jalalabad to Kabul before being shipped to Canada. "This is the hardest part of working with a risky supply chain. It's not easy. This is a road with IEDs, mines," she says. "There may be disruptions. But you have to be patient."

Luckily, the oil arrived intact. Stegemann then invested in the bottles, the formulations, and the packaging to launch a business. She had spent $20,000—all charged to her credit card. But within eight weeks, she had sold $30,000 worth of fragrances and was standing in front of Brett Wilson on *Dragon's Den.*

"I knew we had a business then. I had never believed in charity. I grew up poor, on welfare, and in one of the least-developed parts of Canada. I didn't want handouts. I wanted dignity. I wanted opportunity, and fair pay for a day's work. That's what this business was giving to the farmers in Afghanistan."

Supply chains, she argues, are not meant to be one-sided relationships and simply transactional. "They need to provide dignity," she emphasizes.

With Wilson's help, the business grew, and Stegemann started hearing from suppliers around the world, trying to use business as a pathway to peace. "I call it 'retail activism,' and I've been saying for years that we need a business cavalry to come in and create markets where our leaders have failed us. That's the assured way to end conflict, not war."

A few years later, she journeyed to Rwanda to meet with the Ikirezi group, a social enterprise of farmers growing plants and herbs for essential oils. Rwanda, a post-conflict society that suffered through a genocide of nearly one million people, offered a glimpse of what Afghanistan could look like twenty years in the future, if given the opportunity to rebuild.

In Rwanda, women are the backbone of the economy. During the 1994 genocide, many of them were raped, and thus today struggle with sexual diseases and HIV. Others are orphans who were children during the genocide and are now adults, seeking work, education, and financial independence. These women work as smallholder farmers, working on two-acre plots of land. While Rwanda is known for its coffee, the Ikirezi group is offering another alternative to farmers: patchouli. Not all of Rwanda is suited for coffee, which grows better at altitude. For those who reside at lower elevations, plants whose flowers and other parts can be distilled for essential oils are a better choice.

Patchouli, in particular, is a safe bet because with its musky, earthy smell it is widely used in the fragrance industry. And the bush can be grown easily in hot weather. One of The 7 Virtues' scents, Patchouli Citrus, highlights this smell. It gives the company a stronger, less floral scent that can also be marketed to men.

In 2014, CPL Aromas, a UK-based fragrance company, became aware of Stegemann's work. They contacted her to learn more about her unique supply chain. Since their first interaction, the fragrance house has become an important partner in her business. CPL helped The 7 Virtues rebrand for a younger audience.

But they've also been instrumental in helping Stegemann source ingredients from more social projects around the world. It's been a two-way street: Stegemann shared her unique suppliers with CPL, which the British company is now looking to support. They are especially interested in the Ikirezi group's patchouli, she says. "They're looking to purchase nearly three million dollars of patchouli. They are the beginning of the business cavalry that I was looking for, because the bigger companies need to source from these folks, not just me."

The 7 Virtues itself has been steadily expanding, working with essential oil producers in Israel, Haiti, Iran, and India. "I did not plan for it to become so big, but once the story spread about Afghanistan, I started learning about other communities facing similar circumstances, and seeking business opportunities."

In August 2018, The 7 Virtues products debuted in Sephora stores across the United States. "Sephora in Canada became a great cheerleader for the business and advised me on all the stuff I didn't know how to do: marketing to younger brands, retail, distribution," the founder explains.

For Stegemann, Sephora's support—which came through an accelerator competition for up-and-coming beauty brands—has pushed the company onto a growth path. "I can now finally pay my investor, and moreover, the idea is finally being accepted more widely," she says.

For her first supplier, Arsala, the business with Stegemann led to new ventures. His distillery had doubled in size. He had his own perfume line, called Orzala Perfumes, and had opened a retail shop in Kabul where he sold olive oil and other agricultural products. "He is inspiring to all of us," Stegemann says.

But since the return of the Taliban in 2021, that has changed. And for Arsala to do what he loves—grow these intoxicating florals for their scents—he had to flee the country. Stegemann continues to work with him and is hopeful that he can start a new life in a nearby country, replicating much of his success. Asked if she sees this as a defeat by the very conflict she was hoping to reverse, her answer is an emphatic no. "We were not unsuccessful. We gave farmers for more than a decade a market to sell their oils and that had a ripple effect on their families, children, and neighbors. In those lives, we definitely created a change, and we'll continue to do that—even if it means from a different border crossing. We cannot stop, we will not stop."

THE MOST BALANCED CHOCOLATE

Bringing business to the remote corners of the world, and to indigenous populations that have been detached from global markets, is also Scott Fry's passion. He sees an opportunity to give work to those who live so deeply entrenched in nature and are warriors against extractive industries, like logging. Instead of rose petals, Fry favors Peruvian cacao for his company: Criollo ("native") cacao, which in the long term is more resistant to disease and grows better in the shade of a lush, diverse canopy than the more common cacao.

Its sale enables the indigenous Asháninka community to make a living, while protecting the forest it inhabits. The business model literally has the concept of regeneration built into it. Fry's approach to working so directly with indigenous communities illustrates a desire to transform supply chains, much like the previous examples. For him, it's not just about a chocolate bar but about an understanding that we procure this ingredient from delicate ecosystems. How can he, as an entrepreneur, design a people-friendly cacao supply chain?

The cacao comes from such a remote location in Peru, embedded in the jungles along the Ene River, that even he struggles to get to it on his routine visits to the region. "Last time I went, it was so wet and the rains were too heavy," he says. "I had to settle for the banks of the Ene River where it's collected by the Asháninka cooperative, Kemito Ene."

When not visiting indigenous communities for ingredients, he resides in Melbourne, Australia, the city where he started his plant-based confections business, Loving Earth, in 2007. In 2000, at the age of thirty-one, Fry met fellow Aussie and future business partner Martha Butler while living in India, outside of Mumbai. He would wake up each day at 3 a.m. to practice meditation and study yoga.

He also started learning about the work of Adivasi rice farmers. The term "Adivasi" refers to India's or, more broadly, South Asia's indigenous population, who make up about 8 percent (approximately 104 million people) of the total population of the Indian subcontinent.[13]

In Maharashtra, where Fry was based for eight years, he saw the pull of modernity on the indigenous communities; they were growing rice with fertilizers, but the local market price for the rice barely covered the cost of the inputs. They needed to earn more money to survive. Owing to their vulnerable situation, when they were offered a relatively significant amount of cash for their topsoil by builders from Mumbai, these farmers sold the topsoil to make bricks. This left them with a short-term gain but no long-term livelihood. Once all the topsoil was sold to make bricks, they would be forced to sell their land, Fry explains.

This was Fry's first foray into the tenuous reality between financial struggles, land rights, and preserving a traditional way of life.

After India, Fry and Butler spent three years in Mexico, where he worked with several large indigenous cooperatives. All of these experiences were adding up, giving him the foundation—and the confidence—to launch Loving Earth.

Sourcing from indigenous communities is no easy feat. Recently, Kemito Ene lost $25,000 on a single order when some bandits in the Peruvian jungle held up the team carrying the cash from the bank to pay for a load of Criollo cacao. "These things happen, what do you do?" Fry says. "Law and order can be a bit tricky in such environments. But we've spent years cultivating a relationship with these farmers. They're not going to just drop the ball because of one incident."

The farmers Fry is referring to are members of the Asháninka community in Peru. He spent five years getting to know this indigenous group before going into business with them. "If they were just a supplier to me, I would not have spent so much time on it. But for me, I needed to know that there was local leadership who wanted to improve the economics of their community and be in this for the long haul," he explains.

In 2007, back in Melbourne, when Fry and Butler started Loving Earth, they had one focus: source as many ingredients as possible from indigenous communities and make a health food brand in Australia that was centered around chocolate.

"I realized that if these communities wanted to survive the onslaught of the modern world, they needed to commercialize their products, primarily agricultural products, but they needed to do it in a way that also respected their way of life," he says.

The Asháninka present an interesting case study, because of their precarious position. They reside in the Ene River Valley, an area that has the world's largest production of coca—the raw material for cocaine—and where logging, milling, and Andean migrant farmers are infringing on their land and way of life.

The Asháninka "have been traumatized," he tells me. "Over the last couple decades, they have been sandwiched between the narcos and the government paramilitary. You see airstrips amidst the green. Some of them belong to narcos; some are paramilitary. When you go up the river, you are stopped multiple times in the canoes. Everything is checked by the paramilitary. Some of the Asháninka have been enslaved in camps by the Sendero Luminoso [a Maoist group], who have morphed into narcos."

This is not an easy environment to source from, but that's why Fry is determined to do it. Not only do the Asháninka produce a pure cacao, which he argues is better than the hybridized version that's become more popular in Latin America, but the Asháninka have a lot to benefit from participating in this global trade. "This community has low literacy rates, little education, no land rights till fifteen years ago, and limited medical care," he says. "They were struggling. They need money for some basics, even if they're choosing to live off their ancestral land."

Until customers like Fry came along, as well as the Rainforest Foundation UK, which has been working with the Asháninka since the 1990s, these indigenous communities would settle for what local traders offered for their cacao. "It's like how people would trade three hundred years ago when the Spanish first came through. If they are the custodians to the forests and the jungles, and on the buffer zone between pillaging forces and preservation, we have to empower them to make smarter trade [deals]," he says.

Fry offered to pay a premium to the Asháninka cooperative Kemito Ene for their Criollo cacao: about $2.60 per kilo (2.2 pounds). Currently, Loving Earth buys ninety to one hundred tons of cacao per year. They also offer a contract with the cooperative for the year, assuring the farmers that they'll have a customer when the pods are ready for harvest. "We pay them. We don't tell them what to do with the money. They manage it. They're not selling us a commodity, but a branded story that we then share with consumers through marketing and packaging," Fry says.

The aim of that brand story, according to Fry, is to help the cooperative gain access to more clients—and that is the ultimate goal. "We set the prices at a premium, and so anyone else has to pay those prices as well. So, we know that they're going to be getting a fair price. Otherwise, they can sell to us."

Loving Earth sources several other ingredients from indigenous communities: for example, the *gubinge* plums from the Nyul Nyul community in the Kimberley region of Western Australia and agave from Ixmiquilpan in Mexico.

Fry discovered the gubinge, serendipitously, in Australia itself; gubinge, a sour, tart green plum also known as the Kakadu plum, has a high concentration of vitamin C and grows in the arid landscape of Western Australia. Here, says Fry, aboriginal culture, traditions, and way of life have survived—although they are challenged daily by poverty, substance abuse, and mining. Bruno Dann is an elder who is a member of the Stolen Generation (children who were forcibly removed by the government from their Aboriginal parents). Using Broome, a city on the Western Australia coast, as a base, Dann facilitates the collection of gubinge from December through March when the plant bears fruit. More than one hundred families of the Nyul Nyul community harvest the gubinge.

When Loving Earth started working with the community in 2011, they paid about $30,000 for the gubinge harvest. In 2015, the company had spent just shy of $250,000 in Kimberley for this raw material. In Peru, Loving Earth has been incrementally increasing its purchases from the Asháninka community: in 2015, it was ten tons of cacao for $50,000; in 2016, forty tons; in 2017, sixty tons; and in 2018, ninety tons, adding up to $500,000.

Fry is keen on these markets where communication, infrastructure, and access have historically been limited. "It's a very simple model. But it requires time. It's not the kind of business that happens overnight and you can see change rapidly. Where there is local leadership, and a willingness to improve, and engage, then only can we enter that market."

For a company that started out of Fry's apartment—where he would hand-wrap each chocolate bar and use a bakery during their off-hours—Loving Earth has grown significantly in the last decade. They have expanded into new markets such as the UK with their offering of healthy chocolates while producing more than 2.5 million bars of chocolate annually.

"We aspire to be a model. We just demonstrate how it's done: use compostable packaging, renewable energy in manufacturing, work with indigenous populations, push for regenerative farming. But we recognize that it's not feasible for us to be everywhere or be a big multinational. We'd like to see companies take from our model and emulate it," Fry says.

However, there's still one missing element, he says: capital and finance for agricultural investment. So, Fry, in partnership with the Rainforest Foundation UK, is developing a $3 million "climate-smart" agricultural bond that's focused on aligning the three areas he knows best: indigenous communities, regenerative agriculture, and environmental challenges. "These three issues are common across the tropical zones in Africa, Asia, and South America. And in the Ene River Basin, where we work, the main driver of deforestation is agriculture. The indigenous communities are our allies in stopping this trend," he explains.

Kemito Ene is at the heart of the bond: an association of three hundred Asháninka cacao and coffee producers in the region who have been working with the Rainforest Foundation UK and Loving Earth to improve their yields and the quality of cacao and coffee for over a decade.

"Since the United Nations has been talking about inclusive finance, and finance makes an appearance in the SDGs [the UN's sustainable development goals], this is not a small, isolated issue," Fry says. "We want to show that it can work in one region and then provide a model for replication."

It works like this: The UN Common Fund for Commodities serves as an investor that provides upfront capital to the implementers, such as the Kemito Ene and Rainforest Foundation UK. The activities are verified and audited, and if results meet outlined expectations, Good Energies, a Swiss-based climate solutions foundation, pays the investors. Similar models with social impact goals have already been in effect in the United States for nearly a decade.

"It's not very risky. Loving Earth as a company has already shown that the model works. But to scale it, we need more financiers," Fry states.

They've already put in $100,000 to do a pilot phase, and each sum of capital will be released on the basis of meeting benchmarks. "It's not as if all three million dollars will be handed over all at once," says Fry. "We have to show results."

It's a model focused on the improvement of the supply chain and the ecosystem that the supply chain depends on. It means not only a more resilient source of cacao for Loving Earth, as the company expands beyond Australia but also an opportunity for the Asháninka to diversify beyond Loving Earth. Currently the company buys most of what the Asháninka produce, 90 to 100 tons of cacao annually. The goal is to increase that yield to 250 tons and open it up to more global buyers at the premium prices already established by Loving Earth.

The bond has another added feature: buying cacao from the bond fund implementers directly supports an ambitious project to save one hundred million trees from deforestation.

Of the Asháninka, Fry says, "They really are not just suppliers. They are the answer to keeping the balance between people and the land."

CHAPTER FOUR

WORKFORCE

Building a People-First Company

Putting people first in a business also pertains to our everyday workplaces here in the United States. After seeing headlines of company executives making exponentially more than employees, of workers struggling with rising living costs, and a general sense of indifference to the daily grind and increasing burnout workers experience, it's obvious that businesses need to pay attention to what's happening within the office itself more closely. In this chapter I delve into different ways that companies have broadened their understanding of worker engagement: either by giving them a slice of the pie, by tapping into underserved communities for employees, or by breaking down the hierarchy (and its inequities) between boss and employee. It suggests an evolution in the workplace and in our understanding of how capitalism can operate, extending beyond the elite few to serve a wider community. It's merely a start, I would say. But after a pandemic when burnout became all too commonplace, there's been a renewed focus on how to make work more humane for all. In 2018, US senator Elizabeth Warren, of Massachusetts, proposed a new piece of legislation, the Accountable Capitalism Act. It builds on the groundwork laid by the benefit corporation, a type of corporation that requires companies to report their social and environmental impact as well as sales and growth.

Similarly, the Accountable Capitalism Act would require any company with more than $1 billion in revenue to become federally chartered and develop a model akin to the benefit corporation. As of

August 2018, the benefit corporation was already available in thirty-four states across the United States.

Warren's appeal for change came on the heels of data indicating that most Americans earn a tiny fraction of what upper management makes, creating a divide that fosters inequality and frustration. In 2018, for the first time, all publicly traded companies had to report management's salaries to the Securities and Exchange Commission, including that of their CEO. The results were pretty sad: McDonald's CEO earned $21.8 million—3,101 times the median pay of the company's employees. VF Corporation, a North Carolina–based clothing conglomerate known for brands such as JanSport, Kipling, Timberland, Dickies, Lee Jeans, and Reef, paid its CEO $13,736,655—1,351 times the company's median salary.[1]

These comparisons are not perfect—they include part-time workers and international employees—but the essence of the problem is obvious: top management is earning exponentially more than the people in their workforce. Yet it's both the boss and the worker who make a company successful.

US investors have been fixated on growth, pushing companies to scale and yield dividends. As a result, the US economy, at approximately $23 trillion GDP in 2021, is the world's largest by that measure.[2] But according to the World Economic Forum's Inclusive Development Index, the United States has the highest level of economic inequality among the advanced economies of Europe, Australia, Japan, and Canada, ranking twenty-third out of the twenty-nine countries on the Inclusive Development Index and has the highest poverty rate, 16.3 percent, of any advanced country. Being the largest economy does not translate to inclusivity or equity.

That divide continues to be exacerbated by class and geography. A study by the Hamilton Project at the Brookings Institution looked at how income inequality manifests across the United States, paying attention to specific regions and their economic performance from 1960 to 2016. Although the richer and poorer areas were developing parity with each other, in 1980 that started to change with their economic performance becoming more disparate and pronounced. Another study, by the Economic Innovation Group, introduced the

Distressed Communities Index. It found that fewer than 40 percent of Americans live in middle-class neighborhoods. A surprising 106 million people (32 percent of Americans) live in distressed or at-risk communities, and 86 million (26 percent) reside in prosperous neighborhoods. The gap between the rich and poor neighborhoods has only increased from 2007 to 2017.

To achieve more economic inclusivity, the United States needs to find an economic model that works for its diverse population, spread out over a great landmass with varying cultures and ways of life. Instead of waiting for public policy to adopt measures such as the one Senator Warren is suggesting, the business community has been experimenting with alternative models for more than two decades.

Vermont-based Chroma Technology Corp., an employee-owned company, makes optical filters for the science community. Established in 1991—long before talk of the pay disparity between bosses and regular employees and workforce engagement became common—the company had set limitations on salaries early on, and built a tiered salary system to simplify the ambiguity of pay. "We group jobs into tiers. Each tier has a minimum and a maximum annual salary. Each person in the tier starts at least at the minimum, and each moves to the same maximum," says Paul Millman, president of Chroma.

Originally everyone earned $30,000, but that has evolved to $40,000 to keep up with today's cost of living. Today, the highest-paid individual is the CEO, at $225,000. "In order to recruit executive talent, we raised the top salary from $150,000," Millman explains.

To ensure that everyone benefits from the well-being and growth of the organization, all profits are shared equally and annually; shares are distributed equally, too. Millman notes, "I have still not made it to the top executive tier yet."

In 2007, Technicians for Sustainability, a solar installation company based in Tucson, Arizona, began experimenting with its company structure to give employees a chance at ownership. Kevin Koch runs the company with his wife, and to them it just made sense, particularly for people in the construction industry. "These are not jobs that lead to wealth, traditionally," Koch says. "So, I wanted to not only build a company that reflected the world that I wanted to live in but also [to] contribute to wealth creation for the staff."

The quest for the ideal company structure took Koch nearly a decade. Even in the seemingly noble pursuit to create an equitable structure that empowered everyone, Koch found a variety of dissenting opinions. Perhaps that's why companies are exploring different paths to what each one deems "equitable."

For some, the existing employee stock ownership plans (ESOP) provide the best route, particularly for sizable companies. Bob's Red Mill, an Oregon-based food brand that grew from humble roots in the Portland area, now offers all its employees, after one year of full-time employment, the chance to be an owner through the purchase of company stock. As of 2017 the employees owned just under 60 percent of the shares; by 2020 the company had become 100 percent employee-owned.

In 2010, when owner and founder Bob Moore turned eighty-one, he decided to turn the company, valued at $93 million at the time, over to his employees and adopted the ESOP model. Moore saw the ESOP model as a retirement plan that would enable him to share the profits of the company with those who had made it possible. The ESOP would create more wealth for employees than a conventional retirement plan such as 401(k) accounts. In fact, Moore wanted to shorten the vesting period from six to three years, which made 100 employees eligible immediately for vesting. The decision changed the lives of several longtime employees overnight.

Fundamentally, he was keen to solve the problem of ownership: how to give employees a chunk of the company without burdening them with the tax implications of ownership. "Bob's been thinking about profit-sharing since the 1980s," says Trey Winthrop, CFO of Bob's Red Mill. "He tried with a simple profit share early on."

There are eight thousand to twelve thousand ESOPs across the country, by varying estimates.[3] The aim with this model is pretty clear, according to Winthrop: to help employees build their retirement savings and use them as a long-term investment for their future.

But to many employees, the model has been a new one. Stacey Smith, who runs human resources for Bob's Red Mill, says she was not as familiar with the nuances of the ESOP when she came on board. That prompted her to build out an ESOP committee with twenty-eight representatives who meet monthly to educate employees on the technical side of ESOPs and what it means to be an owner.

"You have a responsibility now, and we have to explain that to people," she says.

Winthrop has also educated himself by attending ESOP conferences. He acknowledges that the company did not get as deeply involved in educating employees until 2015, shortly after Smith joined. Smith and the finance team have come up with a simple ten-page handbook that explains ESOPs, the terminology, and how they affect retirement benefits, among other topics.

"In addition to this," Smith explains, "I make a presentation every quarter to our employees, sharing the financials. We share these details, teaching staff about profit and loss statements, balance sheets. Because we don't want people to be surprised on stock day. Plus, now everyone is an owner. So it's even more relevant."

It sounds like a wonderful way to engage employees and increase retention rates, but does it translate into greater workplace satisfaction and does the plan actually work? According to a 2017 Rutgers University study, the simple answer is yes. The study concludes that employee ownership increases company productivity by 4 percent, and profits by 14 percent.

Moore's office is an ode to all the people, including his wife, who have contributed to the company's success. Photos cover every inch of wall space: in each one he is seen wearing his trademark red vest with the company logo and a paperboy cap—a look that has become the company logo. And in all the photos, he's seen cheerfully embracing people. At age ninety-three, he's still on the road, sharing the business's story with students, other entrepreneurs, and anyone who takes an interest in building an enterprise that, similar to Bob's Red Mill, puts people before profit.

In a 2022 interview with *Fortune* magazine Moore stated, "Companies *could* do this, but because money is the only factor, and the owners and managers are generally looking out only for their own benefit, and what [the] company can do for them, I'm not so sure

everyone cares to do that. Come in, get as rich as you can, get out—
that's their main idea."[4]

A company can also become more fair by becoming more inclusive—by thinking more deeply about whom they hire. Greyston
Bakery in Yonkers, New York, knew this early on, inviting anyone
to work at the bakery without a résumé, an employment history, or
even a background check. Basically, Greyston welcomed as employees people generally deemed "unemployable." In the early 1980s,
when they opened their doors, they didn't realize that what they
were doing is now called building a social enterprise. Today, the
company has more than $20 million in revenue annually and has
been widely celebrated as an example of successful nontraditional
hiring practices.

If you've ever eaten Ben & Jerry's Chocolate Fudge Brownie ice
cream, you've also eaten one of Greyston's baked goods. The bakery developed a relationship early on with Ben & Jerry's, providing
some of the ingredients for their ice cream flavors. That's helped them
create a pipeline of clients who treat Greyston as a business, not a
social project, even though the bakery employs ex-convicts, formerly
houseless people, and immigrants seeking work in a new city. To date,
the company has created job opportunities for more than 3,500 individuals, which, says Mike Brady, CEO of Greyston, has impacted
about 19,000 families. Around 65 percent of their workforce has
been incarcerated.

"The reality is that a lot of people see hiring people facing barriers
to employment as risky. We're still using antiquated capital strategies
that reaffirm and drive both conscious and unconscious biases—we
are filtering out pools of talent who want to work," Brady says.

Brady wants to take the bakery's practices and apply them to
more businesses, helping others adopt an approach that Greyston
has dubbed Open Hiring—Greyston has trademarked the term. To
do so, the company has created a Center for Open Hiring.

"We don't expect companies to take radical action from the outset," Brady notes. "This would seem unrealistic and a huge under-
taking that will likely feel impossible to a lot of leadership teams. We
understand that changing human capital strategies takes time, so we

encourage progressive companies to talk to us and work with us to evolve and tailor the model so that it becomes a reality to apply."

Greyston has inspired others to think beyond the traditional parameters of hiring employees and has built a movement toward a more inclusive workforce. The Last Mile, a San Francisco Bay Area organization, offers classes in computer coding to prison inmates so that they can have a specific skill set before being released. The nonprofit then helps them connect with Silicon Valley companies to get a job when they leave prison. With recidivism rates around 50 percent for federal offenders, employment is essential to keeping people out of prison. A Los Angeles–based nonprofit, Homeboy Industries, has built out a host of businesses over the last twenty-five years to finance their programs for former gang members and offenders: there's a bakery, a café, an electronic recycling program, a T-shirt printing operation, and even a solar installation training program—all in an effort to provide job training and a new path forward.

Not only incarcerated people but also people with disabilities have largely been left out of the economy and cataloged as "unemployable." According to the US Department of Labor, in 2017, about 80 percent of adults with disabilities were unemployed.[5] To be sure, some of these individuals face challenges that prevent them from working, but some are keen to work and unable to find an employer that's willing to hire and train them.

Jim Kales, CEO of Aspire, a nonprofit that supports people with developmental disabilities, says that many people with disabilities want to work but don't know how or where to start their pathway to employment. This motivated Kales to organize a new movement to encourage more companies to reconsider individuals with developmental disabilities as possible employees. In 2018, the Chicago-based organization launched the Career Academy, a ten-thousand-square-foot center located twenty miles outside of downtown, where Aspire can train disabled people for jobs in a host of industries: hospitality, warehouse and distribution, culinary, IT, big box retail, and fitness center administration.

In 2007, when Kales joined Aspire as CEO, the organization had some serious limitations. Aspire had been operating since the 1960s as a nonprofit, but they were heavily dependent on grants to support their programs. "Most of our funding was coming from the state of Illinois. . . . But the state didn't have that much funding, and it was drying up. The morale of the team was low. The organization had accumulated debt. I had to start thinking about how we could sustain this programming without a hefty donor," Kales recalls.

At a team meeting, Kales had an epiphany: coffee. "It [is] a premium product, which would rebrand individuals with disabilities. Typically, they're involved in businesses that resell used items or donated, unwanted things," says Kales. "Instead, here's something that everyone loves to drink, and it's not just any coffee but a great-tasting coffee."

To find that great tasting coffee, Kales turned to a Chicago-based roaster, Metropolis Coffee Company. "We didn't know anything about sourcing and roasting coffee, so we had to find a partner. Metropolis was the second company I called," Kales says.

Metropolis was keen on Kales's vision for Aspire. In fact, Metropolis CEO Tony Dreyfuss says he had been looking for a nonprofit partner for a long time. "The timing was serendipitous," he says.

In 2009, Metropolis and Aspire came together to create a new branch of Aspire: Aspire CoffeeWorks, a revenue-generating social enterprise that sells organic and fair-trade coffee. The packaging tells the story of Aspire and whom it benefits; on the back of the packet is a sticker that gives the name and story of the person who packed the coffee.

One of these people is Ben Rankin-Parker, who, alongside five workers from Aspire, packages coffee daily in Metropolis's facilities. Diagnosed with Fragile X syndrome, a genetic condition that results in developmental disability and cognitive impairment, he struggles in social settings, such as an office. For him, the coffee roastery is a more comfortable spot where he can excel in repetitive tasks, such as scooping and bagging coffee and labeling the bags.

For Dreyfuss, this is not just a feel-good endeavor. He says the Aspire workers are solid employees, standing on their feet for eight hours a day and completing all the tasks asked of them. But the added effect, he says, is that it "reminds us we're all part of something bigger."

It works both ways: "The relationship is symbiotic: Aspire has the roasting partner they need to be successful, and in turn, Metropolis has the opportunity to create a more inclusive workforce and tap into a skilled and underutilized labor pool."

There is one shortcoming of the coffee collaboration: it can employ only a few people. Thus, it became important to Kales to find other businesses that could also incorporate people like Rankin-Parker in their workplaces. "I didn't want to place people as one-offs: . . . when you just hire that one person to make a statement, perhaps."

But the coffee business succeeded as a good starting point. Essentially, Aspire had to become a matchmaker between individuals with disabilities and jobs they can do. Finding a person with disabilities a job means figuring out what settings work for each disability. For that, Kales had to reimagine the HR process: "I realized that when many people go in for an interview, part of what we do is just small talk to get know one another," he says. "But someone with autism would do better if you just placed them on the warehouse floor and asked them to complete a task. Small talk is much harder for certain people. Plus, [putting them in a realistic job situation is] a better assessment of whether or not they can do the job."

The answer for people with disabilities lies in the newly built training center west of Chicago, he says. Here, individuals with developmental disabilities who want to work can come and train for jobs in a host of industries. It benefits both groups: individuals learn a practical skill set, and it gives Aspire a pipeline of people who are trained and ready for the workforce. Then, they can offer a group of people to a company for consideration, not just one individual.

"I wanted to make sure that these were not charity jobs but real jobs that anyone else would do," Kales explains.

Companies such as Hyatt Hotels learned about the model and agreed to work with Aspire on job placement. Since 2015, Aspire has helped more than seventy career-focused people with disabilities obtain jobs. Ninety percent were placed into jobs in their communities and 90 percent of these have retained their jobs for at least twelve months. "Our goal is to position ourselves where we are helping upwards of one hundred people annually to connect to career opportunities over the next two years," Herb Washington Jr., the chief innovation officer of Aspire, says.

"People have the impression that hiring someone with a developmental disability will be difficult," says Kales. "I would argue otherwise. [People with disabilities] tend to have less turnover, and if it's done right, you could end up with a great, loyal employee who is thrilled to go to work every day."

Aspire is not alone in this effort. Toad&Co, a clothing company based in Santa Barbara, California, has employed a similar model, working with a Chicago-based nonprofit, Search Inc., to train and provide work opportunities to adults with developmental disabilities. In 1997, the two organizations came together to cofound Planet Access Company, which manages not just Toad&Co's inventory but also the inventories of a number of other brands. Since 2004, more than three hundred people have participated in job training and employment programming at the warehouse. In 2001, Toad&Co added another element to their program: a chance for these workers to experience the outdoors. Set up as a nonprofit, Search for Adventure takes adults with disabilities on trips to enjoy natural beauty, like the Appalachian Trail or the beaches of the Bahamas.

These companies have realized that work can be more than just work. It can be a learning experience for both employees and employers. The concept is global: Groupe SOS, a French conglomerate of social enterprises, has been using this inclusive model for decades, going back to the 1980s, when they started to employ marginalized members of society. Veja, the shoe brand based in Paris mentioned in chapter 1, selects people who at first might seem unemployable and come from underserved neighborhoods of the city to run their warehouse and ship out their shoes.

An employable person is not one who looks good on paper, but one who helps the company through his or her service, Kales says. "That's based on performance. And we should be more open to that idea."

In crafting a regenerative business, these companies are all showing that the parameters set by society are malleable; in fact, they ought to be altered to make way for employment that truly welcomes all.

INVITING MORE YOUNG MINDS TO THE LAND

In the Netherlands, a farmer created a program for young people who have no other place to go; they either have developmental disabilities or otherwise sit on society's sidelines. Piet van Ijzendoorn, a seventy-year-old farmer, came up with the program on his organic farm in the year 2000, arguing that farmwork is healing to the soul and rigorous enough to create discipline. Not only do these young people work on his farm, but they're offered housing as well.

Van Ijzendoorn grew up in an agricultural family and witnessed the rise of large-scale farming and the introduction of chemical fertilizers. He started working on the farm in his childhood at the age of nine. That instilled in him a work ethic, he says, that he has carried through life, in addition to a curiosity to learn more about agriculture. In 1975, he graduated with a degree in environmental science, with an introduction to biodynamic farming. Six years later he established his farm, Zonnehoeve, at the time a barren piece of land north of Amsterdam.

Today, it's a lush landscape, framed by wind turbines and the flower fields of neighboring farms. On the farm, numerous activities take place simultaneously: a bakery operated by people with developmental disabilities, stables that local residents can use to house and train their horses, a dairy farm with sixty cows, and a market garden.

Van Ijzendoorn walks through the bakery, now shut for the day, talking with some of the young men cleaning flour off the floor and sorting the last few bread loaves of the day. He says twenty people reside on the farm, which in the Netherlands is referred to as a "care program" for youth who have developmental disabilities and need support and a place to live. They help with the farmwork: feeding horses, cleaning stables, preparing crop beds, planting, weeding, harvesting, milking cows, and repairing things on the property. There's no task they're not qualified to do. That's the way he prefers it—learn it all, and if there's a task someone particularly enjoys, he's happy to have that person concentrate on it.

The bakery, which the members of the care program run, now sells its products to more than forty health food stores in Amsterdam, Utrecht, The Hague, and the Gooi region. Van Ijzendoorn sees food-based businesses as a therapeutic way to address challenges in life. "Baking bread can be like meditation but it's also work, and something you have to do every day," he says.

Twenty-one-year-old Mario—who struggles with autism and aggression and has panic attacks—has worked at the bakery for seven years. The daily rhythm and structure of working in a bakery has been helpful for his mental health, he says, handing me a loaf from the day's production.

Van Ijzendoorn says, "He has really changed from a scared, aggressive, and insecure youngster to a confident adult who functions very well in a structured working environment. He's pleasant to work with and enjoys working. In fact, his increase in confidence enabled him to pass his driving license test."

In 2006, at the age of fifty-eight, van Ijzendoorn earned a master's degree in educational science. He wants to use Zonnehoeve not only as a farm but also as a space for people of varying backgrounds to come together and develop individually. That's why the farm also has a multi-use building: a barn structure that converts into a music hall, a gathering place for meals, and a crafts center. Here, members of the Zonnehoeve community come together for events and invite members of the public to join them.

"Life on the farm makes for a good life where people can learn from the animals, nature, and each other," he says.

Van Ijzendoorn wants to inspire the new generation to farm in a regenerative manner. The name of his farm, Zonnehoeve, means "Sun Farm," a nod to the essentials of farming: ample sunshine, rich soil, and hardworking hands. He pines for more voices in agriculture deeply concerned with soil health, environmental impact, and the long-term vitality of the farm.

"Unfortunately, it's true that more and more small farmers who take care of their soil are out-competed. In the Netherlands, every day, approximately six farmers quit farming," he says. "This is a great pity, because not only is their land taken out of production but also the farmers' experience is lost. Nowadays, approximately 1 percent of the population claims farming as an occupation, compared to 25 percent after World War II."

The Netherlands is an interesting anomaly in farming; though a small country, it is one of the largest exporters of food in the world.[6] Much of that food comes from greenhouses where crops are grown in a high-technology environment. Some greenhouses do not use soil—only recycled water or rainwater. About thirty-six square miles, or the size of Manhattan, is covered in greenhouses, some lit by LED lights to maximize growth. Drones closely monitor how much water is provided to the plants, and they also track growing conditions. The Netherlands' agricultural industry is hoping to help famine-struck nations with its bounty of produce. While this progress is being celebrated by global media and the technology sector, van Ijzendoorn is skeptical.

"Farmers who are in direct contact with their land discover new things in their perception and experience. Wherever agriculture is checked and controlled by computers, no real new things are discovered. But we are in an age of industrial agriculture," he says, driving through the fields of flowers farmed nearby, which, he points out, have all been cultivated with a heavy dose of chemical fertilizers.

"Organic farming is still small in the Netherlands. Too small," he says.

To get more young farmers into the mix, particularly those who believe in his regenerative style of farming, van Ijzendoorn has opened up Zonnehoeve to a model of community ownership. The capital of the farm stays in the farm and is used for further improvements.

"All owners are responsible for the total system of the farm, not just a fraction of it. I want all the parts of the farm to stay together," he says. "We've written [that] in our vision and mission. When you work together, you grow. We, as a society, live in a culture of taking, but we need to transition to a culture of giving and community."

RESTRUCTURING A BUSINESS

Getting a job is often the first step to sorting out one's life. Then, it's the task of accumulating savings—to have a safety net, to buy a home, to take care of a family. Yet, as more Americans feel pinched by the cost of living, how do they do this, working hourly jobs or at stagnant pay grades?

A female coffee farmer handpicks coffee cherries in the beautiful Rwenzori mountains of western Uganda. UK-based Falcon Coffees works directly with farmers to encourage better farming practices and help improve yields, which increases their incomes as well. © Graeme Williams/Falcon Coffees

Hand sorting coffee parchment at the Gisaka washing station in eastern Rwanda. Washing stations such as this serve a community of coffee farmers who live nearby. Typically, women from the community are employed by the station to do sorting during each harvest. © Falcon Coffees/Rwanda Trading Company, 2015

Workers at California Safe Soil's factory sort through excess and old produce, which will be converted into organic fertilizer and sold to California farmers. © Esha Chhabra

At a UK brewery, bread slices from a local sandwich manufacturer are added in a mash tun, a vessel used to mix grains and water to make beer. © Tom Moggach/Toast Ale

Toast Ale's Craft Lager is a crisp, hop-forward beer made with surplus fresh bread, malted barley, and European hops. It's sold in major retailers in the UK such as Waitrose, Tesco, and the Co-op. ©Mark Newton/Toast Ale

Technicians for Sustainability extended the opportunity to its staff to become co-owners in the business. Today, the small business has grown to having over twenty co-owners, some of whom are gathered here outside their Tucson office in Arizona. © Technicians for Sustainability

Wild rubber trees are native to the Amazon and can live to be over one hundred years old. The French shoe brand Veja works with *seringueiros*, or rubber tappers, to harvest wild rubber from these trees, instead of resorting to clearing the land for cattle farming. © Esha Chhabra

Veja chose to keep their supply chain mostly in Brazil to cut down on their carbon footprint. Wild rubber from the Amazon is transported to their factory in Porto Alegre in southeastern Brazil where it's pressed into the soles of each Veja shoe. © Esha Chhabra

Veja's classic canvas shoes are made with organic cotton sourced from farms in northern Brazil and wild rubber from the Amazon. © Studio Veja

The picturesque Aurlandsfjord is a branch of Sognefjorden, the "King of the fjords," in Norway. Because of its natural beauty, it's been a hot spot for cruise tourism. © Montag

Boutique hotel 29|2 Aurland invites travelers to slow down at their lodge and take in the scenery by foot or in rowboats on the fjords, reducing the footprint of travel. © Montag

In addition to being a poaching target for their ivory, elephants have been at the heart of the human-wildlife conflict in the Serengeti region, as local farmers try to keep them out of their fields. © Singita

With the help of technology, Singita, a safari company, has built a robust conservation program in which animals under threat, such as elephants, are tagged and monitored to protect them from poachers. © The Grumeti Fund

Wandera "Collins" Urthur, of Entebbe, Uganda, became an above-the-knee amputee after he found a cancerous tumor in his knee at just twenty-one years old. With an eighty-dollar prosthetic knee, provided to him by Equalize Health, he's now mobile and working as a dentist. © Equalize Health

Osomtex transforms recycled fibers made from used textiles, without additional water, dyes, or chemicals, into socks. Founder Patricia Ermecheo has been collaborating with brands such as Stella McCartney and Nike to incorporate recycled fibers like these into a broader array of products. © Patricia Ermecheo

Kevin Koch, CEO of Technicians for Sustainability, in Tucson, recognized early on that certain industries that require manual labor such as farming and construction are difficult professions for employees to move up the ranks or build wealth in.

Thus, when he took the helm of the company, which installs solar energy systems on residential and commercial buildings, he wanted to see how he could democratize the system. Turns out, it was harder than he thought. "I spent nearly a decade experimenting with various models before I landed on the current model. Even when I thought I was being democratic, the feedback I was getting was that I was not," he says.

Koch is something of an accidental entrepreneur. He finished graduate school in 1997, and after volunteering at local nonprofits in the Tucson area, he was still unsure what he wanted to do. One day he attended a talk by an employee of the Sacramento Municipal Utility District, which was installing residential photovoltaic systems. "It was a proactive, positive way that people could address energy use in their homes and urban centers. It made sense to me," he recalls. "I heard that talk and was off to the races. I knew it was what I wanted to work on."

He applied to every solar company in town, but they were all working on battery-based systems. Koch didn't see that as the answer. "I wanted to work on on-grid solutions, not off-grid."

In 2001, he began independently offering classes and workshops to those who wanted to learn about solar system installations. He would educate people through the classes, and they would provide labor for the installation. He then met a Frenchman, Jean-François Camson, who had started Technicians for Sustainability as an electrical company; Koch came on board as a partner, providing solar expertise. In 2006, Camson left the company; that marked the start of Koch's journey to find the right employee ownership model.

Initially he tried business models that took into account tenure at the company and any sweat equity that someone would have contributed. "I didn't have a sense of what I might call the 'entitlement of capital.' I started in this company through bootstrapping. The value that's delivered to the startup, I believe, comes largely from labor," he says, adding that he didn't come from an MBA background. His approach to business has been to learn on the job.

"I know many companies raise capital, hire people at market rates, and then try to make a go of it. I really saw labor as the means to build the company up. I felt that labor should get a share of whatever came out of the company."

Koch started with profit sharing, offering 20 to 40 percent of profits to employees for their contributions. The amount they earned in excess of their wage was measured by three factors: the hours worked at the company, tenure (how many years they had been there), and, most important, the value they brought to the company. Sometimes that last element trumped tenure.

"One year we had an employee who had only been at the company for a year. But he got a larger sum through the profit share because he had revamped the efficiency of our packing process when we're preparing for jobs, which was really helpful to us."

Then, as Koch started to develop an employee ownership model, he looked to some of the stalwarts in the industry: Namasté Solar and PV Squared are both solar companies that offer employee ownership, and they introduced him to the South Mountain Company, an employee-owned architecture and energy firm on Martha's Vineyard, in Massachusetts.

Koch tried to build a rubric of how to invite employees into membership. As a bootstrapper who believed in long, hard hours and risk taking, he wanted to give sweat equity to those who had been at the company longer. At first he offered $15,000 common stock to his employees for ownership. There was only one type of stock. But he made a "sweat equity discount" for employees who had been at the company for a few years.

"I thought I was being fair and generous to those who had been committed to the company. But instead, people wanted something that was equal across the board. It turned into a collective angst: everyone was unhappy, myself included."

In January 2017, he tried again. This time he lowered the entry point to a $10,000 common stock. But running a capital-intensive business, he wanted to ensure that the company would always have enough capital for upfront costs of a job, so he tweaked the standard employee-ownership model to fit his needs.

"I created a program where you could double your profit share: if you left about 75 percent in the company, it would be reinvested into the company as a long-term five-year loan," he explains. "If you had $10,000 in profit share, you would put $7,500 into the company."

The profit share then helped employees buy ownership into the company. All but one of the owners used several years of profit-share funds to purchase the common stock share at $10,000.

"I felt that it was important to have a sweat equity method [to buy stock]. We don't offer a loan. Instead, you can put in some time, build up the profit share, and then buy stock if you don't have cash. Or go get a loan elsewhere. But I needed to keep some of these employee-created profits in the company to have enough capital to be successful."

After the conversion to an employee-owned company, the profit-share program changed from a long-term loan to the company to a purchase of preferred stock with a five-year vesting schedule. These preferred stocks earn dividends but do not go beyond a target rate.

In addition, he introduced an internal capital account (ICA) for co-owners. After a portion of the profit is distributed companywide in profit shares and dividends to stockholders, a portion of the remaining profits are allocated to each co-owner's ICA. This is referred to as a "patronage dividend" in cooperatives. This allows co-owners to build assets and allows the company to retain that capital for future use.

For instance, if the company made $10,000 in profit, then 20 percent needed to be paid out as per regulations. But the remaining 80 percent, or $8,000, can stay in the company and be allocated to each owner. If an owner leaves, they can cash out their share, according to the vesting schedule.

"That way we're not shocking the company with major capital outflows when people leave the company," Koch says.

But why did he even do it? Koch says it was an idealistic vision: "I wanted to create a company that represents the society I want to live in, where labor has access to profits just like capital and entrepreneurship. I'm looking at what a company [should] look like in my version of utopia."

But it's also translated into real-life scenarios: most clients, when they meet an employee who goes out on a job, are also meeting one of the owners of the company. And an owner of a company is more interested in problem-solving. "That produces a pretty positive work culture," Koch says. "People are bought in. They don't want to let things fester."

The company now has fifteen owners, with an age range from late twenties to sixties. Anyone who works at Technicians for Sustainability full-time for one year can become an employee owner. All potential owners are voted in by existing owners. "We've tried to make it as democratic as possible, and I think we've finally got there," Koch says.

CHAPTER FIVE

WOMEN

Bringing Women to the Forefront

I n India's northern state of Uttarakhand women are farming on the terraced fields. They're collecting mint, nettle, and rosemary from their one-acre plots. In the eastern state of West Bengal, Nepali women are hugging the sloped tea estates, plucking tea leaves. In Kenya, they're picking through tea estates in Kericho. In Uganda, it's bananas. In Nicaragua, it's coffee.

"Women are not only the lifeblood of their families and communities, but they also happen to be the backbone of the coffee supply chain," says Noushin Ketabi, one of the cofounders of Vega Coffee, a company educating female coffee farmers to become roasters and coffee specialists in Nicaragua. "However, they've historically lacked the same access to resources as their male counterparts. The only way to achieve gender equity in the coffee supply chain and beyond is to truly recognize women and to work toward tearing down any barriers that stand between them and the opportunities that they so richly deserve—to learn and advance, create a bright future for themselves and [their] families, and shape their world," she says.

The problem of women's restricted rights is not limited to the coffee sector. Many rural women work on farms where they do not even have rights to the land. According to the United Nations, less than 13 percent of the world's female agricultural workers have land rights.[1] Yet in many regions, such as South Asia and Sub-Saharan Africa particularly, 60 percent of women work in agriculture.[2] Women in the developing world are a strong force in agriculture, yet they need some support to be given a voice.

One of the UN Sustainable Development Goals is gender equality. It underpins many of the other goals: education, helping the environment, fighting hunger, and financial inclusion.

Just as in the developed world, women in developing countries run their households, feed their children, and look after the health of the family. The context is merely different: the developing world is where the impact of climate change, hunger, and inequity is more acute.

If companies invested in empowering women, they could address half of the Sustainable Development Goals in one sweep. Women hold the key to their family's health, financial prosperity, and the vitality of the land they work on.

It's a ripple effect. If women are able to farm their land organically—and to take care of it from season to season with regenerative practices like mulching, intercropping, and using cover crops—they'll have healthier land in the long run. That translates to less erosion from heavy rains, better odds at dealing with drought because healthier soil traps and holds more water, healthier foods for them, and a safer environment to work in. Plus, they don't have to spend as much on fertilizers and add-ons, resulting in cost savings. Basically, they can use what's there to enrich the soils and harvest seeds each season to plant in future seasons—a cycle that's financially beneficial for them and their families. With more money in their pockets—and organic products fetching higher prices—women can invest those funds in their children and in their own futures.

That could be the saving grace for mitigating climate change. Driving up into the hills of Uttarakhand in India, you'll spot women working small plots of land—bent over, dressed in saris and wrapped in shawls to ward off the chill of the wind coming off the Himalayas. They tend to fields of amaranth, rye, and barley. But many are alone: the men have left for the cities to find paying work—or are sitting idle in the village center, drinking. It's a trend that development experts have referred to as the "feminization of agriculture."

By necessity, the women are managing the family's finances, and doing it well. A comprehensive study of 350 microfinance institutions

(MFIs) in seventy countries led to the conclusion that women have higher loan repayment rates than men and thus are less risky for the lender. According to the study, "More women clients is associated with lower portfolio risk, lower write-offs, and lower credit-loss provisions. . . . These findings confirm common beliefs that women in general are a better credit risk for MFIs."[3] This is what Dr. Muhammad Yunus of Grameen Bank and the microfinance community established nearly two decades ago. Yet we're still struggling to adopt these ideas widely.

Women are savvy with money not because they are frugal or overly cautious but because they see their family's expenses firsthand—school fees, health bills, trips to the market for food and fuel—and they tend to think long term.

Kalyan Paul and his wife, Anita, are Delhiites who nearly two decades ago saw the trend of farms being run by women. In the state of Uttarakhand alone, nearly six hundred thousand women struggled to work farms with increasingly depleted soil quality and little support. That led the Pauls to create a foundation devoted to the development of the women of the region and the preservation of the forested slopes they call home.

"This is not an easy fix. We've got young people going to the cities. We've got girls in the schooling system here that are not being taught about the local ecology. And the average age of the farmer is a fifty-plus-year-old woman," Kalyan Paul says. "How are we going to save the forest?"

The Pauls employed women to build nurseries and grow saplings of indigenous trees and trained the women how to look after them. This led to the development of a cooperative so the women could earn money from their organic farms and handicrafts. Women from more than two hundred villages across the Gagas and Kosi river basins have come together to form the Mahila Umang Producers Company, a cooperative of three thousand women made up of small self-help groups of ten to twenty women each.

Within these smaller groups women discuss family matters, ways to earn more money, the water shortage in the region, and their own health. They've been able to increase their incomes and spread the word about organic farming. Moreover, they've planted over one million native tree saplings and shrubs in the river basins to revive the forests. Each year, members plant another five thousand fruit tree saplings, whose fruit they can eventually harvest and eat or sell for additional income.

At their headquarters, tucked in on a hillside about a ten-hour drive from Delhi, they sell the fruits of their farms: dried herbs, grains, pomegranate seeds, jams, jellies, and pickles. And recently they've developed a website that has allowed them to reach all of India.

"We have to find a balance between economics and ecology," Kalyan Paul says.

Women should be a part of the answer. In developing countries, women take on the brunt of the work: working in the fields, collecting water, gathering cooking fuel and food, and then looking after the well-being of the family—they're seeing and experiencing climate change firsthand, arguably more than the men of the community. When women work in agriculture, they see the effects of erratic rainfall, drought, high temperatures, storms, and a shortage of water. It affects what they till every day. Listening to women, and giving them the resources they need, could help mitigate many of these challenges.

However, it goes beyond women's role in conserving the environment to recognizing women for their skills and potential. Businesses such as Divine Chocolate, Nisolo, Vega, and Soko have highlighted what women can do if they're given that nudge of support, training, and a general confidence that "we've got your back." Going forward, regenerative businesses celebrate the strength, wisdom, and resilience of women, instead of shying away from it.

ADDING THE FEMALE VOICE

London-born Sophi Tranchell saw this firsthand on her trips to Ghana as she built Divine Chocolate, a partially farmer-owned chocolate company. Raised by parents and grandparents who were campaigners for social issues, Tranchell developed a passion for social justice in her teens, which compelled her to protest against apartheid by campaigning about the choice of goods and services people buy. In

1999, she was recruited as the managing director for a new chocolate company. Divine Chocolate was created when Twin Trading, a UK-based nonprofit that had already helped build Cafédirect, and a Ghanaian cocoa farmers' cooperative, Kuapa Kokoo, collaborated to establish a chocolate brand that had its roots in fair trade and would give consumers a new way to express their values with their purchases.

"At that time, awareness around fair trade was under 10 percent," Tranchell says. "Now, it's at 90 percent in Great Britain. Young people want to know more about where their products come from, [and] how and what change they're making in communities."

This new consciousness has worked in Divine Chocolate's favor: it is 44 percent owned by cocoa farmers in Ghana, and it's been nudging women into leadership positions in the cooperative and on the company's board of directors since the beginning.

Divine Chocolate works primarily with Kuapa Kokoo, a cooperative of around one hundred thousand farmers of whom one-third are women. Since its founding in 1993, the cooperative has encouraged women to be a part of business discussions from the outset. If five members were on a local committee in the cooperative, two would need to be women. Over the years, that nurturing of women's voices and leadership has grown. Hundreds of women have stepped up to leadership roles in their own districts, ultimately serving on the National Executive Committee and even becoming presidents and vice presidents of the organization.

"Thirty-five percent of membership [in Kuapa Kokoo] is women; probably only 30 percent of cocoa farmers in the country are women. To be a member, you have to own a farm, so it's impressive to see so many women in the cooperative. That's how you shift culture," Tranchell explains.

In 2007, Tranchell invited a longtime cocoa farmer, Comfort Kumeah, to join her in Washington, DC, to announce the launch of the company in the United States. Kumeah, who had not traveled much beyond her village in Ghana, was given the opportunity to speak and share her story.

Kumeah, sixty, the mother of five children, joined Kuapa Kokoo more than a decade ago when she, like many other farmers, noticed that the scales the cooperative used to measure the cocoa gave an honest weight—they weren't designed to cheat the farmer of her income by underweighing, as was often the case. "If someone would have told me that twelve years later, you will be the national secretary of Kuapa and chair of the Farmers' Union, I would have laughed," she says. Kumeah also has an educational role, speaking to women in the cooperative about becoming active and diversifying their income streams in the off-season—because cocoa is a seasonal crop.

In 2014, the cooperative elected women to 40 percent of village leadership positions: 12 percent were presidents, 80 percent vice presidents, 90 percent treasurers, and 13 percent secretaries. In 2010, that number had been just 14 percent overall for women in leadership positions. The educational training and support were working.

Despite all this encouragement for women to get involved, the cocoa cooperative saw that some women still were not applying for leadership positions. The reason was because they're not able to read and write easily.

"Women also make more sensible choices when they are literate," Tranchell adds. They can then make informed decisions about health, education, and the financial futures of their families, as well as participate better in organizations outside the family sphere.

Divine Chocolates, Kuapa Kokoo, and Twin Trading commissioned a study to determine the results of the training programs. They found that equal training for women in cocoa-farming practices helps women improve farm productivity and cocoa quality. Furthermore, having women serve as recorders—responsible for buying the cocoa from farmers, weighing it, and paying the farmers for their crop—helps them earn extra income. The women with extra income funneled it to their children, allowing their daughters and sons to attend school longer than families without extra income.

Women, though not traditionally involved in cocoa production, have now become an integral part of it and help drive Divine Chocolate's growth and success, Tranchell says.

The farmers receive a fair-trade premium on all the cocoa they sell to Divine Chocolates, and they get to decide what to invest it in—focusing on education, health, and community improvements. In 2006, after seven years in business, the company became profitable and started sharing these profits with farmers, an income they have invested in their own businesses. As of 2018, Divine Chocolate had an annual turnover of about $18 million (£14 million). Every year, Divine Chocolates invests 2 percent of the turnover in farmer-led projects that support women such as literacy programs, which women actively participate in. Once literate, women feel more comfortable speaking up, Tranchell says.

"I've gone out of my way to ask these women to come and share their story here in the United Kingdom and in the United States," she says. "Because not only is [it] a good story for us—to connect women buyers with women farmers—but also, these women have gone on to become leaders in their own farming communities when they go back home to Ghana. They've recognized the potential of the organization—of what a chocolate bar can do."

WALKING IN HER SHOES

When Patrick Woodyard started Nisolo, a Nashville-based company, he was disgruntled with development. As a student at the University of Mississippi, he'd focused on two areas: business and economic development. Between semesters, he spent time building a nonprofit in Uganda and volunteering in Argentina. "This was pre–social entrepreneurship, or everyone knowing about it. I just wanted to know how market forces could help in some of these situations," he says.

In 2010, after graduating from college and having learned Spanish, he signed on to work with a small microfinance organization in Trujillo, the third-largest city in Peru, teaching women business skills and financial literacy. "At that time, microfinance was a panacea, or at least some people viewed it that way. But I wanted to get some hands-on experience," he says.

Going from home to home, he offered women assistance with their accounting and helping them find ways to save and spend better. On a home visit with Doris Ortiz Quispe, she invited Woodyard to meet her husband, a shoemaker. "Turns out, her husband was making these beautiful leather shoes," he recalls, "sitting on a dirt floor in their home. And I just thought, *Here's someone with talent and skills, and no real market for it.*"

Willan Ulloa Sanchez, Quispe's husband, originally from the foot-hills of the Andes, had learned the art of shoemaking from his father. His father had learned from his father. Now Sanchez worked alone or in tandem with a few other shoemakers in the city. With manu-facturing having shifted to Asia, the once-renowned shoe industry in Trujillo was struggling.

"I met so many artisans like Willan who were making leather shoes on the outskirts of this city, but few had enough working cap-ital, design understanding, or links to markets to sell them beyond their corner of the world," Woodyard says.

It was a conversation with Sanchez that triggered the idea of an artisan-based shoe brand, though Woodyard never forgot about Doris and the women like her who sold bits and bobs but didn't have their own connection to the shoemaking industry.

After completing his work with the microfinance organization, Woodyard returned to the United States and educated himself about the shoe industry. "I had no design background, and I didn't know anything about making women's shoes," he jokes. "So I had to find a partner."

Fortuitously, he met Zoe Cleary, a fashion buyer with a design background who was working in New York City. They met through mutual friends, and when Woodyard shared his vision of building a brand that worked with artisans like Sanchez, Cleary jumped on board. "I couldn't offer a full-time salary, but Zoe was ready to hop in because she saw how little billion-dollar companies cared about their producers," he explains.

Woodyard chucked the idea of grad school and instead dove into building a shoe brand. The two launched Nisolo—Spanish for "not alone"—in 2011. Cleary designed modern classic footwear using leather available to artisans in Peru. It was not all smooth sailing.

Most of Trujillo's shoemakers were men—leather cutting was traditionally considered men's work—but Woodyard didn't forget his original commitment to working with women and seeking to help them improve their small businesses. After some success with Nisolo, Woodyard and Cleary began to look for ways they could incorporate women into the male-dominated industry. They decided to take a proactive approach by bringing women into the factory. By December 2017, about a quarter of the staff was female. As of summer 2018, that number had risen to 41 percent. The goal, says Matt Stockamp, impact leader at Nisolo, is to get that number up to 50 percent. "I'm very excited about this, as it's been an ongoing objective of ours to hire more women."

The company provides training and workshops; they are keen to make their staff as skilled as possible, Stockamp says. In a society where leather cutting has been a man's domain, not really appropriate for women to do, Nisolo has been challenging that preconception by training women in more "hard" skills. Carmen Maximiliano Tumbajulca, a single mother, joined Nisolo and started on the sewing desk. They taught her how to cut leather. "Without my job here, I would not have stable work, and I would not be able to maintain my household or daughter," she told Stockamp.

That's been one of the challenges for Nisolo from day one. When they started, they partnered with individual artisans working from their homes or workshops. It became hard for them not only to manage so many moving parts but also to ensure that each individual was benefiting from the growth of the company. They started with fifteen shoemakers, and the model worked till 2014. But as they grew to more than fifty artisans, Woodyard and his team wanted to formalize the structure.

So they invested in a factory in Trujillo, where women such as Tumbajulca come to work. Here, they're provided more than just a living wage. They're also given company-paid health care, free weekly financial literacy sessions to help build their savings, free English classes for the staff and their families, and workshops on psychological health and interpersonal skills to help them develop a holistic set of skills. Each employee is also entitled to fifteen days of paid vacation each year.

Women have seen their incomes jump drastically, as much as 123 percent. In Peru, the average wage for an individual is 942 Peruvian soles a month, or about $280. The men and women manufacturing the shoes in Nisolo's Trujillo facility earn on average 1,370 soles, about $415, per month.

The extra cash, and the assurance that it'll be there each month, has been instrumental for Nisolo's workers. Ana Rosa Aguirre Vazquez is a sewing specialist. A mom of three, the thirty-six-year-old appreciates the stability. Before she worked for Nisolo, "I was pregnant with my son, there was a complication with the pregnancy, and I needed to have four operations done in eight months. I couldn't work or do anything really because I was bedridden. All of this got me thinking that when we have the possibility and ability to do what we love, we should do it," Vazquez says.

Once her health recovered, Vasquez decided to find work. She discovered Nisolo through a friend, applied for a job, and was hired as an *ayudante*, or helper, fulfilling small tasks required in the day-to-day activities at the factory. "Since the moment I started, I began to feel the relief of having a stable job," she says. "You don't have to be concerned about not having work because of a lack of demand or raw materials, and therefore you don't have to be concerned about not being paid. The stability here changes our situation a lot."

Her eldest daughter is a university student, and Vazquez wants to support her as she completes her degree. Seven years ago, when Vazquez was bedridden due to complications from childbirth, her daughter, then ten years old, had to rise to the challenge of helping out. "She had to mature quickly and assume a lot of roles in our home [while] my husband had to work," Vazquez explains.

Now, says Vasquez, her work at Nisolo enables her to pay for her daughter's education costs. "I always tell her that it doesn't matter what she does after school so long as she has completed her education. From there, I hope she will help me encourage her younger siblings so that they can also have good careers."

The domino effect of investing in one woman, even if she didn't have a specific skill set when she applied to Nisolo, is already coming to fruition. From Vazquez's earnings, her daughter, who is studying social work, will complete her education. From there, that daughter may continue to work in the social sector and encourage other women to pursue employment and education. Female inclusion is not an overnight story; it's a slow push for equality.

Vazquez wants to see more women working in the Nisolo factory. "Of course, because it's a big support for us as women to be able to develop ourselves."

Vasquez is not the only one excited about having more women at the facility. Yamila Robles Llamos, a twenty-one-year-old who is working and studying at the same time, does leather stitching at Nisolo. Llamos too didn't know much about the craft when she arrived three years ago but went through training. Since she doesn't have financial support from her family, the job is the only way for Llamos to pay for her education. In fact, Llamos has done better than that and is able to take some of her earnings home to her father and stepmother. "I've had the opportunity to support myself and my family financially. This helps me a lot because I didn't have a stable job before," she says.

Having taken part in the workshops at the factory, Llamos wants to see more women involved in this industry. "Because there are some women," she says, "who have to function as the father and mother at the same time. There are families with single mothers, and they could really benefit [here]."

Stockamp says that company already prioritizes hiring women who are single mothers, have school-aged children, do not have access to health care, and have never worked in the formal economy with benefits. "We definitely want to get as many women on board" as possible, he says.

In the United States, the Nisolo team, based largely out of their headquarters in Nashville, has been two-thirds female in recent years. But it's not just about adding to the statistics. Woodyard wants to challenge practices in the fashion business, which employs thousands of women in factories across the world but in questionable conditions. Even Stockamp, who joined Nisolo in 2015, said he did so partly because of what he had seen elsewhere. "I got passionate about the fashion industry in 2014 when I spent a summer in India listening to the stories of factory workers who had been abused in the workplace," he says. "We are proud to be challenging gender norms in a shoemaking industry and doing it in an ethical manner. You think about how little [of the profit] goes to the producer, only about 1 to 3 percent. Imagine if consumers were given the choice to just spend marginally more, it might just be another 1 percent on a shirt or a pair of shoes [to give the producer more]."

While that may seem like a small increase, if scaled across factories and across the industry, it could have a profound impact. Woodyard is not interested in merely preaching to the choir about the need for an ethical system of production. "We want to make a product that's comparable to the biggest brands in the footwear industry and compete on price as well so that it is affordable enough to buy," he says.

With more and more women applying for jobs at their factory in Trujillo, Nisolo is hoping that consumer demand will enable them to have the kind of social impact they envision. "I wanted to start a brand that values the producer as much as the consumer," Woodyard says. Nisolo's management takes the name of the company—"Not Alone"—seriously. "Our lives are interconnected; a decision here has a direct impact there. You and I have the power to shift the fashion industry."

BUILDING MICRO-ENTERPRISES

Women are not just relegated to lower-level jobs in the cocoa and footwear industries. They're also not as involved in the jewelry industry, particularly when it comes to designs that involve metals, stones, and bones. Though women design this type of jewelry, getting them to take part in the manufacturing process is a challenge, because they lack the needed skills. Yet, two Americans and a Kenyan woman are encouraging women to think beyond beads and get excited about soldering.

In the passageways of Kibera, a sprawling slum in the heart of Nairobi, Veronicah Adhiambo Rachiedo runs a small jewelry-making business. Her creations are sold by Nordstrom, Anthropologie, Reformation, and Amour Vert, and at over six hundred retailers, thanks to Gwendolyn Floyd, Ella Peinovich, and Catherine Mahugu, the founders of Soko, an artisan jewelry company in Kenya.

Soko is doing something more than just marketing artisan-made products to US consumers; they're building technology to streamline the whole process, cut down on deadstock, eliminate the need for massive inventory storerooms, and incentivize entrepreneurs like Rachiedo who want to build workshops of their own. Plus, their designs are on-trend, modern, and minimalist while paying respect to their origins.

"We didn't want people to buy this as a charity buy. [We wanted them] to buy it because it's a beautiful piece of jewelry, made to last, and at a price point that's reasonable. The story is probably the third factor in their decision-making process, after aesthetics and price," Floyd says.

Soko's headquarters in Kenya is situated in a residential neighborhood where bumper-to-bumper traffic is the daily norm. What looks like a residence slowly reveals itself to be a business as you meander through the corridors and small structures sprawled about the property: a testing lab for new products, a small inventory room, a design team, a tech team, a quality-control crew, a tiny showroom, a workshop with machinists.

Josephine Olwamba, a supply chain manager, oversees much of the process. A soft-spoken Kenyan, Olwamba joined Soko after working as a social worker. She was not impressed with the aid model. "Most of the time in Africa, people want to give goodies and leave. That's not a sustainable model. If you give someone a machine to make jewelry, they're not going to care if it breaks down. But if you give them opportunity to buy one and then use it to make money, they will take care of it if it breaks down."

Olwamba discovered Soko through Kotsanai Matereke, the company's COO, a Zimbabwean who is one of the few men in the office.

Although a team of fifteen works in the United States on marketing and sales, Soko is very much a Kenyan operation with more than sixty employees, more than half of whom are women, in their Nairobi headquarters.

As the social entrepreneurship movement grew in the region, East Africa welcomed many Americans and Europeans who wanted to solve social problems with their solution-driven businesses. This top-down design approach has sparked debate and invited criticism, as many of these companies failed to deliver the social impact they had promised. Floyd, who had worked as an industrial designer before cofounding Soko, has been acutely aware of this.

A Texan by birth, Floyd started college at Brown University but dropped out to build her first company in her early twenties. That took her to Amsterdam. From there she's been hopping around the globe throughout her twenties and thirties, living in Germany, China, and Cuba, building systems for development projects and consulting with governments and businesses. Floyd is well traveled and aware of the nuances—and hypocrisy—of doing business in a country that's not her own. "I don't go in with the answers. I go in with the intention that here are the resources available—how can we fit them to serve people better, using what's here," she says.

When Floyd arrived in East Africa in 2010, it was at the height of the mobile money revolution. At the time, mobile phone penetration was at 50 percent in Kenya. By 2018, it had skyrocketed to more than 90 percent of adults subscribed to a cell-phone service.[4] With the rise of telecom operators like Safaricom, mobile money quickly followed. Kenyans were exchanging digital money years before Apple Wallet debuted.

Enchanted by the seemingly limitless capacity and capability of the mobile phone, Floyd partnered with Mahugu, a software engineer, and Peinovich, an architect who also had a systems design background. This was very much a women-led company from day one, Floyd says, looking to harness their tech, engineering, and design experience into a business that could have social impact.

Established in 2014, Soko did what no artisan company had done to date. Whereas many artisan brands were simply selling artisan-made products into a marketplace or a selection online, the Soko co-founders, working with local Kenyan developers, built an app that would become the foundation of their business.

It's this technology that helps Olwamba coordinate the flow of 45,000 pieces of jewelry every month. Soko doesn't stock pieces; instead, artisans receive orders on their mobile phones, design them, and get paid through the app as well. "That's really the innovation," Floyd says. "Because there are other companies working with artisans, yes. But few, if any, are using this model."

The process is simple yet tackles several big issues with ethical fashion. "For too long, ethical fashion has been written off as too ethnic, earthy, [and] not high-quality. This model changes that. And it's fast enough to compete with fast fashion," Floyd explains.

Whereas most fashion companies design twelve to eighteen months in advance, trying to forecast trends, Floyd designs products just weeks before they're offered to the market. Then, as orders are placed, artisans are sent assignments. Soko has built up a network of more than 2,500 artisans in Nairobi and the surrounding area. Each artisan works as a micro-entrepreneur. When Soko receives orders from its retail clients, it allocates the order to one or multiple artisans and gives 25 percent of the revenue to the artisan in advance to cover the costs of material and labor. And at times, that can increase to 35 percent. "Compare that to other fashion or jewelry companies. The producer would get 2 to 3 percent at most," Floyd says.

Crafts constitute the second largest industry in the developing world, but the production of craft items is fragmented and disconnected from lucrative markets.[5] Floyd wanted to solve that problem, send more profits to artisans, and streamline the industry. "I never planned on being in the jewelry business," Floyd says, "but jewelry is a great way for me to harness the skills that I saw and make them profitable for Kenyans." Three years into the venture she continues to design all the jewelry herself.

Even though jewelry is a woman-led business with a woman-centric product, women are underrepresented in the jewelry manufacturing workforce. For example, out of the 280 workshops that Soko sends work to in Nairobi, only about 20 are women-led—less than

10 percent. That's because jewelry manufacturing requires skills like welding, cutting, and coating metals. So as Soko grew, and the office side of the business kept hiring women, Floyd and her cofounders made a concerted effort to draw more women into manufacturing.

By providing free training sessions to women, they caught the attention of people such as Beatrice Akinyi, a thirty-three-year-old mother of three. She learned needed skills from her brother, attended classes, and experimented until she was comfortable handling the metalworking equipment. Operating from a small workshop in the heart of Kibera, which she rents for $20 a month, she's able to garner orders worth $1,000 a month.

Her business has grown to the extent that Akinyi can employ an assistant, who sits next to her as they polish upcycled brass. She sources the materials, most of which are repurposed metals, locally. Horn and cow bone come from the meat industry—a waste material that would otherwise be thrown away.

Maureen Naftal, head of field staff at Soko, says, "I love to see women like Beatrice empowered, because she's producing some stuff that's even better than her brother's and is now employing more people."

Just a few workshops down from her is Rachiedo, who has become something of an all-star entrepreneur. Rachiedo has been making jewelry for more than a decade. A college graduate and fluent in English, Rachiedo has been able to expand her business, bringing in more employees and even traveling to New York City to meet other artisans and learn new skills. "I'm trying to get more women on board," she explains, "but many do not stick with it because of the nature of the work. It can be messy, dirty, and loud."

"We had to seed fund this process," Floyd says, referring to the free trainings and workshops for women artisans. "Otherwise, it would not have happened. Some companies might see that as cost-prohibitive. But we saw it as a long-term investment. Women are better business owners. It's not philanthropy; it's just savvy business sense."

Though Kenya is far more developed than some of the other nations of East Africa, limited access to land and capital has kept women out of the workforce; they make up about one-third of the formal wage jobs.[6] On the financing end, Soko has launched asset-financing programs, which helps artisans purchase equipment for their work-shops. Floyd hopes that as the company continues to grow, it'll be able to provide an even more supportive structure to the female artisans.

ROASTING IN THE FIELD

Women in agriculture have different challenges from those of urban women. Unlike in the skilled trades that Soko and Nisolo require, where they have to learn specific techniques in order to perform these jobs, women have been working in agriculture since the beginning of human agriculture. They do the work, but it's often unpaid. They're essential to a farm's success yet often lack land rights. And they're rarely seen on the business end of the farm; husbands, brothers, and sons negotiate pricing with middlemen.

These factors play out in the coffee industry, so much so that the Coffee Quality Institute, a nonprofit that works on improving the quality of coffee around the world, developed a program specifically for increasing gender equality in coffee production. In 2015, the institute produced a report, *The Way Forward: Accelerating Gender Equity in Coffee Value Chains*, which has become the go-to reference in the industry.[7]

According to the report, more than a hundred million people worldwide are involved in the production of coffee. The bulk of the coffee—80 percent—comes from twenty-five million smallholder farmers; half of this workforce is women. The Coffee Quality Institute argues that women need to be more deeply involved in actually running these farms than they currently are, not only for social justice but for the sake of the coffee business itself. When women spend the bulk of their time looking after the planting, harvesting, and processing of coffee beans, the end result is a better-quality agricultural product, which in turn can fetch a higher price.

Robert Terenzi noticed this effect of women's engagement on his visits to Nicaragua. After completing his undergraduate studies at Boston College in 2005, he signed on to work with a women's coffee cooperative there for two years. Though he didn't know it at the time, this experience would provide the foundational learnings of his business, Vega Coffee, a woman-centered coffee company.

"I'll never forget the first time I saw [a woman] stirring green coffee in an open pan over a flame. Seeing the magic, the 'transformation,' as farmers refer to the roasting process, was incredible. It suddenly brought the whole process into light and how much women contribute to the process of taking a seedling from nothing to the amazing cup of coffee in front of me," Terenzi recalls.

He was young and still wanted to complete more schooling, so after spending two years in Nicaragua and coming to understand the nuances of the coffee industry, he returned to the United States to earn a degree from Fordham University in law and international development. At Fordham, he met his wife-to-be and future business partner, Noushin Ketabi, who was studying the same issues: how the legal system could alleviate poverty, include more women, create eco-friendly solutions, and encourage beneficial development as a whole.

In 2011, Ketabi earned a Fulbright scholarship to Nicaragua, where she studied renewable energy policy in the country, looking at the role and scope of solar power. It gave the duo more time in the country; meanwhile, Terenzi had begun bringing small groups of savvy coffee lovers to Nicaragua to watch the farm-to-cup process. Yet, once again, they didn't stay for good. Ketabi returned to the United States to work for the State of California on energy policy. Terenzi joined a Bay Area law firm that was consulting big players in the tech industry. It was a far cry from Nicaragua and coffee farmers.

Although these work experiences had little to do with coffee, the future Vega founders were learning about startup culture, legal systems, and the third-wave coffee trend—emphasizing high quality and connoisseurship—that had hit San Francisco by then. Most of all, Ketabi jokes, "We were drinking hipster coffee and seeing that customers were willing to pay three to four dollars a cup. Yet we knew that so little of that [price]—perhaps pennies per cup—would go back to the farmer."

That frustration ultimately led them to quit their well-paying jobs for a more adventurous career in coffee. They brought in a longtime friend, Will DeLuca, who had a tech background. The trio raised

$40,000 on Kickstarter to fund a unique business model in the coffee sector.

Unlike most boutique coffee brands that buy green beans from exporters and then roast the beans after they've been imported at their own facility, Vega Coffee roasts the coffee in the country of origin before shipping it directly to the customer's home or workplace. And 91 percent of their roasters are women.

"In Nicaragua, women do about 70 percent of the work," Ketabi says, "but they've had little ownership of the business, the land, and understanding of how to turn that agricultural product into something that can work for them."

Vega used the startup capital from Kickstarter to establish a roastery in Estelí, Nicaragua's third-largest city and the hub of all things coffee in the country. Ketabi helped the team build an eco-friendly roaster, which is operated almost entirely by women.

As Ketabi and Terenzi spent more time in Nicaragua, they also saw a local appetite for good quality coffee. With tourists coming to enjoy the beaches, warm weather, and laid-back culture, they spotted an opportunity. "Most cafés and hotels were serving instant coffee," Ketabi says. "I know, it's crazy—in a country that grows great coffee. But the thing is that most of that great coffee gets exported as a raw product. Hardly anyone roasts in-country."

Their roastery in Estelí is near the Pan-American Highway, which makes it easy for farmers and visitors to access. It's also easy to get coffee to the airport in the capital city, Managua. That way, it could be at a customer's doorstep in Florida, California, or New York within five days of roasting.

Part café, part roastery, this facility became the hub of the company. Vega worked with co-ops, representing upward of four thousand farmers, many of whom are women. In 2015, when they opened their roastery, they trained five women to lead the roasting team. In one year, that number increased to twenty, and it has been growing consistently ever since.

Vega's mission was to add value to the product for the farmers in the country of origin; thus, instead of fetching $1 a pound when they sell it as is, the farmers could get $4 a pound, increasing their incomes by 400 percent, Ketabi says. The coffee is referred to as "farmer-roasted."

"As Vega developed, we never set out to become a women's-only organization," Terenzi says, "but it was always the women farmers who showed up for community informational sessions, it was the women who wanted to learn about processing, had a talent for cupping (taste testing the coffee), and who every day, rain or shine, big production or small, persisted and showed up to work. We are a women-driven company because women power us."

One of these farmers is Heydi Indira Gamez. Her family farms organic coffee in the Miraflor Natural Reserve, located just north of Estelí. Gamez started young, working as a *cortadora* on the farm, plucking coffee berries during harvest. "I enjoyed working closely with the plants, but the entire time, I had to endure these negative, sexist comments that reflected society's expectation—that working on the land is the job of men, and the woman's responsibility is to stay at home and raise children."

Gamez didn't care about those comments, and now she's working at Vega and studying at college. The income from Vega as a farmer-roaster has given her some peace of mind, she says. "My family and I have more financial freedom."

Gamez wants to use her education both from Vega and school to invest in more innovative farming practices, and she's still keen on being a coffee producer. The roasting helps her understand the bean better. Gamez says, "My favorite part is differentiating roast levels. Before, we didn't really know how to roast in a way to highlight the quality of the bean and bring out its natural flavors."

When Ketabi and Terenzi decided to set up a roastery in Nicaragua, they did have coffee critics who said that it couldn't be done there. "We definitely had our share of cynics who said that roasting is not so simple and needs to be done carefully to not destroy the bean. They questioned the talent of the farmers. But I think we've proven them wrong," Ketabi says.

In fact, the couple were even more ambitious, albeit a bit naive, in their original vision. When they originally returned to Nicaragua to establish the company, they wanted to put the roastery in the heart of the coffee farms. Terenzi had worked with a women's cooperative named Nuevo Amanecer in 2006. He discussed the idea of a roastery with Mayra Velásquez, the director of education for the co-op, and tried to install a coffee roaster on her farm, situated in the Sontule-Miraflor region. Ultimately the roaster didn't make it; the remote location and rough roads to the farm made reaching the site impractical from a business perspective. But Ketabi and Terenzi sold Nuevo Amanecer's coffee as their first offering through Vega.

The Sontule-Miraflor region has been growing coffee for decades. Nuevo Amanecer, a thirty-two-member co-op, came about in 1994 because many of the women, like Velásquez, didn't know what became of their coffee after it left the farm. Since the group consisted only of women, banks were not willing to provide them with a loan, and so they didn't have enough money to buy the land. Ultimately, they met a man from Germany who lent them $5,000. They would repay him in coffee for the next three harvests.

The other cooperative that Vega likes to support, SOPPEXCCA, is managed by a woman, Fátima Ismael, an agronomist who once worked for the Department of Agriculture in Nicaragua. As the subject of documentaries, and having given speeches at fair-trade events in the United Kingdom, Ismael has put her 650-person cooperative on the map. She is adamant that the machismo culture in Nicaragua has contributed to fatherless families and set back the progress of women looking to own their own plots of land. About one-third of SOPPEXCCA's members are women. Established in 1999, the group produces fair-trade-certified shade-grown coffee.

Ismael worries that coffee, especially shade-grown, is under threat as Nicaragua and neighboring countries experience higher temperatures and the other effects of climate.

Ismael's leadership has helped create a host of programs specifically for female coffee farmers ranging from access to credit, to free screenings for cervical cancer, to schooling for their children. The last is a long-term investment: children become literate and also advance the tradition of coffee farming in the region, and young children learn from an early age that girls are equals of boys. She argues that it may reverse the local culture of machismo if this fact is drilled into them for years.

Ismael has also made women farmers stewards of the land: the cooperative does not use chemical fertilizers and is investing in soil health to ensure that during hurricane season, the most fertile soil is not washed away by heavy rains.

By giving women access to this knowledge, and lines of credit to afford land, Ismael is reversing Nicaragua's long-standing dismal statistics on gender equality. In 2017, Nicaragua ranked 124th out of 189 countries on the Human Development Index, developed by the United Nations Development Program, which ranks countries by a combination of indicators such as life expectancy, education, and per-capita income.

"Stories like these are abundant in the coffee world," Ketabi says. "That's why we don't want to limit this model to Nicaragua. We want to take it to as many coffee-growing countries as possible and continue to source from both cooperatives and smallholder farms directly."

In 2018, Ketabi traveled to Colombia to replicate the same model there: incorporating farmers in the roasting process, and thus increasing their wages. This time, instead of Kickstarter, Vega had backing from the Mercy Corps Social Venture Fund. With the added capital, they opened a roastery, which works with a cooperative of 1,800 farmers. Social Venture Fund partner Timothy Rann referred to Vega's model as a potential "fourth wave of coffee: a more equitable and empowering coffee market for smallholder farmers."

In Colombia, Vega is starting in the Cauca region in the south, working with Mujeres Rurales del Cauca, the Rural Women of Cauca—nearly two thousand members who are a part of Caficauca, a larger coffee cooperative of more than twenty thousand growers.

Beyond adding more countries to their supply list, Vega partnered with the Goizueta Business School at Emory University in Atlanta, which runs a "women in coffee" program. Their advisory board of four women includes Ketabi and wants to empower women in the coffee movement. A three-year incubator, the program aspires to help women in the coffee sector get a bigger share of the market by connecting them with international buyers and advising them on how they can improve their operations.

The program is headed by Professor Peter Roberts, someone who, Ketabi says, is "widely respected in the coffee industry due to his deep commitment to cultivating transparency in the coffee supply chain." That's why Ketabi joined. "The real cost of coffee is hidden," she says. "I'm glad that someone's taken it up to force people to think about the actual cost."

As the company expands, Terenzi, Ketabi, and DeLuca want to ensure that their farmer-roaster model works effectively in each country. Customers in the United States expect beans at their doorstep within five days of roasting. "Even though we have a strong social mission, we have to deliver on taste and compete with other coffee subscriptions on speed and freshness. I'm quite aware that people will not support the company just because of our mission," Ketabi acknowledges. That's why Vega is sourcing coffees that are shade grown, without agrochemicals, and that rank high on the coffee grading scale (above 83).

While they respect the efforts of organizations such as Fair Trade Certified to suggest frameworks for pricing coffee, Ketabi notes that Vega actually pays more than what these certifications outline. "If you look at the price that consumers are paying for a cup of coffee to how much farmers are earning, they're going in opposite directions. Coffee prices are going up, yet farmers are making less," she says. "That has to change, and we will change it."

In 2018, they raised an additional $100,000 investment from Village Capital, a venture fund that has keen interest in agricultural development. As of 2019, Vega had raised a total of $2 million—a small sum compared to other startups. But Ketabi is not concerned. The point is not just to raise money but to create industry change. "It's time someone took on this broken system and created one that works better for coffee farmers and drinkers alike, one that is based on equity, gender inclusion, fair and livable wages, transparency, connection, exquisite coffee—and of course, love," Ketabi says.

CHAPTER SIX

TRAVEL

Thoughtful Tourism

A s I stand amid three hundred thousand acres of protected land east of Serengeti National Park in Tanzania, it's hard not to feel insignificant. Giraffes leisurely stroll by, elephants slowly make their way through the grasslands, and a large herd of water buffalo crosses the only dirt road, which cuts through waist-high grasses. Life happens at a startling slow pace.

It's perhaps one of the few places left on the planet where travelers are unlikely to see another human being for hours. Such landscapes—their beauty, their romanticism, and their vastness—lure travelers from around the globe.

Yet through their visits, humans are pushing natural spaces to the brink. In neighboring Serengeti National Park, the Seronera airstrip has been seeing increasing activity: in 2017, they reportedly had 3,742 aircraft land on the barren runway. Approximately 350,000 people visit the park each year.[1] Despite hefty park fees and the not-so-cheap airfare to East Africa, visitors are flocking to the park to see its wildlife.

The challenge for the tourism industry, be it in East Africa or other areas of natural beauty, is to find a balance between humans and nature. Too many people encroaching on a fragile ecosystem can be disastrous—destructive of the very landscape that attracted them in the first place.

In the Philippines, for example, a popular tourist beach, Boracay, was closed in 2018 because the once-beautiful clear white sand beaches had been polluted by too many tourists and related development. The beach remained closed for six months, time to restore some semblance of balance.[2]

Thailand, too, in spring 2018, had to shut down a beach that had been popularized by a Leonardo DiCaprio movie, fatefully titled *The Beach*.[3] Maya Bay, on Phi Phi Leh island, located in the Andaman Sea, will now remain closed for four months each year. The island's coral reefs and sea life had been damaged by the onslaught of tourists—four thousand a day were keen to see a landscape featured in a Hollywood film. When the beach reopens, the authorities cap the daily limit at two thousand tourists and no longer permit boats to anchor offshore.

Tourism is not only challenging the ecosystem; its overall carbon footprint is also damaging the earth's atmosphere. Though it's wonderful to travel, explore other countries, and engage with different cultures, companies will have to find ways to offer a more environmentally friendly tourism experience. Everyone doesn't need to stay home, but carbon offsets (that actually work), truly eco-friendly hotels, and more selective travel need to become more widespread.

According to researchers at the University of Sydney, the United States takes the prize for having the biggest carbon footprint from travel, followed by China, Germany, and India.[4] Scale clearly matters here; big economies with large populations account for the bulk of the carbon emissions. The United States produced 1,060 metric tons of emissions from Americans traveling, and 909 metric tons of emissions by people (American and foreign) traveling to US tourist destinations. Chinese travelers produced about half that, 528 metric tons and 561 metric tons, respectively.

To conduct the study, the research team spent more than a year examining more than a billion supply chains to determine their impact and emissions. The outcome: tourism accounts for 8 percent of global climate emissions. An industry that contributed $7.6 trillion to the global economy in 2016 will only continue to grow as wealth increases, flying costs become competitive, and social media sites popularize certain destinations. It's possible for that statistic to creep up to 10 percent in the next decade, making it one of the most destructive industries if not managed correctly.

According to the UN World Tourism Organization, one in ten jobs in the global workforce comes from the tourism sector—about 290 million jobs.[5] Aside from its environmental footprint, tourism is important because it affects jobs and security, and also influences the preservation of history and biodiversity. Tourism touches many different components of life and therefore has the potential to make positive social and environmental impact in communities.

However, there's a big hurdle on the environmental front: flying, particularly long distance, is one of the largest contributors to greenhouse gases, particularly CO_2 emissions. While hotels have been adopting eco-friendly practices, and some are even building brands around it, the aviation industry has been slow to move toward using cleaner-burning fuels. It's estimated that the aviation industry alone contributes 2 to 3 percent of global emissions of CO_2.[6] While several airlines have been dabbling with biofuels, the industry primarily runs on fossil fuels. That's likely to change as jet fuel prices continue to increase. In fact, Indian carriers have started considering biofuels for this very reason: jet fuel prices reached new highs in 2018, increasing by almost 50 percent, and then again in 2022, skyrocketing and overshadowing the world's return to travel after two years of a pandemic. SpiceJet, one of India's low-cost carriers, did a test run from Delhi to the Dehradun, a city at the base of the Himalaya, using 25 percent biofuel.[7]

Other carriers around the world, such as Virgin Atlantic, Virgin Australia, Alaska Airlines, and United Airlines, have been experimenting with biofuels for several years.[8] In December 2021, United had its first flight with one hundred passengers on board, from Chicago to Washington, DC, using 100 percent SAF, sustainable aviation fuel, made from bio-based waste and materials. United also bought a $30 million stake in Fulcrum BioEnergy, a California company that has built a plant near Reno, Nevada, where it will convert household garbage into what Fulcrum calls "low-carbon transportation fuels."[9] The company estimates that it can turn 175,000 tons of household garbage into 10.5 million gallons of fuel annually. In 2018, United Airlines also announced that it will cut its greenhouse emissions by 50 percent by 2050.[10] Alaska Airlines' fleet had the best fuel efficiency among the American carriers in 2015 and 2016 and has been experimenting with biofuels made from scraps from the logging industry in the Pacific Northwest.[11]

Long heralded as an effective and eco-friendly way to move large numbers of people, trains are getting revamped with newer technologies. In 2018, Germany debuted the world's first hydrogen-powered train, built by French train manufacturer Alstom, also known for producing the high-speed TGV (*train à grande vitesse*) trains that connect major cities in France.[12] Although, so far, only two hydrogen-powered trains have been put into service in Germany, plans are in the works to ramp up production and have more than forty trains in service from 2022 onward. These trains run on fuel cells that use hydrogen and oxygen to generate electricity; only water and water vapor are emitted. They can travel six hundred miles using just one tank of hydrogen—comparable to the range of a diesel train.

Obviously, transportation is a major element of travel. Another is hospitality. Industry veterans like Accor, Hilton, and Hyatt hotels have all adopted some level of sustainability practices—reducing linens used, doing laundry less frequently, opting for more eco-friendly lights. But it's smaller establishments such as the Green House Hotel in Bournemouth, on the south coast of England, that have meticulously thought through every aspect of a hotel's environmental footprint and have taken significant steps to reduce it.

SMALL FOOTPRINTS

I arrive on a wintry December evening, the hybrid car I rented at Heathrow having survived the sleet and snow en route to Bournemouth, Dorset. Over two hours southwest of the airport, the Green House Hotel is just a block from the coast, occupying a cream-colored Victorian-era building. There are just thirty-two rooms, a dining room, a lounge, and a multipurpose room—no spa, salon, or fitness center. That knocks it down from a five-star to a four-star, says Olivia O'Sullivan, the general manager. "The difference is not about luxury or quality, it's merely about facilities," she explains.

At this time of the year, just a few days before Christmas, the hotel charges about £80 a night for a standard room, or about $120. That rate goes up to approximately $200 a night in the spring and summer when the days are longer and the weather more suitable for visiting some of the nearby sites, such as the New Forest National Park, a beautiful woodland with blooming rhododendrons on warmer days.

The Green House Hotel's foyer is decorated with a Christmas tree made from paper and recycled materials. The ornaments draped on it are reminiscent of a bygone era, consisting of dried fruits and paper cutouts. There is certainly an understanding of simplicity and elegance: the lifestyle motto "less is more" would be suitable to describe the Green House. It has everything a traveler needs but none of the extra frills and waste.

I arrive at my room, the English Oak. It's a double standard with an en suite shower. The walls are covered with Forest Stewardship Council–certified wallpaper designed by art students at the Central Saint Martins school in London and printed with vegetable inks. The carpet is 100 percent wool, the furniture is made from fallen timbers, the linens are organic cotton, the temperature is controlled by the hotel (to avoid having Californians like me turn up the heat), and there is practically no plastic. Water bottles, with "House Water" written on them, are filled every day. A few homemade cookies in a cookie jar accompany tea and coffee. The shower and faucet heads conserve water by aeration, and the toiletries are made locally from nontoxic, natural ingredients. Linens and towels are not replaced daily.

O'Sullivan says that she and her team have spent a lot of time thinking through each aspect of the hotel. "For instance, we wash our linens on site. One, because we use nontoxic soaps, free of damaging chemicals, and because [the linens don't] have to travel. So again, smaller footprint."

It's not just about the materials used. It's about where they come from, she says. "We tried countless beauty products before we settled on this [line] because it's made locally. It was a combo of source and ingredients."

For O'Sullivan, who has spent years in the hospitality industry, it was these nuances that really caught her attention when she first spoke with Christopher Airey, one of the owners of the Green House Hotel. "I've worked for the big hotel chains, the ones that talk about sustainability. They don't care about anything but money. I was really getting tired of the industry and its ways before I came here," she says.

The Green House Hotel was conceived with the intention that it would be great for corporate clients who care about environmental issues. But it turned out, O'Sullivan says, that corporate clients often rely on rewards programs and have limited vetting. "It's very easy for a hotel to fill out a form and send it to a potential client, citing all these eco-friendly practices," she says. "No one is checking, though, to see if they're actually doing it."

Yet instead of becoming a mecca for sustainability-aware corporate travel departments, the Green House has resonated with tourists and savvy business travelers, according to O'Sullivan. "We definitely get people who like what we're doing and want to support it and enjoy it. There's only about 10 percent of guests I would say who have no clue or interest in the eco-friendly practices."

We walk on the unvarnished floorboards (varnishes are generally made with chemicals) to the dining and kitchen space. In these short, cold days of winter, the solar panels and a CHP (combined heat and power) unit generates nearly half of the hotel's electricity. A boiler kicks in as a last resort. They also work with Ecotricity, a UK-based company that offers home and business owners the option of sourcing their electricity from wind and solar power; the company uses these revenues to support the development of new renewable energy sources.

In the morning a simple continental breakfast is laid out—juices, fruit salads, croissants, toast. A traditional hot English breakfast, brought to the table for guests who request it, includes options such as a vegan British breakfast: meat-substitute sausages, beans, tomatoes, toast, and potatoes. They also offer traditional fare that, wherever possible, is sourced from local producers and organic and biodynamic farms.

"We work with some small producers who sometimes don't have certifications. But their farming practices are as in-line as a certified producer," O'Sullivan explains. "We're also happy to use wonky fruit and veg, the misshapen stuff that gets thrown out by farmers because it doesn't comply with supermarket regulations."

The hotel even helped fund a local social entrepreneur to create community gardens in the city. Sarah Watson runs Bournemouth & Poole Sustainable Food Cities. Four years ago, O'Sullivan got a note from her asking whether the Green House would be willing to help her set up Bournemouth and neighboring Poole as a sustainable food city. She connected Watson to a local organization, Green Goals, which was working with the local council and businesses in the city to promote eco-friendly practices. The Green House ended up supporting Watson financially, and soon the community garden grew enough produce that they could even sell some of it to local businesses like the Green House.

The local vegetables are cooked in the hotel kitchen, where all the appliances are as energy-efficient as possible, which translates into hydrocarbon refrigeration, induction burners, a hot fill dishwasher, sensor taps, and sensor grills. All the food that's served during breakfast, lunch, and dinner is made from scratch, including the breads offered with each meal.

Andy Hilton, the head chef, came to work at the Green House when the hotel opened in 2010. He was a sous chef then and was quickly promoted. He likes to serve "uncomplicated" food that tastes good and is sourced locally—satisfying and what Hilton calls "relatable." The food waste from the kitchen is separated and sent to a plant in nearby Piddlehinton, where it's pumped into an anaerobic digestion unit, which produces biogas that can be converted to electricity and heat.

When Airey drummed up the idea of an eco-friendly hotel with his business partners, Harish Sodha and Sarah Burrows, their intent was to make something that balanced environmental concerns with practicality and affordability. "I was aware that there were eco hotels, but they were less mainstream. I wanted to make this the norm, a hotel that attracted the corporate market and those just looking for a nice place to stay. Not a cabin in the middle of the Amazon. Those kind of eco resorts exist. But what about for everyday needs?"

In 2006, the three partners started to look at properties in the London area. "Everything we found had a queue of people waiting [who were] willing to pay twice what it was worth," he jokes.

To find something within their budget, they broadened their search to nearby cities that served as hubs for offices and were destinations for holiday goers—Bournemouth checked both boxes. When they came upon the Grade 2–listed heritage property—meaning that it cannot be pulled down—it was not love at first sight. "We loved the building. But it was a tired three-star hotel," Airey says.

Nevertheless, they purchased the aged hotel, then closed it down for nearly a year to refurbish it and install more energy-efficient systems. They hired a mechanical and electrical consultant for advice on the latest technologies that would work in the historic structure. "But I didn't want to turn this into a showcase of the latest eco-technologies," Airey continues. "I wanted it to be beautiful, and comfortable, and within the period."

They also spent a fair amount of time looking at embedded energy generation. They toyed with the idea of a biogas boiler, which would use bio-pellets. While it was certainly eco-friendly, it required deliveries of bio-pellets every day because there was nowhere to house a month's supply. "And that just seemed wasteful to have a truck coming daily or even every few days," Airey says.

The vision was, and continues to be, to create a hotel business that could be replicated elsewhere in the United Kingdom. "It had to be a viable business model. That's why we didn't just go for every environmental technology on the market then."

A carbon trust grant offset some of the upfront costs of using more expensive materials and technology. "It definitely costs more in the beginning," Airey says. "But as a result, we've bought things that have lasted longer and are higher quality." Many hotels are refurbished every six to eight years, but the Green House Hotel is a decade old now, and no major renovations are planned; everyday maintenance seems to be working in combination with higher-quality materials to preempt costly refurbishing.

For Sarah Burrows, an interior designer and a partner in the business, the project enabled her to source materials from suppliers around the United Kingdom that are often neglected in the race for the cheapest option. "The reality is that when you go to traditional suppliers in the hospitality industry, much of [the products are] coming from

Asia, and it's not natural materials and [it's] treated with chemicals," Airey says.

Instead, Burrows looked to the Scottish island of Bute, home to about seven thousand people and scores of sheep, for wool fabrics to furnish the hotel with carpets. Over a decade later, they're holding up well. For the hallways she used paints from Farrow & Ball, a company fifteen miles from the hotel that produces eco-paints with linseed oil and clay. The wallpaper comes from the UK company Graham & Brown and comes wrapped in natural starch, not cellophane packaging. It's details like this that distinguish Green House from its larger competitors.

Corporate clients tend to go for the well-known hospitality brands, but Airey may have an alternative in mind. "Hotels are wasteful by nature," he says. "That said, the hospitality industry has started to adopt better practices, and better technologies. But it's not mainstream yet. What if eco-friendly hotels had their own rewards system, and they could come together to support it? Because many of them are independently run."

Pushing the collective effort of entrepreneurs like Airey forward sounds like a smart idea. "It amazes me that there are not more Green Houses in the United Kingdom today," he says "If we don't end up making this more mainstream, I'm sure someone else will. It's only a matter of time."

What has kept Airey and his partners from developing more hotels like the Green House is the fact that hotels are not cheap endeavors, requiring large sums of money upfront. "It takes an extra three to four years to see your returns when you've invested more upfront," he says. The hotel is now a profitable venture, and their investments are reaping returns. Perhaps that's a sign that Airey, Burrows, and Sodha are still keen on scaling their business model and will be back in the real estate market, searching for their next project in the United Kingdom.

SLOWER TRAVEL

Tone Rønning Vike and her husband, Bjørn Vike, share the same sentiment in regard to running a restorative travel company. "The whole experience and operation need to be on board, not just one element of it," Tone says.

Situated in the heart of a UNESCO World Heritage site, near Aurlandsfjord in Norway's Aurland Valley, the Vikes' ten-room operation is a fifteen-minute drive from the village of Flåm, which sits at the very tip of the Aurlandsfjord. While it's only twelve miles away, it seems like a different world.

Flåm is on a lot of bucket lists, and a convenient stop for cruise ships showcasing the beautiful Norwegian fjords. That means a village of three hundred people is transformed overnight into a town of five thousand whenever a cruise ship docks in the harbor. And the huge vessels dominate the view: guests staying in fjord-facing hotel rooms wake up to a surprise: a massive ship, blowing its whistle and blocking the majestic views of the fjord.

"No kind of tourism pollutes more per passenger than cruise [ship] tourism," Tone says. "Imagine a floating city—the amount of waste, and how little they contribute to the local economy, is jaw-dropping."

Research is beginning to back up these claims. According to the Norwegian Center for Transport Research, the number of cruise visitors went from two hundred thousand to seven hundred thousand between 2000 and 2015.[13] In the villages of Geiranger and Flåm, where most tourists go to see the fjords, nitrogen oxides in the air have reached levels considered toxic to health. The *Aftenposten*, Norway's largest newspaper, asked the Norwegian Institute of Aeronautics to examine the air quality at Geiranger. The results were surprising. On days when several cruise ships docked at the small town, air pollution, particularly nitrogen dioxide, reached levels comparable to that in London, Barcelona, Glasgow, or Munich—surpassing 180 micrograms a day. Since many of the cruise ships were built before the year 2000, they are not operating with the latest systems. Plus, they navigate through waters surrounded by steep mountains where there is little wind, so the polluted air just sits in the narrow fjord, hanging over Geiranger. The government is looking at various ways to curb the pollution and minimize the impact on towns such as Flåm and Geiranger. Tone argues that it's not happening fast enough.

In 2018, the Vikes' hotel hosted a walking festival where they invited guests and visitors to walk through the Aurland valleys and waterfalls. "We want to give slow adventures, organic, local produce, and show that this can be the walking heart of the world," she says, preparing a pot of tea in the hotel's kitchen, from which guests can see waterfalls in the distance.

Tone and her husband are oddballs in the tourism industry. They're from Bergen, where Tone worked as a journalist and even made a documentary about pollution in Norway's fjords. But middle-class life in Bergen was beginning to bore her. "I felt all the conversations revolved around 'proper clothing for the kids,' and 'how to redo your kitchen (for the third time),'" she jokes. "Having worked as a journalist for most of my adult life, it felt like it was about time to do something. I wanted to do, do with a capital D."

The opportunity presented itself in the form of a farm that Tone's husband had acquired from his family. He had stayed at the farm as a child and his mother had grown up there. His aunt and uncle worked in the fields, growing hay and carrots. Since Bjørn's aunt and uncle didn't have kids of their own, in 1996 they passed the property on to him. In 2014 the couple decided to turn it into a boutique hotel.

In neighboring Flåm, there are three or four hotels with en suite accommodations. None of them are terribly cheap—starting at $250 a night. After all, this is Norway, one of the most expensive countries in the world. The Vikes offer ten rooms for similar prices.

The difference in the experience, though, is unmistakable. The Flåm hotels are situated right on the fjord, which means they have views, but they also have thousands of cruise visitors ruining the views, to the extent that the experience can often be overpowered by the ships that moor right in front of the hotel balconies.

The Vikes instead have created a slower, gentler approach to visiting the fjords. At their hotel, named 29|2 Aurland—the address of the property—a variety of small structures house the ten rooms. They're configured as singles, doubles, and suites to accommodate guests traveling in various-sized groups.

What's most notable about the space, though, is its heritage. The rooms encapsulate the history of Bjørn's family and the various visitors they've had over the years. The fisherman's cabin, where they hosted their first guests in 2014, is one of the oldest structures in Aurland itself, dating back to the early eighteenth century. Fishing is a common theme throughout the property. Framed images of the fly fishermen adorn the walls, including an image of Bjørn's grandfather, who preferred to fly-fish wearing a suit, not his farm clothes.

The rivers and waterfalls that run through this corner of the world are important to the Vikes. Because she had investigated environmental issues affecting the region in her journalism days, Tone is well versed and outspoken on what's happening around her.

"We look at the waterfalls as the veins of the country. As 99 percent of the electricity used in Norway comes from hydropower, we have seen too many rivers dammed—among them, our Aurland River. It severely influences the ecosystems of the river and the fjords, and that, combined with the many salmon farms in the Norwegian fjords, have caused a severe decrease of the wild fish population," she says.

While Tone is taking guests on hikes to see the waterfalls close up, Bjørn is also active in preserving as much open space and dam-free rivers as possible. He is the leader of the local river owners' association. Every year he brings together fly fishers and researchers to a gathering in the Aurland Valley. Needless to say, he's also happy to teach guests fly fishing. There are rules though: only one fish is allowed to be kept per day, and salmon fishing is catch-and-release only. And each year, at the beginning of the fishing season, the duo donates a one-week stay at their hotel to the annual auction, held by the North Atlantic Salmon Fund to support its environmental program.

Typically, cruise-ship visitors just make a quick stop in Flåm, go on a tour, and then move on to the next fjord with their ship. The Vikes, instead, invite their visitors to stay a few nights and enjoy the area at their leisure—and largely on foot. Fishing, hiking, visiting waterfalls, and rowing boats on the fjords slows the pace. For guests who would like a little cultural immersion, they organize a picnic with a local writer or artist.

"It's about the simple things we take for granted," she says. "In Norwegian, there is a word, *friluftsliv*, which refers to an outdoors attitude. We feel a bit unfulfilled if we have spent a weekend without hiking or skiing."

For her, the average day includes driving her children to school, overseeing operations at the hotel, taking guests on a hike up to a waterfall, and then picking up the kids and doing chores around the home as well as ensuring that guests have what they need. She admits that it's a lot of work, yet she's happier than she was in Bergen. "Many kids nowadays grow up without ever having seen the Milky Way due to the light pollution. We are very blessed to have this natural treasure chest around us."

By working with travel operators who celebrate a similar slow-travel mindset, the Vikes are able to keep their hotel occupied. In fact, it's sold out from May to September. Guests come to 29|2 Aurland for a pristine environment of natural beauty, not a hurried tour of the fjords. "I've had guests from Hong Kong and Singapore who wondered if they were really allowed to pick the wildflowers," she says. "They've grown up in cities where everything is manufactured."

To celebrate the handmade elements of their community, the Vikes have brought together local artisans and business owners to create an organization called Sakte—"slow" in Norwegian. They try to support one another by using each other's businesses wherever feasible. For instance, 29|2 Aurland sources all its organic bread from Krutt & Kanel Bakery in Aurland. They take guests on guided tours of Aurlandskoen, a handmade-shoe factory, and offer guests a visit to Rein Glass, a glassblowing workshop. The Vikes also employ students from the local organic agricultural school as gardeners to look after the hotel's vegetable patch.

"Norway sells nature," Tone says. "Not lineups [of cruise ships]."

KEEPING OPEN SPACES WILD, AND OPEN

Keeping natural spaces open, and the wildlife in them free to roam, is essential to ecotourism—be it in Scandinavia or in East Africa. Just as tourists flock to see the raw beauty of Norway, hundreds of thousands travel to view the wildlife of Africa. But it's a catch-22: tourism needs tourists; but too many tourists spoil what they are there to see, until the destination itself begins to disappear.

Luke Bailes has spent his entire life in the African tourism industry, and it has made him less interested in droves of tourists and more keen on using tourism as a tool to fund conservation work. As founder of Singita, a South Africa–based safari and conservation company that has more than one million acres under its management, he wants to continue the high-value, low-impact model he pioneered twenty-six years ago in South Africa.

"Africa will need to regulate its tourism. Otherwise, we end up with too many safari vehicles, leaving tracks, and tourists usurping precious resources like water. It's not good for the animals, the environment, and it's not the best experience for visitors," he says.

In Tanzania's Grumeti Reserve, Singita has leased 350,000 acres from the Tanzanian government on a thirty-three-year lease. The goal is to bring back wildlife that was previously hunted and poached in the region. Bailes got into the safari business by accident. Born and bred in South Africa, he often went on low-budget safaris with his family in the bush. When friends asked if they could join him, the idea of building a travel lodge became a viable business option. Given that the Bailes family had access to land just outside South Africa's Kruger National Park, he started to fix up an old property and use it for a safari experience.

Bailes's grandfather, James Fawcett Bailes, bought the land located in present-day Sabi Sand Game Reserve in 1925. It was a thirty-thousand-acre hunting concession. When Luke Bailes started the company in 1993, Singita's first lodge, Ebony, debuted a new approach to safaris—one that was comfortable and luxurious.

Twenty-six years later, Singita has become a familiar name for luxury safaris. They entertain guests from well-to-do backgrounds—primarily Americans—at their fifteen lodges in South Africa, Tanzania, Zimbabwe, and Rwanda. The price tag is high, starting at $1,500 per person per night all-inclusive of meals, airport transportation, and safaris.

Singita has developed a conservation approach that makes them unique in the crowded safari market. They see their lodges and their hospitality business as means of conserving wildlife from poachers, protecting biodiversity on the continent, and improving the lives of people living near the reserves through education and small business development. Yes, it's expensive, but it's a once-in-a-lifetime experience. Many of the guests go there to celebrate momentous occasions—weddings, retirement, or a significant birthday. These are holidays that they've saved years for.

That works in Singita's favor: the price point helps the company regulate the number of visitors they host and consequently helps keep their environmental footprint to a minimum. Bailes also has a policy that the company will not build a new property unless it offers something better than is currently provided and creates an opportunity to conserve wildlife.

The Singita lodges in the Grumeti Reserve in Tanzania—a vast swath of the African bush dotted with acacia trees and abundant wildlife where the Grumeti River flows free—is perhaps one of their best success stories. In 2002, a philanthropist investor, Paul Tudor Jones, established the Grumeti Fund and acquired the land; Singita came on board later to establish lodges. The Grumeti Fund team had a challenge: to convert an area known for intensive hunting and poaching into a space where wildlife was protected. Owing to the density of poachers in the region, much of the wildlife stayed to the west, within the Serengeti National Park.

Poaching was a rampant problem until the Grumeti Fund arrived; particular targets were elephants and rhinos, whose tusks and horns have value on the global market. The Great Elephant Census, one of the more comprehensive studies conducted specifically on elephant poaching, found that Tanzania had seen a rapid 60 percent decline in elephant population in the five years before 2016. Along with Mozambique, Tanzania had the largest decline in elephant population in eastern Africa. Now, the elephant herds are thriving on the Grumeti Reserve, and many other species have returned to the game-rich area.

Poaching is not limited to elephants: lions, leopards, rhino, buffalo, wildebeest, pangolin, and vultures are also targets. Elephants have been at the heart of several wildlife campaigns because they tend to enter the fields of local farmers, and human-wildlife conflict follows.

The elephant deaths are a mix of poaching and locals protecting their land and livelihoods.

"Human-wildlife conflict is one of our biggest challenges," says Wesley Gold, who worked for the British Army for a decade before joining Singita. Originally from South Africa, Gold organizes the law enforcement and anti-poaching efforts for the Grumeti Fund. "It's not every day that a tourism company has an anti-poaching squad," he jokes while driving through the bush in one of Singita's open vehicles and swatting tsetse flies away from his face.

It's the first week of July and everyone is waiting for the wildebeest migration to begin. Light rains in the morning keep the animals from congregating around the watering holes and tsetse flies are everywhere. This is the beginning of Gold's work season. Soon the drier months will follow, the grasses will get drier and shorter, and the wildebeest will make their way through the reserve.

"Though a lot of the focus has been on poaching larger animals, like elephants, much of what is poached, particularly at this time of the year, are wildebeest," he says, driving up to his headquarters, located near Singita's largest lodge in the reserve, Sasakwa, an Edwardian-style manor with open views of the savanna.

As the wildebeest migrate through the reserve, poachers place snares in the bush. Strapped on tree branches and hidden in vegetation, the wire snares blend in and trap the animals by the neck or the legs. Gold estimates that hundreds of thousands of wildebeest are poached each year—20 percent of the 1.2 million animals that migrate across the Serengeti-Mara ecosystem.

He collects these snares and throws them on the poles in front of his office. It's early in the season so the poles are empty. "But in a few weeks, sadly, these three poles will be filled with hundreds [of snares]," he says.

Though still a tourism company offering a luxurious camp or lodge safari experience, the company's mission has steadily broadened, Bailes says. "We've recently revamped [our hundred-year plan] to reflect where we're headed, focusing even more on the conservation work in our messaging. We're replicating the model in Rwanda, where we are excited to open two lodges on the edge of Volcanoes National Park."

Simply put, the hundred-year vision, he says, is for Singita to preserve and protect large areas of land on the African continent. "The world's population is increasing; the demand to see nature and wildlife will increase too. Yet we also have to leave nature to itself and ensure that man does not interfere," Bailes says.

In 2006, Bailes met the American philanthropist, Paul Tudor Jones, who had acquired the Grumeti Reserves from the Tanzanian government. They partnered up to create the current Singita offering of five properties: Singita Sasakwa Lodge, Sabora Tented Camp, Faru Faru Lodge, Serengeti House, and small glamping accommodations referred to as Singita Explore. Each lodge has completely different characteristics. The largest lodge, Sasakwa, is referred to as home base. There visitors enjoy the impressive panoramic vistas of the savanna. The Sabora Tented Camp has a 1920s-era feel, enabling guests to camp in tents fitted with four-poster beds placed on rugs, surrounded by vintage suitcases, lanterns, and old English furnishings. Animals occasionally meander through the site. Meanwhile, Faru Faru Lodge has just ten rooms in a more modern and minimalist style with floor-to-ceiling windows, framing views of the Grumeti River; the dining space overlooks a watering hole where lions, monkeys, impalas, and baboons come for a drink.

The lodges are furnished with upcycled and recycled materials wherever possible. Accent pieces and glassware at Faru Faru come from the Shanga Shop in Arusha, a social enterprise company that employs disabled individuals to repurpose glass into homeware and décor items. Several of the properties already run on solar power or are being converted to solar. (One of their South African lodges just introduced Tesla Powerpack batteries, which power 90 percent of the lodge.) Singita eliminated 90 percent of single-use plastic from the lodges, and 80 percent of the food is sourced from nearby villages where Singita operates community development projects.

The staff is also a familial bunch with brothers and sisters working in different components of the business. Gendi Gohebo Gorobani, for example, works at the Faru Faru lodge, taking care of guests. A tall, seemingly always happy chap, he greets guests when they arrive, and then stays by their side throughout their stay—providing, essentially, a friendly butler service. A Tanzanian, he extols the virtues of chai at breakfast, shares his favorite local fare with dinner guests, and bounces from room to room taking care of any personal requests, working long hours most days. Coming from a nearby village, Gorobani is happy to be working at Singita: "I get to meet people from all around the world. That is the best part." Despite his long days at the lodge, he's offered support that would have been hard to find elsewhere: he started as a trainee in the staff canteen and now is the face of the company for so many visitors. And he has a family member nearby: his brother, Pascal Gohebo Gorobani, works as a scout with Gold in the anti-poaching squad.

The numerous community development programs—from farming and a community culinary school to preserving wildlife and biodiversity—are all managed by the Grumeti Fund, the not-for-profit conservation partners of the safari company. Stephen Cunliffe, a South African who had worked for other conservation efforts on the continent, came on board to run the Grumeti Fund in 2015. "Aside from just overseeing the various projects within the fund, we also have to liaise with the government. If we're going to improve road conditions, change any of the dynamics here, operate machinery, we need to work [with the] Tanzanian government and other stakeholders," he says.

The fund employs 165 people, the biggest component of which is law enforcement and the scouts who help Gold with his anti-poaching program. During the dry season, which lasts from about May to October, they hire another sixty individuals to help with seasonal activities like fighting fires. Cunliffe also spends time thinking about how to manage other, less-publicized issues facing the region, such as the possible damming of the Mara River, which could, he says, have a "catastrophic impact on the ecosystem."

One of the least-discussed environmental concerns is the invasion of non-native species. Plants such as the Mexican sunflower and prickly pear have been introduced in villages or other lodges in the park and have spread easily, their seeds carried for miles by animals, insects, and the weather. Now, they pose a threat to existing vegetation and can be poisonous for some animals to consume.

But the biggest challenge is poaching and human-wildlife conflict. According to a survey conducted by the Grumeti Fund in 2016, 86 percent of households and eighteen of twenty village leaders named wildlife intrusion, particularly by elephants, as their key concern. A full 80 percent of households said that they had already been impacted by human-wildlife conflict, and 77 percent blamed elephants invading their crops and causing damage.

"This is going to be the hardest challenge because you've got [Lake Victoria] right here, villages are on the boundary of the protected area, and every year [they're] encroaching [more] because of the [villagers'] need for space for cattle to graze. The fact that there is no fence, the conflict grows exponentially," says Cunliffe.

The Grumeti Fund is tackling this problem with the anti-poaching squad led by Gold and his right-hand man, Gotera Gamba, who is the head of the fund's law enforcement operations. Gamba knows the problem intimately. He used to hunt the very animals he now hopes to save. At eighteen he started poaching, but after years of hiding out in the bush to capture animals, he called it quits. "The conditions were really bad. It was dangerous, hard, and I just got tired," he recalls.

Even though his work requires long days—waking up at 4 a.m., patrolling for five hours, making a long drive back to base camp, training and late-night missions—the forty-year-old says it's worth the hard work and risk. Risk is a given in this line of work. "I've had a few arrows, that had poison, just miss me," Gamba says. "I also saw one man from our team get shot by an arrow."

So far, Gold and Gamba have lost only one of their men. It is a sad reality they live with: "We signed up for this work. We know what it entails," Gold says.

The members of the Grumeti Fund's law-enforcement and anti-poaching squad come primarily from nearby communities, individuals who understand the geography and the local players in poaching. The scouts operate from twelve camps, observation points located throughout the reserve that enable them to keep a watchful eye. They also take that knowledge and learning from the field and share it with friends and families in their communities. Gamba has six children, and he's hopeful that the next generation will have a different outlook on animals. The most resistance he's faced has been from an older man in his village. "I grew up with this man. He cannot walk. I go over and help him get around. But he says the animals are God's gift to be hunted."

"And he even helps him financially," Gold adds, shaking his head. "The work he does at Singita enables him to look after [this old man]. I don't think he's won him over yet, but it's good that they can have this dialogue."

Changing human behavior is the hardest thing to do. "You have to remember that people have lived in these areas for generations and used bush meat as a local protein source. It's very easy for someone like me to say it's wrong. But these people have always been hunters," Gold says.

I ask Gamba if he's still a minority in the community. He nods. "Yes, I'm one in a few. And I've only been able to change the mindset of fifteen people or so. Not many in all these years." He shares his dream to educate children at the schools in the villages about animals. "That is how we solve the problem for the future," he says.

The other option—fencing off the reserve—is contentious and hotly debated among conservationists in the region. "'Fence' in the Serengeti is a swear word," says Gold. "Sometimes people sitting in the United States or Europe, who are distant from the problem, don't understand the nuances of it."

But then how do you ensure that the eighty thousand people who live on the periphery of the Serengeti and the reserve will not run into conflict with the animals? "For many of these farmers, they don't see an elephant as this wild, beautiful thing," Gold says. "They see it as a threat because it came and ate through their crop, or ripped up the farm, and then maybe even trampled on small animals as it was escaping."

Next to Gold's office is a room filled with monitors and tracking devices, much of it donated by Seattle-based Vulcan Inc., led by the late Paul Allen, who was a keen supporter of Singita's work. That may be the best answer for now: keep an eye on the elephants, geo-tag them, and study their behavior. From here, staff can monitor the activities of animals, particularly elephants, throughout the reserve. They can collect data on where snares were placed, where poached animals were found, where conflict arose, and use these findings to predict future movements by hunters and poachers.

Most guests do not see this side of Singita, unless they sign up for a participation safari, one of Singita's latest offerings. Hopefully, it will become a growing revenue stream for the Grumeti Fund's conservation work. In 2017, Singita was able to host the first group of participation safari guests; in 2018, an additional eight guests helped collar elephants with GPS-enabled satellite collars and witness conservation work firsthand. For this privilege they pay $25,000 each, which supports the Grumeti Fund's conservation projects.

Cunliffe explains that the idea behind all these experiences—for guests to see the antipoaching unit, help with the elephant-collaring project, see their specially trained K9 police dogs sniff out hidden contraband—is to offer people a glimpse behind the scenes. "Plus, we can then engage a group of individuals with high net worth who will hopefully become longtime supporters of the fund," he says. One of the guests did just that, donating $350,000 to a K9 unit. This is a concept that Singita had introduced in 2012. The dogs scare off poachers, who, when they realize they're being tracked and followed by these dogs, are less interested in entering that part of the bush to hunt.

These types of "immersive safaris" are designed for travelers who want to get involved, are more conservation-minded, and have the money to enjoy such experiences. Some critics may dismiss these safaris as experiences available only to the 1 percent, but Bailes sees it differently: he is keen on channeling more of these tourists' money to much-needed conservation work.

In safari tourism, the balance between humans, development, and wildlife is a difficult one to strike. "Some would like it if we don't have any lodges or any people in these ecosystems," says Bailes. "But then how do you attract the funding needed to support the program?

The pressure on pristine wilderness is like never before, and we have to take that seriously."

The word "safari," after all, means "a journey" in Swahili. "And traveling to Africa," Bailes says, "can be a really powerful journey. Many have said it's a spiritual one—to be in such a landscape where you are not the focus."

CHAPTER SEVEN

HEALTH

Health Care for People, Not Profit

The health industry ought to be the easiest one to marry mission with business: the purpose of any health company should be to elevate the health of their clients. So why do health companies fail so miserably at this? The answer is greed. If health care is to be private, like it is in the US, there is an inherent risk: profit over people. Plus, there is an added challenge in the US—the poor health of our nation's citizens. Ideally, health care should go beyond providing medications to helping people lead more holistic lives, where their general health is the result of their lifestyle, their diet, their sleep, and their overall quality of life. Businesses are beginning to tap into these needs now, looking at health care through a wide-angle lens. What is required may be not just a pill or a quick remedy; it may be a long-term lifestyle change. That is, after all, the regenerative approach: nature heals slowly and seasonally, and each aspect of nature has a role to play in its overall productivity.

Thus, it's hard to provide a broad overview of the challenges in public health; each country has its own nuances. In the United States, the problem is that health care is provided by entities focused on profits, not patients. In many countries in the developing world, the lack of a robust public and private infrastructure poses a different problem: it is challenging just to improve quality of life and increase life expectancy. In the coming pages, we look at innovations in both to illustrate how business can work toward health care for all.

Public health facilities are available in the United States, but most people turn to private care. In 2016, 27 million Americans were uninsured.[1] That's the first hurdle: getting everyone health insurance. Despite the passage of the Affordable Care Act, approximately one-tenth of the US population remains outside the health insurance system. The primary reason? Money. Nearly half of uninsured adults said they were uninsured because it was too expensive. With the freelancer economy growing steadily each year—in 2017, 57 million individuals in the United States worked as freelancers—more and more Americans will not have an employer to provide health insurance for them.[2]

Yet being insured does not guarantee medical care. Even with insurance, patients are expected to pay a fee, called a co-pay, when they visit the doctor. Also, many services fall outside of insurance coverage, or they require an additional fee. So what do people do? They avoid going to the doctor unless it's absolutely necessary—simply to save money. The health care industry gives a discouraging message to Americans: you can receive good care only if you can afford it.

Some county hospitals and public clinics have open-door policies and provide care if a patient is in need without being referred for treatment by a primary-care physician. But they still send a bill afterward. If the patient does not qualify for government-subsidized programs, that bill is his or her responsibility to pay—essentially, it's a debt.

The kind of care that's provided in health care facilities is another topic altogether—typical treatments options rely on a push for antibiotics, steroids, and short-term cures for long-term problems. And treatment is not cheap. According to one study, in 2016 the United States spent about $9,400 per capita on healthcare, 17.8 percent of GDP. That's almost double the average of other comparable developed nations: the United Kingdom, France, Germany, Canada, Australia, Japan, Sweden, the Netherlands, Switzerland, and Denmark spent on average about 11 percent of GDP on health care. Australia had the lowest percentage, 9.6 percent, and Switzerland, the highest, at 12 percent—still significantly lower than the United States.[3]

The study also found that Americans spent more per capita on pharmaceuticals and that US physicians made significantly more money than their international counterparts. On average, general practitioners earned $218,000 per year in the United States; in the other countries the annual salary ranged from $87,000 to $154,000. With all that spending, one would imagine that Americans are in great health, but Americans' life expectancy was the lowest, 78.8 years, in the group, and the highest infant mortality was in the United States.

What may be at fault here is the emphasis on money-making in a profession that should not be profit-driven. In healthcare, purpose-driven companies ought to be a given. Yet it has not proved to be the case for some of the country's biggest players in the industry. The Hospital Corporation of America (HCA), most infamously, has faced scrutiny and hefty fines for its misconduct. In 2003, the company paid more than $2 billion in penalties for overbilling and kickbacks to medical professionals.[4] It's not alone: Tenet Healthcare also paid $54 million to settle a case involving doctors giving patients unnecessary heart treatments in a Northern California hospital.[5] Despite the lawsuits and heavy fines, these companies seem to continue with their ways. In 2012, HCA again faced allegations of medical misconduct and unnecessary procedures ordered by doctors at its hospitals.[6]

The complex web of money and healthcare has made more players want a piece of the pie. The drugstore chain CVS is looking to add clinics that do more than just provide flu vaccines. Humana and the retail giant Walmart are joining forces. And UnitedHealthcare, one of the largest insurance providers in the country, is buying medical groups to provide more doctors "in network."

Yet few are talking about the underlying issues that make Americans some of the sickest people in the developed world: poor diet, an agricultural industry that promotes large-scale farming whose products provide little nutrition, long work hours, few holidays and no federally mandated maternal or paternal leave. As a result, the onus is falling on private companies to find solutions to the crisis in American healthcare and Americans' health.

Digital clinics, the latest wave of healthcare startups, offer quick online diagnosis and medical care at little to no cost. But just prescribing meds is not the answer. And many doctors worry that if patients are not seeing at least one general physician in person regularly, the doctor assessing them through a digital screen may not have a complete view of the patient's health.

FOOD, NOT MEDS

Dr. Andrea Feinberg is an internist who, after spending ten years working in Los Angeles, moved to central Pennsylvania to serve as the medical director at the Geisinger Medical Center in Danville. "We don't want you in the hospital," she says. "I wanted people to get back to basics and be less dependent on the meds and technology in hospitals. That's not the way to manage health long-term."

When she relocated to Pennsylvania, she volunteered with a local food program for low-income households: children were provided a box of food each weekend to ensure that they'd be well fed while not at school.

"But we were giving these kids foods that I would not give my kids. It was very high-calorie, high-sugars, processed foods," she recalls. Dr. Feinberg didn't feel comfortable sending the kids home with foods that would encourage chronic illnesses.

She reached out to the Central Pennsylvania Food Bank with an alternative approach. "At the food bank, the idea was any food is better than no food. But we in the medical field say, 'Above all, do no harm,'" she says. "I asked if we could send the kids home with more fruits, vegetables, and whole grains and recipes on how to prepare the foods."

The food bank staff were open to the idea, if she could prove that it worked. Dr. Feinberg did a pilot study in 2015 with five patients who had diabetes. "They were very sick, constantly in and out of the hospital," she says. Each of the patients got a regular box of nutrient-dense foods and twenty hours of nutritional education about diabetes: how to treat it, how the medicines work, and what lifestyle changes can help control the condition. They were sent home with a box of food and recipes for the week for themselves and their families. "They're much more likely to do it if everyone is on board," Dr. Feinberg says.

Within one week the patients' sugar levels dropped. Within three months, the tests showed that they were healthier overall. The program was working, so she reached out to philanthropic organizations to help fund it. With the Geisinger Medical Center paying for 50 percent of the cost, and grant funding covering the rest, in 2017 she was able to scale the program to six hundred people. Her goal is to serve 1.5 million meals.

Next, she put together a randomized control trial to build out more scientific proof that the model works. Ultimately, she sees health care insurers paying for it. "We can't keep writing grants. I have to find a sustainable solution to it. The majority of Americans who are not food insecure—lacking access to fresh, healthy, affordable foods—also have these illnesses and can benefit from this knowledge. They get tricked into buying foods that are tasty but not good for them. And the costs from the majority can offset the costs for the smaller, food-insecure population."

The program sparked interest from hospital groups and health care systems around the United States. Every week Dr. Feinberg spends a few hours speaking to those interested and seeing how the Geisinger Medical Center can fuel a new movement. Recently, the center absorbed a medical school; the medical students will be given nutritional training, which historically has not been covered in traditional medical training.

"Some doctors don't take very good care of themselves, and others just get dissuaded when they see that patients are not able to keep up the lifestyle changes. It's easier to throw a pill at it. That's the American way, isn't it? Just take a pill," Dr. Feinberg says.

When she applied for a grant from a drug company, she was denied because her model focused on lifestyle changes and didn't include prescription drugs. "Drug companies want to keep you on the drug. That's how they make money," she says.

However, patients getting off medicines and reducing the number of hospital visits has reduced costs for Geisinger. Patients who took part in the pilots were "expensive and sick patients," Feinberg notes. "We saw a two-thirds drop in claims data early on. We are currently obtaining financial claims data on our enrollees, and we are seeing what seems to be a 25 percent reduction in ER visits, [and] a 45 percent reduction in hospitalization."

Overall, patients with type 2 diabetes reported that their levels of hemoglobin A1C, a measure used to track the severity of diabetes, went from 9.6 percent to 7.5 percent. Even though the hospital is providing extra services like dietary counseling, wellness classes, and nutrition workshops, their costs are still lower. The problem, she argues, is in the system: "Medicare doesn't pay for [services to reduce] diabetes, heart disease, and improvement of health. We're in the sick-care system."

This "Farmacy" solution requires less money, and more thought, and doctors will have to spend more time engaging with patients. They'll need to guide them through the process, encouraging them if they don't see results immediately. "It takes more time from us as practitioners. It's not as simple as meds. But that's what we need. We need a paradigm shift in medicine."

EXPANDING THE REACH OF NUTRITIOUS FOODS

Thrive Market, an online health food store, is trying to get more nutrient-dense foods to consumers beyond the coasts. Though based in Los Angeles, 50 percent of their customers are actually located in the Midwest and South, where health food stores are fewer and harder to locate and can be pricier.

When cofounder Gunnar Lovelace thought up the idea of an e-commerce platform that made health foods available with a Costco-style membership fee, no one wanted to invest in the idea. "Every investor I went to was in San Francisco or New York City. And they all were in walking distance of a Whole Foods or a similar offering," he says from his Ojai, California, home. "They did not understand how the [food] landscape looked beyond that."

That was back in 2013, long before Amazon had become ubiquitous and taken over Whole Foods, and similar companies were few and far between. But studies had confirmed the existence of food deserts—neighborhoods where access to fresh fruits and vegetables are scarce—in the United States, and a lack of knowledge about nutrition compounded the problem.

Nick Green, a social entrepreneur and investor at Launchpad LA, a startup accelerator in the city, had seen 750 pitches for various startup ideas. "None of them excited me enough to get personally involved," he says. "I wanted to do something at scale and with a very clear purpose. When I finally saw [Lovelace's pitch], it hit the nail on the head," he says, seated in Thrive Market's office in Marina del Rey, California.

Green and Lovelace decided to join forces and put in their own personal funds before seeking investor money. They even tried to build a version of the e-commerce platform with an agency, but it was a $150,000 experiment that didn't work. Knowing that they were going to be an online company, reaching consumers through their platform, they decided to bring on third cofounder and chief technology officer Sasha Siddhartha, who could build a robust website and app.

"It was a bit of a crisis moment for us. We had been rejected by about fifty VCs [venture capitalists] who were affluent and disconnected from the problem. The first iteration of our website didn't work. We needed a different approach and Sasha brought it," Green says.

In late 2014, the concept of Thrive Market finally came to fruition, with the help of investors far from Silicon Valley. The cofounders turned to health and wellness influencers—people who ran blogs, had built an online presence, or were active on social media. Instead of asking them just to get the word out about Thrive Market, they invited them to become investors in the business.

"We raised about $8.5 million in small checks from dozens of mission-aligned influencers who got the vision and knew there was demand for what we were building," Green says. "That was really the genesis. That's extended now. We give back to our employees, giving them equity in the business. One term we use a lot is 'stakeholder-driven.' We want as many people as possible to benefit from this business."

Green, who grew up outside Minneapolis, Minnesota, recalls how his family shopped at the local Sam's Club, where most shoppers were stocking up on cases of A&W soda. "The biggest barrier I saw was information. We didn't know much about health."

But Green and Lovelace saw value in the Costco and Sam's Club membership model and gave it a modern spin: families purchase a

$59.95 annual membership to Thrive Market, which enables the company to offer discounted prices on whole foods. Each membership purchased also provides a low-income family with a free membership. And fundamentally, the membership gives Thrive Market the funds they need to operate the business, and the national platform lets smaller, mission-driven brands get a spot on the "shelf."

The Thrive Market cofounders are looking to break down three fundamental barriers. "Organic and healthy foods can be more expensive," Green says. "So, price needs to be competitive. Secondly, huge swaths of the country are health-food deserts, even in urban areas. And third, we need to increase awareness. [Health food] can be intimidating, and overwhelming, not knowing where to start."

Though Green and Lovelace were acutely aware of these issues, Siddhartha was not. His mother worked as a diplomat, enabling him to travel, try different foods, and grow up in a household where most meals were cooked from scratch. "When we first met, I have to admit that I didn't realize the extent and scope of the problem," he says. "I didn't really have to think about price when I walked into a grocery store."

As Siddhartha learned more about the food-insecure populations in the United States and the food deserts that exist even within cities like Los Angeles, he began to share Green and Lovelace's conviction that they needed to challenge how the government dispensed food subsidies. In 2016, Thrive Market appealed to the US Department of Agriculture (USDA) to rethink its food stamps program to allow use of the stamps for Thrive Market purchases of healthy foods. But the USDA rejected Thrive Market as a viable shopping option for food stamp users, prompting the trio to start a petition in 2016 asking the agency to reconsider. Over 310,000 people signed it. In September 2016, the USDA agreed to the request, implementing a new pilot program that allowed recipients of SNAP (Supplemental Nutrition Assistance Program) to use their benefits online. But it was geared toward larger e-commerce platforms, like Amazon.

"We are still waiting for participation in the pilot," Green says, noting that there's been little transparency with the project. "Ironically, we helped compel the USDA to start the pilot, but they've proceeded very slowly and started with larger businesses while leaving us waiting."

Lovelace and Green began by pushing for non-GMO foods (foods free of genetically modified organisms). That is their baseline definition of healthy foods. Thus, Thrive Market has become the largest retailer of GMO-free foods in the United States. For Lovelace, this is an essential aim: "The fact that 90 percent of Americans are testing positive for the chemical glyphosate in their urine is troubling. As for GMO [foods], we should not be rushing these things to market without proper knowledge, testing, and understanding long-term effects. It's jeopardizing our health."

As a result, the company has promised to buy only from companies that uphold these standards and has developed its own private label for products they get from farmers and producers directly. When Thrive Market launched in 2014, they sold zero products under their private label. Now, they offer more than five hundred products under the Thrive Market brand. Their latest are sustainable meat and seafood and what they call "clean" wines—wines with minimal additives from grapes grown using sustainable farming practices. It may seem odd to deliver meat or wine by mail, but Green says that for many Americans across the country, the options for high-quality meat or affordable wines are few.

The same day I visited their offices in Marina del Rey, they were hosting ranchers from Chile who are raising grass-fed cattle. "In America, 'grass-fed' can be grass-fed pellets, but these animals are grazing on pastures freely," Green says. The ranchers' collective is raising these cattle and selling meat directly to Thrive Market. That, he says, is the vision for the future: to source directly from farmers. "It's more value for farmers and more value to customers."

Similarly, the Thrive Market brand olive oil comes from a single family-run farm in Greece that has been practicing organic farming for decades, unlike many other brands that blend olives from different farms, and even countries. Working with one family is more challenging logistically and more expensive but also provides a greater level of transparency and traceability.

"Direct-to-consumer is a really incredible innovation," Lovelace says. "The implications of that are barely hitting the economy."

The backend of all this is quite difficult, though. "Maintaining really high quality in every step of the supply chain, with thousands of products, and then all the way to the delivery to the customer, while incorporating all these environmental factors, it's not easy," Siddhartha chimes in. That's why so many companies cannot, and do not, do it: the profit margins are slim.

Since 2016, Thrive Market has been aggressively looking at how they can minimize their waste and create a zero-waste packaging facility; they're inching closer and closer by repurposing cardboard waste, asking suppliers to be conscious of how they send products to the warehouse, and using primarily recycled and compostable material in shipping boxes to customers. By 2020, the company was B Corp–certified, and by 2021 it was certified as zero-waste for its fulfillment centers.

Soon Thrive Market had competition in its niche: when Amazon bought Whole Foods in 2017, the race to provide health foods to more Americans heated up. But neither Lovelace nor Green were shaken by this. "We look at it as a massive validation," Green says. "Amazon believes the future of food is going to be in the health food business. But the difference is that Amazon is not a stakeholder-driven business, with the planet as one of those stakeholders. If you order fifteen things, they may send you fifteen different boxes. We send one box from a zero-waste facility, [and the box is] recyclable, with compostable packaging."

The Thrive Market founders have spun the buyout of Whole Foods to their advantage, focusing on a curated selection of brands that live up to their company values and prioritize the health of the consumer and the planet above everything else. "You don't need to pick from forty different nut butters, right?" jokes Green.

But it's not just the overwhelming selection, Lovelace adds. "[John] Mackey, the founder of Whole Foods, wrote the book on conscious capitalism but the leadership has eroded in recent years, due to economic pressures. Now, Whole Foods is selling Honey Nut Cheerios by General Mills . . ."

This deep-seated desire for transparency and cleaner foods drove Green and Lovelace to start Thrive Market in the first place. "We want to support some of the smaller brands that are really inventive, building the future of business and food, not old-school corporatization," Lovelace says. Brands featured on Thrive Market get national exposure, with as little investment as $50,000 in inventory, he adds. "You need millions, to do it [through Whole Foods], he says.

Today, Green says, the business is resonating with more and more consumers who want to live healthier lifestyles. Thrive Market's customer base is more than 50 percent in the Midwest and Southeast. With over one million paid subscribers, that's more than five hundred thousand customers between the coasts who order at least once a month with an average order coming to about $80.

"This whole idea of my health, the health of the community, and the health of the environment are ones that didn't exist ten years ago. It's not just people in New York City and Los Angeles who are rich and foo-foo and can afford to think about it. Now you have moms in the Midwest who want their kids to be healthy and think about their carbon footprint."

GOING BEYOND THE UNITED STATES

For the rest of the world, public health needs vary drastically. One distinguishing factor between the developed and developing world is a massive gap in basic infrastructure. Potholed roads, broken buildings, limited supplies, and inadequate human capital immobilize public health care in much of the world.

For the past decade, for-profit health care companies—no matter how good their intentions—have struggled to deliver care to those who need it the most. Getting to patients who live in remote corners or beyond paved roads, ensuring that clinicians show up and perform their duties, and finding price points that are affordable has been a challenge when the target customer is someone living on $2 to $5 a day in a remote area.

One of the most revered models in global public health has been that of the Aravind Eye Care System, a rare success story of a mission-driven enterprise led by a visionary clinician. Started by Dr. Govindappa Venkataswamy, a fifty-eight-year-old ophthalmologist who was too restless to retire, Aravind Eye Care System has become an institution that's been studied by universities, written about by journalists, and examined by health care practitioners around the world. Though it's not perfect, and addresses primarily one condition, cataracts, which can be treated effectively in one procedure— Aravind Eye Care has introduced an alternative model in health care and served millions of individuals.

Dr. Venkataswamy—commonly referred to as Dr. V—came from a small village in South India. He had health complications in his own life, suffering from rheumatoid arthritis starting in his thirties. This exposed him to a broken health system and the need for compassionate care. At nearly sixty, he began offering "eye camps" in the southern Indian state of Tamil Nadu, in schoolhouses that were converted into clinics.

Although Dr. V started with the intention of giving free eye care to everyone, Aravind Eye Care evolved into a more nuanced approach with tiered pricing to provide revenue streams. What began as a humble mission to help those around him has turned into an institution, now over four decades old and running strong, with more than thirty-two million patients treated, most of whom have paid little or nothing for their treatment.

His idea consumed his whole family. Dr. G. Natchiar, Dr. V's younger sister, took the reins in his later years. "Everyone who has eyes must have sight," she says, recalling her brother's perspective.

The business model, which essentially charges only patients who can afford to pay and funnels those profits toward patients who cannot pay, practices a certain frugality, discipline, and innovation that today's large health care companies have lost. The full price treatment allows for a private room and more elaborate meals—though still very rudimentary when compared to the United States. Those who cannot pay are taken care of with kindness but asked to rest and recover in rooms with possibly ten other patients, seated on blankets on the floor. Despite the tiered pricing, the medical treatment is the same for all three tiers.

Innovations such as enabling doctors to work on two patients at once minimizes the doctor's time spent between surgeries. This lowers the overall cost and increases scale: in one hour, a doctor can perform eight surgeries. Between March 2017 and March 2018, Aravind conducted nearly five hundred thousand surgeries and laser procedures, and had more than four million outpatient visits. Since cataracts account for more than 60 percent of blindness in India, they're making a serious dent in the problem.

The model is now referred to as the "Aravind Way," consisting of the following values: making eye care accessible to all, quality and continuous improvement in care, patient-centric, self-reliance, staff centric, frugality and sharing. Hospitals and health organizations around the world have been trying to replicate it. Aravind shares its procedures, software, financial systems, and learnings: they are an open-source blueprint that others can draw from.

In 2006, after seeing his eleven-bed clinic scale to a revered global institution, Dr. V passed away. His family and closest supporters have kept the vision going, and the organization has trained thousands of ophthalmologists to build a cohort of qualified staff and hopefully inspire a new generation.

Despite having revenue streams, Aravind has remained a nonprofit. It is associated with Aurolab, a for-profit manufacturer started by Dr. V that produces intraocular lenses used in cataract surgeries and has been selling the lenses since 1992 to markets around the world that seek more affordable pricing.

Before starting Aurolab, Dr. V had approached manufacturers in the United States and Europe to source a cost-effective lens but couldn't find a supplier that was willing to budge on price. Some generous donors offered to give lenses in order to build a scalable model, but Dr. V argued for self-sufficiency. He decided to manufacture them right there in Tamil Nadu: lenses initially priced at 10,000 rupees ($150) were instead manufactured at Aurolab for 500 rupees (less than $10) without any difference in quality. All the funds generated from the sales of the lenses, surgical equipment, and paying patients is transferred to a general fund. Those funds then allow Aravind to perform more eye surgeries.

Motivated by compassion, the organization grew, drawing immense interest from around the world. One of Dr. V's oft-cited statements is "When we grow in spiritual consciousness, we identify ourselves with all that is the world. So, there is no exploitation. It is ourselves we are helping. It is ourselves we are healing."[7]

The Aravind hospitals are simple, clean, and basic. There are no luxuries. Rather, the funds are spent on high-quality equipment and talented clinicians; this has enabled them to have clinical results that are on par with and occasionally superior to those in the United States.

Some critics have written off the Aravind model as assembly-line health care, which, they say, doesn't work for more complex treatments and long-term care. But perhaps they have missed the most important detail about this organization: the spiritual foundation on which it was started and which continues to drive it. The mission is very much to provide each person with the best care possible, and to never turn anyone away.

This obsession with equity is also what has kept Krista Donaldson going for the past decade.

As CEO of Equalize Health, a nonprofit organization that designs products for the developing world, Donaldson has experienced similar frustrations. "Health care is very much a human right. I'm always thinking about health equity," she says. "I meet individuals from for-profit health companies who talk about impact, but also share that their bosses will not allow them to run a project or sell somewhere because it's not profitable. You cannot be in this game to maximize profits."

In 2009, Donaldson joined Equalize Health, then called D-Rev, shortly after the organization had been founded by Paul Polak and Kurt Kuhlmann. A development veteran, she had worked in places such as Iraq during the country's reconstruction period, where she saw the shortcomings of aid. The US government had spent $2 billion on electricity infrastructure in the country, but to little effect.[8] She says, "I was having tea with a local one afternoon, and he said to me, 'You can put a man on the moon, but you cannot make my lights work?'"

It was a light-bulb moment, literally. She knew that top-down initiatives didn't work. Yet the alternative to aid was a conviction that business can solve the world's problems. Health care is trickier than other industries because there are customers who cannot pay for even the cheapest option, yet all people deserve medical treatment. Thus, a more fluid and hybridized model is needed where nonprofits and for-profits work together, she says.

But it's been a rough journey for this small organization, even if its intentions are well-meaning. Equalize Health, for instance, works with for-profits, local manufacturers, and distributors at the grassroots level who administer its two most important creations: a replacement knee and a blue-light device to treat babies with jaundice. Philanthropic funding covers most of their annual $2 million budget for a team of about twenty-two, spread out in India, East Africa, and South Africa.

"There are not a lot of donors who want to fund med devices for poor people," Donaldson says. "Yet there is a gap in care." The gap is largely due to the fact that it's not a lucrative enough market for a for-profit company, given that their target "customer" lives on less than $5 a day.

An added problem is corruption in the medical sector. Equalize Health has seen irregularities with distributors. For instance, in one country in sub-Saharan Africa, the government opted for a more expensive product that was not as effective. Why? Kickbacks, Donaldson says. That means that Equalize Health doesn't just have to design low-cost knees and jaundice-reversing devices, it also has to work closely with hospitals and experts in emerging markets to overcome this kind of corruption.

In India, Equalize Health works with Phoenix Medical Systems, which sells neonatal equipment to hospitals. Brilliance, one of Equalize Health's product offerings, uses blue light to reverse jaundice in infants. In the United States, a similar device would cost about $3,500 or more, says Donaldson. However, in India, Equalize Health capped the price at $400. But the actual ingenuity came from Equalize Health restructuring the licensing so that Phoenix made more money selling to smaller, rural hospitals and clinics than to large, well-funded ones.

Equalize Health couldn't just deal with product design—a challenge in itself—but had to focus on marketing and distributing as well.

"The last mile," a term used in development to describe distribution challenges at the point where the product actually reaches the end-user, has become a Equalize Health focus: "It's not enough to just create a low-cost product," Donaldson says. "You have to get solutions in the hands of people. Global health is tricky; the experts setting development policy are not always well connected to the needs and markets of the patients that they're trying to serve."

"Health and health delivery have not traditionally been a very innovative space and can get swayed in one direction or the other," Donaldson says. "It's an uphill battle when you're trying to do something truly groundbreaking in this space."

That said, Equalize Health's technologies, primarily Brilliance and the low-cost knee replacement device, ReMotion, have reached more than 650,000 individuals since the organization's inception. Brilliance is sold in fifty countries and ReMotion in thirty. In some countries, the government health departments have taken charge: Rwanda, for example, installed 106 Brilliance units in forty-six public hospitals.

Abhishek Sen is trying to find solutions to the same problems of getting health care to people in developing countries. He was a college student when he cofounded Biosense, a low-cost medical technologies company in India. When they started out in 2008, he says, "we really didn't know anything about business, distribution, or manufacturing. We were just good at building products."

A decade later, he had learned that building a health technology business is unlike any other, particularly in a country where manufacturing facilities are limited and distribution can be a nightmare.

When Sen and three friends—Myshkin Ingawale, Aman Midha, and Yogesh Patil—started Biosense they were all still in college, building ideas for medical devices that were cheaper but just as effective as their Western counterparts—all from their dorm room. On the side, Sen was working in primary health care centers across the western state of Maharashtra, where he got a dose of reality: despite India being a technology powerhouse, smaller cities and villages had little access to medical technology to diagnose patients quickly and accurately.

"About 80 percent of these devices used for diagnostics were, and continue to be, imported from Western counties," he says.

The realization that there was a lack of homegrown solutions put him and his three colleagues on a quest to democratize health care in their country. The first device they built tackled the anemia problem in India. According to the 2017 *Global Nutrition Report*, worldwide 614 million women between the ages of fifteen and forty-nine are affected by anemia, and the country with the largest number of anemic women is India, where more than half of reproductive-age females have this condition.[9]

"One of two women in the areas we worked in had anemia," Sen recalls. "And yet in most cases, it's completely treatable."

Biosense created a noninvasive, low-cost anemia detector. "No pin prick on the finger because everyone is scared of a needle and blood," he says. Instead, the handheld device can take images of the conjunctiva of a person's eye, of the nail bed, and of the tongue to determine whether the person has anemia. The results are provided within a minute.

The device is now used in 1,100 villages across the country. But with a fragmented health care system, getting the device to the market was a real challenge. "We don't have a clear distribution system here, like you do in the United States or Europe," Sen says. In the United States, he explains, there are three to four major distributors that are responsible for disseminating medical technologies, whereas in India, one distributor would only work in a local area of about forty square miles. "That's really small, and that means you have to engage with so many different distributors."

The only way to make Biosense financially viable, Sen argues, is to create a basket of products—not just one medical technology.

So they developed two more products: a strip for diabetes patients to measure their glucose levels and a urine analysis device. Bioscience's products cost a fraction of the price of their Western counterparts. For example, Biosense's glucometer, Sen says, is about half the price of a comparable device manufactured by Johnson & Johnson and sold to diabetes patients.

The key to making more medical technologies at lower pricing is to bring manufacturing closer to home. "But manufacturing anything here is painful," Sen laments. "Manpower is challenging, and infrastructure is not there. It's certainly not easy, and that's why the medical technologies have not taken off."

He said this the day before Biosense opened its first manufacturing facility in India, in the southern state of Andhra Pradesh, which has carved out a medical technology zone. Companies like Biosense that choose to set up their factories here have some advantages, Sen says. "You get an entire ecosystem including ancillary and testing units in the same campus, subsidized prices for long-term leases, and inclusion in a preferential purchase policy for Andhra Pradesh public procurements."

The Andhra Pradesh MedTech Zone is the first medical devices manufacturing park in the country. The zone has allocated 270 acres to support specifically medical technology manufacturing. According to Sen, India lacks adequate space designated for medical technology manufacturing, and this has kept the country behind neighboring China. Though Biosense currently sources its glucometers from China, they plan to use programs like this one to manufacture everything in-house in India.

Another difficulty, after distribution and manufacturing, is financing the whole venture. Biosense has received funding from the Lemelson Foundation since its early days. Lemelson is a Portland-based philanthropic organization named after Jerome Lemelson, an American inventor who had nearly six hundred patents to his name before he passed away in 1997. The foundation wants to find and invest in inventors like Sen who are looking to improve the quality of life for low-income individuals. The Lemelson Foundation funded Villgro, an Indian incubator for social entrepreneurs, which has gone on to fund more than 100 innovators in the country. Biosense was one of those early grantees.

In late 2017, Biosense ran into a different kind of finance problem: a shortage of working capital. "We were growing faster than we were aware," Sen says. "Loans in India were hard to come by, because of demonetization and some of the new policies put in place by the government. We had interest from doctors and clinics, but we were struggling to meet the demand because we simply couldn't manufacture fast enough."

The Lemelson Foundation provided debt-financing to address that problem. In total, Biosense has raised just over $2 million in equity funding during the last decade, a small amount compared to typical Silicon Valley investments in tech companies churning out apps. The financing for medical technologies in chaotic economies like India's continues to be too risky for many investors who have yet to see these ideas and innovations morph into profitable businesses.

"It all goes back to the distribution and manufacturing problem," Sen says. "That's why we knew we had to be one of the first companies to start making these diagnostic tools at home."

Biosense's business consists of three elements: 40 percent is selling to doctors and small nursing clinics located primarily in tier 2 and tier 3 cities—areas beyond Bangalore, Mumbai, and Delhi, which are classified as tier 1 and have better infrastructure and more resources than most Indian cities. Since the startup's goal is to get more afford- able diagnostics in the hands of clinicians and patients, they want to extend their focus beyond these urban centers.

The second part of their business, about 30 percent, entails pro- viding diagnostics to pharmaceutical companies. And the final com- ponent of their business, about 20 percent, serves the public sector in rural India, where people are served by government health facilities or large international NGOs.

"Here, we are talking about people who do not have enough money to pay for health care services. Food and shelter [are] their focus," says Sen.

Yet serving this latter group is tough, because government agen- cies take time to finalize a contract, and then they ask for such large orders that companies like Biosense lack the working capital to de- liver. "Plus, you don't get paid for another six months," Sen laments.

Despite the hurdles, he found a way to access this market. Ev- ery primary health care center has a small annual budget of about

50,000 rupees ($675) available that can be spent at the discretion of the medical officer at that clinic. "We've had to prove ourselves to them, accuracy-wise. They want to be sure that [our devices] work. Once they're convinced, then it's 40 percent cheaper for them," he says, explaining their sales pitch. "Plus, we tell them that we are an Indian company, and any issues with product are addressed within seventy-two hours." This level of response is something that the large distributors cannot provide as easily.

The combination of affordability, quality, and customer service is resonating. According to Biosense, nearly eight million children have been screened using one of their devices.

In India, there are about seven hundred medical technology companies, but two-thirds have annual revenues of less than 10 crores ($1.5 million), making them too small to make a big difference in India's health care, Sen argues. "Until we solve the un-sexy problem of distribution and manufacturing, these ideas will not make it out in the market and the industry as a whole will not reach its potential."

Though a decade and a half into the venture, Sen has no desire to slow down or veer off in a different direction. While two founders, Ingawale and Midha, have moved on to other ventures, Sen is in it for the long haul. "The opportunity and need here is huge," he says.

CHAPTER EIGHT

ENERGY

Clean Energy for All

The thirteenth UN Sustainable Development Goal is to take action against climate change. This is one of the most important of all the goals; if this goal does not succeed, the rest cannot work, or exist given the speed at which humanity is altering the earth's climate.

In 2018, the UN's Intergovernmental Panel on Climate Change released the most damning report yet on the environment—*Global Warming of 1.5° C*—warning that the global community has only about twelve years to keep global warming at a maximum of 1.5 degrees Celsius. Another half a degree could push the balance of the entire planet's ecosystem in a new, dangerous direction, characterized by worse droughts, floods, and excruciatingly hot summers, conditions that would result in poverty, famine, displacement, and increased migration. More than ninety scientists from forty countries contributed to the report, which collates the results of six thousand scientific studies, making it one of the most comprehensive global assessments on climate change ever published. In 2022, the IPCC followed it up with another report, *Climate Change 2022: Impacts, Adaptation and Vulnerability*, suggesting that some of the impact is irreversible, and that more than 40 percent of the world's population was "vulnerable" to the effects of changing weather patterns.[1]

It should be a no-brainer that our energy sources need to be diverted from fossil fuels to cleaner options. Some countries and states have been proactive about this: Scotland, for instance, announced that it wanted to move to 100 percent renewable energy by 2020 and was able to achieve 97 percent by that deadline.[2]

The United States is now the second-largest emitter of greenhouse gases—in first place is China. In 2018, US carbon dioxide emissions rose by 3 percent after three years of continuous decline.[3]

Some energy companies have ignored the divisive political rhetoric in the United States and created a market for renewable sources and continue to invest in more eco-friendly solutions. That's in keeping with the goals outlined in the United Nations report: by 2050, the IPCC advises that the use of coal for electricity needs be reduced from 40 percent to less than 7 percent, whereas renewable sources like wind and solar, currently at 20 percent, need to become the dominant fuel of economies—at least 67 percent.

As of 2018, alternative energy, like wind, is now as affordable as coal.[4] Community solar projects have taken off, but household solar remains sluggish because it requires a hefty up-front investment by the homeowner in solar panels. Private, public, and regional government sectors are driving the movement forward: by December 2017, 117 companies had made a public commitment to 100 percent renewable power. Similarly, 222 mayors pledged to build 100 percent renewable energy cities and towns in the United States. Some states, such as California, have outlined independent plans to transition to 100 percent renewable energy by 2045.[5]

This is a good foundation for the next industrial revolution of cleaner, more planet-friendly energy sources. Some countries have already put this into law, ensuring that future generations will abide by the same philosophy. Bhutan, a small Himalayan kingdom of fewer than one million people, for instance, has written into its constitution that 60 percent of its land will be kept as forest. It's also the only country in the world that's not just carbon neutral but carbon negative, meaning that it sequesters more carbon than it produces. Although it's largely been undeveloped for decades—most of its population still works in agriculture—the leadership has committed to offsetting its emissions with its thick forests as Bhutan develops. This progressive mindset extends beyond energy emissions: the country aims to be 100 percent organic and completely waste-free by 2030.[6]

That's a far cry from the United States. With a population three hundred times larger, a legacy of coal as a fuel source, and an industry that's still advocating for carbon-capture technology despite falling wind energy prices, can the United States move in Bhutan's direction, despite the differences?

ADIOS, COAL

Kiran Bhatraju is from coal country. After spending his post-college years in Washington, DC, trying to go the policy route to bring about change in the energy sector, he started a business instead. "Energy is a pretty old, stodgy community. And business just made more sense because the market for renewables is only increasing, while [the market for] coal is not. I'm not sure politics is where you go to effect change. It might be better done in the private sector."

Bhatraju grew up in Kentucky, the heart of America's coal industry. The history of coal mining in Kentucky dates back to the early 1820s, but the hunger for coal has dropped steadily since the 1950s.[7] In 2016, the state produced forty-three million tonnes, 30 percent less than the previous year and the lowest production level since 1954.[8] Companies that have manufacturing plants in the state, such as Toyota, GE, and Ford, have been transitioning to alternative sources to meet their energy needs. "It's definitely not the future. Business has moved on," Bhatraju says. "People in Kentucky also want to be a part of something new. That's why we're seeing solar projects crop up. People are looking at what's next."

But to understand the need for renewable energy, it's worthwhile to backtrack and look at how the US built its electrical grid. In the late 1800s, Thomas Edison and George Westinghouse competed to electrify American cities. Edison focused his experiments on direct current, or DC. Westinghouse, who worked for Nikola Tesla, found the answer in an alternating current, or AC. The ability to control the voltage, and downgrade it, gave birth to the modern AC grid system. High-voltage wires run like highways throughout the United States; the voltage is lowered for residential or commercial use.

There's one problem with this system: it relies on centralized energy sources to provide the power. The heavy infrastructure meant that this was a capital-intensive system to build. In fact, many American farms were cut off from electricity until the federally supported Tennessee Valley Authority installed power lines under Franklin Roosevelt's watch. Generating electricity has required hydropower (through damming rivers and coal). That system didn't change for decades, although nuclear energy was added as a source in the 1950s.

Introducing alternative energy sources, namely wind and solar, as entrepreneurs like Bhatraju want to do, creates a challenge. Because electricity has to travel in the power lines that are already laid out, it's nearly impossible to track the source of that electricity: nuclear, wind, coal, solar, hydro—they all come together to travel the same electrical highways.

Instead of trying to rebuild the energy system, Bhatraju looked to a virtual solution that could drive more households in America toward wind energy. According to analysts, one megawatt-hour of wind energy costs $45 to produce. Compare that to nuclear at $148 and coal at $102.[9]

Even though wind power seems like a no-brainer, there is no way for a household to ensure that its electricity actually comes from wind because it all gets combined in one pot with electricity that's generated by nuclear and coal. As a result, the industry uses renewable energy certificates. Every megawatt-hour of power that is produced from wind energy is recorded. This traceability enables companies like Bhatraju's to assure households that their dollars are supporting renewable energy. With more RECs, Bhatraju says, there will be greater demand for new wind farms to be built.

Bhatraju's company, Arcadia, based in Washington, DC, started by letting homeowners sign up for 50 percent wind at no additional cost. For those who want their monthly bill to entirely support wind power, there's an additional cost of five dollars for the renewable energy credits. Arcadia now has more than three hundred thousand households signed up, so they've been able to amass some purchasing power.

Although private sector giants like Google and Amazon have been buying up wind farms, Bhatraju says, "a wind farm is not going to talk to you or me, because we don't have purchasing power. We're too small. So, we wanted to see if we can get the hundred million

American households that pay a utility bill to basically drive demand for wind energy by coming together."

Wind farms are appearing throughout much of the United States, with Texas taking the lead. In 2017, the United States produced 89 gigawatts of wind energy; this amount is likely to climb as more off-shore wind projects get underway. Wind energy in 2017 made up about 6 to 7 percent of the grid. In fourteen states that number is higher, with 10 percent of electricity coming from wind.[10]

Wind is one of a growing list of alternative energy sources, but the industries are hard for the public to understand, maneuver in, and take part in, Bhatraju says. "I wanted to build one platform that would simplify all this. We're breaking down all the options and giving it to you based on where you live and your energy usage. There are so many companies selling products that can make homes energy-efficient, but they have upfront costs. How do we make that accessible?"

Once households sign up, the Arcadia dashboard shows customers their energy usage, how much of that is contributing to wind energy growth, and other Arcadia Power programs available in their state or county, such as community solar.

Solar, though one of the most obvious choices for residents living in the sunny swaths of the West and Southwest, has struggled to get on neighborhood rooftops because of stringent installation requirements, binding contracts, and the upfront costs. With panels costing anywhere from $5,000 to $20,000, rooftop solar is a substantial investment. There's also the politics: Nevada, a state that gets a heavy dose of sunshine, has been rigged with regulations preventing the spread of solar.[11]

Community solar is the simple solution of numbers to create buying power and allow residents to tap into solar projects scattered throughout their neighborhoods. It's open to everyone, homeowners and renters. The solar panels are hosted on sites such as a school for disadvantaged students, a clean-tech incubator, a police department, office buildings, and multifamily apartment buildings.

Arcadia provides this option free in a number of states—New York, Rhode Island, Illinois, Maryland, and Washington, DC—with an up-front price tag in others because of state policies. These solar programs have traditionally required credit checks, cancellation fees, and paying two bills, but in an effort to make it easier, Arcadia doesn't require any of that. This model has been resonating with customers who don't want to deal with the hardware as city-dwellers or renters but want to support solar energy: Arcadia sold nearly four thousand solar panels in its first run and then signed on with Boston-based solar company Sunwealth to add another eight hundred panels to the program.

Again, this is not a perfect solution. It requires some investment for a very marginal return, but what it does do is give individuals the power to align their values with their dollars. One Arcadia customer who was defending his decision to fund a community solar project wrote on Twitter: "I can't get solar at my house (too many surrounding trees) so I'm putting my money where my mouth is."

"I don't think the answer lies in just one technology. We have to include all of these to get some overall impact and change," Bhatraju says.

In 2018, Arcadia signed on with Amazon to bring some eco-friendly tools to the home in a more convenient manner. Though smart thermostats have been on the market, they're pricey, Bhatraju argues, and not everyone can shell out the cost at once. So, Arcadia divides the sum into affordable monthly payments and covers installation costs. Packages include LED light bulbs, smart thermostats, Wi-Fi–enabled smart plugs, and more. Again, these products already exist, but now they are in one package that includes installation, and the cost is spread out with monthly installments rather than a one-time high bill.

Bhatraju says this tech-focused minimalism with an à la carte model is what distinguishes his company from others. "With tech, we're trying to make it more user-friendly. People want choices. They want clean energy. Here's how you can back that."

When Bhatraju started in 2014, he had five years of policy experience and had spent three years working at American Efficient, a for-profit company focused on energy-efficient solutions. Even though he had been immersed in the issues for years, starting up his own company "was not easy. Also, because we were trying to do something across America, not just in one state or region. And utility companies don't have easy-to-access APIs"—application programming interfaces, a set of tools, definitions, and protocols for integrating application software and services. On the electric grid, APIs connect a variety of power sources.

Before diving in, he looked to the United Kingdom and Australia for some lessons. Here he found companies that had a more user-centric approach. "Electricity companies looked more like consumer brands, where the customer had options and utility companies were selling not just the utility but hardware that made for more efficient, eco-friendly homes. That was inspiring," he says.

When Bhatraju launched his company, he relied on family and friends to get the word out and eventually collected $250,000 in startup capital from supporters. Since then, the idea has caught on with investors: in 2018, the company raised $25 million. Most of Arcadia's customers live in California, New York, Ohio, Florida, and Wisconsin. As of 2019, the company has users in all fifty states, and they've accrued over three hundred thousand customers.

"In early 2016, we were at the fifty-thousand-customer mark. But we knew that the industry would take us seriously only if we had enough customers. Now, we're a licensed broker in every market," Bhatraju explains.

Changing customer behavior, he admits, has not been easy. "[Paying] your utility bill is something you've done your whole life in a particular way. So, why change now?"

At first, the company struggled to acquire new customers. When they started offering 50 percent wind energy for free, that all changed. "We just made it stupidly simple for the customer: sign up, connect, pay by credit card, auto-enroll, everything your utility offers—but also support wind."

In comparison to Bhatraju's political career—where the emphasis was on talk—this is a tangible solution. "It's not this existential, big thing, beyond your control," he says. "It's a small step that each American can do to clean up our collective footprint."

FROM ACTIVIST TO ENTREPRENEUR

Emmanuel Soulias has been taking that same message to residents of France. Soulias was the recent managing director of Enercoop, a cooperative in France connecting energy producers to consumers directly, bypassing the energy market and distribution channels. The difference in customers' energy bills is less than $11 a month, he says, "but the impact is huge."

Unlike Arcadia's model, where energy is purchased from wind farms as an offset, Enercoop's sixty thousand customers can find out where their energy is coming from directly. They like to call it the "short circuit" model.

"But we're very small still when you think about the thirty-five million potential customers in France who need energy," Soulias says. This is true; after a decade in the business, Enercoop is still a tiny player. Yet he's excited by the recent public interest in sustainability and the push to reduce the country's environmental impact.

Started by environmental activists—including Patrick Behm and Julie Noé—renewable energy players, and citizen associations, the company did not emphasize growing the business, Soulias says. "Enercoop was created by quite alternative people that were working on an alternative system to the capitalist, centralized system—it's not part of their culture, or their motivation."

As a result, the first years of the business were "low-profile," as Soulias puts it. "And that was a choice. It has changed now. We are more willing to develop ourselves and promote the business."

Soulias's transition to leading the organization corresponds with that change. He first discovered Enercoop as a customer. In 2008, he joined the advisory board of the organization, and in 2014, he became the CEO. "I didn't have training in renewable energy. I was in telecommunications and insurance before," he says. "But I was always interested in the environment."

Since he took over the leadership role, the cooperative has been expanding, gaining more producers and growing its customer base. In 2007, the French electricity market was opened to competition. That allowed for smaller players to compete. But as of 2017, the biggest player in the energy market in France, Électricité de France, still had a monopoly, controlling about 85 percent. Other companies, like Total, ENGIE, and Casino Group—twenty-nine in all, including Enercoop—compose the remaining 15 percent.

Now, says Soulias, as consumers are becoming more conscious of their environmental footprint, the French public "is interested, awake, and listening."

Enercoop's electricity comes from idyllic French villages that have wind turbines and solar panels as well as hydropower stations. Together, there are 180 producers who are grouped into smaller, regional cooperatives serving the surrounding areas. There's a reason for this, he explains. "The weather in the Champagne region is not the same as in Provence or the south of France. You need to think about what kind of technology you put in."

In France, nuclear power has been king: about 75 percent of France's energy comes from nuclear power plants.[12] Politicians have talked about decreasing that to 50 percent by 2035. Électricité de France oversees nearly sixty reactors in France, and an additional ten beyond its borders. Enercoop has steered clear of nuclear, focusing on wind, solar, hydro, and biomass. They are decreasing their emphasis on hydropower, aware of the growing environmental concerns with dams. Enercoop doesn't encourage building new dams or changing river ecosystems, but if the infrastructure has already been built, the company will use it.

The second reason for this shift away from hydro is slightly ironic: unpredictable weather. "If we have too many hydropower producers," he says, "we are too dependent on the climate. For instance, in 2017, the rainfall was quite low, so hydro facilities underproduced. Too much dependence on the climate is not smart. It's good to diversify because the weather can be unpredictable."

What distinguishes Enercoop is not just its focus on renewables but also its structure, relying entirely on the cooperative model, as its name signals. Though its electricity rates are 10 to 15 percent higher than market rates, Soulias says it's a marginal difference. "The other players buy electricity at the cheapest rate possible and then turn around and sell it for a profit," he says. For them, "The goal is the profit, not quality or source of that energy."

Enercoop prefers to invest its profits in the various energy producers throughout the country and help them increase their energy output. Each member of the cooperative is given a voice, and that ensures that the decisions around reinvestment are made democratically.

"Enercoop is seen as a way to deal locally, to find local alternatives. It's about recreating a local link that is all but tenuous today in rural territories," says Zacharie Ter-Minassian, an energy officer at Enercoop whose role entails vetting each producer candidate and helping them understand and meet French regulations. Most of the producers, Ter-Minassian says, are driven by the desire to live sustainably, which leads them to energy. For example, Guy Giraud, an organic milk producer in Saint-Cyrles-Vignes in the Loire region of France, signed on with Enercoop in January 2018. He had already taken advantage of a government subsidy to invest in solar photovoltaic cells. He can generate 240 megawatts per year on his farm, for an income of about $165,000. Giraud has started running the farm as an educational site, inviting students to visit and learn about organic farming and renewable energy production.

With a pipeline of interested producers, Ter-Minassian is trying to speed up the process to get them approved. While solar is usually an easier sell to local authorities, wind can take longer to get the necessary permissions; previously projects have been rejected because wind turbines disrupt idyllic countryside views. Some of these wind projects, he says, can take up to five to six years to obtain the necessary approvals from local authorities.

That's why Enercoop has agreed to work with hydropower producers such as Frank Adisson, CEO of Nouvelles Énergies Hydrauliques, who has been with Enercoop since 2016 and is now a member of the company's board of directors. He signed on with Enercoop because the cooperative offered a three-year contract—other large energy companies work on shorter contracts. In 2019, Adisson will produce 75,000 megawatt-hours for Enercoop, yielding about $3.3 million (€3 million).

Other Enercoop producers are very citizen-led. For instance, a group of residents in Aubais in the Languedoc-Roussillon region of southern France bordering Spain and the Pyrenees raised $243,000 (€220,000) to build a community-sized solar plant that can generate about 500 megawatt-hours each year, enough electric power for 170 families. The solar farm is housed on an old landfill, a derelict site that had no other apparent use. The project, which is now called the Citizen Watt Plant, came about because a group of individuals came together to fight fracking and drilling for shale gas. That activism led them to find a solution, instead of just opposing something they didn't like.

This model of connecting producers to consumers is resonating with civic-minded and eco-friendly companies. Of Enercoop's sixty thousand customers, five thousand are from the private business sector. "Most of these companies are coming to us because we're not on the stock exchange. They are not there by chance; they know exactly what they're paying for," Soulias says. "They want to be associated with this model."

One of them is Veja, the shoe brand mentioned earlier. Sébastien Kopp, Veja's cofounder, wants to see more people sign up with Enercoop. He's looking to partner with Soulias and have people sign up at one of their Paris stores. Centre Commercial, Veja's flagship store situated on the Rue de Marseille in Paris, already curates brands from around Europe and the United States that are environmentally conscious. "Why not add electricity to it?" Kopp says. "We make it easy for people to sign up and convert over."

As it is, changing electricity providers is not a cumbersome process, Soulias says. "There's no hardware, infrastructure, cables, or anything involved. But it's just about taking the time to do it and be[ing] willing to pay a bit more."

France, though not as significant a polluter as the United States, has struggled with pollution in the capital. In 2016, Paris saw some of the worst pollution the city has experienced to date. Two years later, in 2018, the French ecology minister confessed that the country had failed to meet the carbon-emission reduction targets outlined earlier. In fact, as of early 2018, carbon dioxide emissions rose 3.6 percent over the target amount of 447 million tons.[13]

Enercoop is one of more than a dozen cooperative energy providers in Europe (so far it is the only one in France). The REScoop is a European federation for renewable energy cooperatives that is growing steadily, with more than 1,500 co-ops that serve more than one million citizens. In neighboring Germany, there are over 1,700 cooperative projects (not all are part of REScoop), with 90 percent of the owners being private individuals.[14] In fact, Germany and the Netherlands lead in terms of the number of citizen cooperatives, and England is close behind.

Soulias is now looking across borders to collaborate with other renewable energy cooperatives in Europe to accelerate Enercoop's growth and bring in more producers. A financial tool, he says, is in the works, which he built in partnership with co-ops in the United Kingdom, Spain, Belgium, and Germany. "This will help European cooperatives raise money from citizens. We are not just exchanging ideas, we are mutualizing investments," he says. In addition, they're mapping out services that they can provide to their customers. Like Arcadia, Enercoop wants consumers to be able to monitor their electricity usage and use technology to reduce consumption.

Soulias is finding traction at home with government agencies as well. The cities of Paris, Lille, and Nantes have signed on with Enercoop to power schools, libraries, and community centers. "I would like it to go faster. We have thirty electricity providers in France; we are the only one with the status of a general interest [nonprofit]. It would be better if governments, or public institutions that are there to represent the general interest, would work with us," he adds.

"Cooperatives in energy have proven themselves as a viable business model," Soulias says. This citizen-centered approach led Enercoop to also buy a wind farm with Énergie Partagée and Neff Investissement in 2014. Built and operated by Valorem, the wind farm is located in the Loire-Atlantique region, twenty-five kilometers (fifteen miles) inland from France's west coast. Valorem's employees have 18 percent ownership of the wind farm. But with the financial support of Enercoop and its partners, citizens of that area have acquired part ownership.

The three wind turbines can produce 17,000 megawatt-hours of electricity per year, enough to meet the electricity needs of more than 6,000 households and eliminate 2,500 tons of carbon dioxide per year. This is the next wave—the closed-loop model—that Soulias has been advancing: citizens are not just end-users—they are involved in the production of renewable energy projects.

To expedite some of this growth, Soulias turned to lenders in 2016 to raise $5 million (€4.5 million) from socially responsible banks. "This was to help us invest in our information system and hire more people on the operation side," he explains. "It's a question of speed to market and scale. We could do it without this added capital, but it would take much longer."

Ter-Minassian agrees. "Sometimes we have [a need] for [more] energy from our individual producers, but they're not able to generate enough. It's definitely a balancing act as we grow this."

The urgency is evident. Since Enercoop spent the first ten years developing the model and gaining a foundation, now the organization is ready to put the foot on the accelerator under new leadership.

CHAPTER NINE

FINANCE

Investing in Humanity and Nature

C apitalism is messy. It's hard to address toxicity in finance as we would do in the food, beauty, and clothing sectors. In food, the focus has been on eliminating bad ingredients that are toxic to our bodies. In beauty, it's the same: the goal is to eliminate the fillers and preservatives that can disrupt endocrine systems. In clothing, we target chemicals that are toxic to the environment. Yet, getting rid of the problematic players in finance is more complicated when their dollars are invested in so many pots. The tentacles of capitalism are so far-reaching, and often under the radar, that the world of finance is almost always connected to the moneymakers of the world who invest in socially and environmentally damaging projects. Money, after all, is the ultimate tool that can transform a landscape, literally and figuratively. Financiers who see the long-term vision of a regenerative business are the ones who will work in sync with such a business. Investing for positive impacts is called impact investing.

In Paris, on the opening day of the 2018 Global Impact Investing Network Investor Forum, the leading impact investing conference in the world, Marilou van Golstein Brouwers, the then managing director of a Dutch investment firm, Triodos Investment Management, said, "We can no longer ignore the fact that all investments have impact. . . . There is no such thing as a neutral investment."

Just as all consumption has an impact, including the most planet-conscious efforts, so do all investments. And despite the rhetoric by global players to support the next generation of entrepreneurs looking to change the system, the funding to do so often comes from the most paradoxical sources; for example, PepsiCo's launching "healthy" beverages and investing in entrepreneurs behind these new brands—after selling sugary drinks for decades.[1]

The hypocrisy is, sadly, typical: those who do harm come back and fix it later through their philanthropic dollars while making sure to loudly announce this news to ensure the public is made aware of their efforts. Often there's a vested interest: large financial entities advocate for financial inclusion not merely out of generosity but because they're interested in the data and a potential new customer base. Business is business—it's always about the bottom line.

But could finance operate in a different way, one where a company would lend to or provide financial services to those who don't have bank accounts or collateral? Could investors sit patiently and wait for a company to mature slowly over fifteen years? Could investors be organized in a manner that the capital that flows back into a business is lent out again to create more people- and planet-friendly businesses, not just to pad the wallets of a select few?

It goes back to the fundamental question presented in the introduction of this book: How much is enough? Several of the entrepreneurs interviewed in these pages built their businesses from their own coffers because they wanted to do it slowly and with integrity. They didn't want the pressure of taking on someone else's capital—and expectations for success. In fact, many of the entrepreneurs featured took their time to build their business, possibly a decade or longer, because it had to be fed slowly, with sales revenues.

But using personal finances is not always the answer. When it comes time to scale, it's necessary to invest in infrastructure or inventory; or when entering new markets, it is necessary to get financial backing on a large scale. So where does one turn? The retail banks that most of us use every day to house our money have been investing in fossil fuel, coal, and other damaging industries.[2] Though the divestment movement has begun, it will take a new finance paradigm to bring down the old giants. Currently, credit unions, co-ops, and small, local banks cannot offer customers the same convenience and suite of services as the giants.

To accomplish the United Nation's SDGs, the world will certainly need financiers. It's far too idealistic to think that it can be done only with bootstrapped models. Yet the focus of these financiers cannot be solely on growth.

Even though so many startups turn to Silicon Valley for fundraising, there are other avenues, which are explored in this chapter—even if one is going after venture capital. It's imperative to stress that what works for one company may not work for another. For instance, Veja, discussed in the first chapter, has been growing using their own cash flow all these years. That was a model the founders were keen to use because they wanted freedom from investors. However, that may not work for a company looking to scale more rapidly. Thus, finding the right investor is crucial. What's unique about the investors discussed here is that they're all looking at finance through a more nuanced lens, driven by values as much as by market potential. After that, it's like getting into marriage—make sure it's the partner that you want to work with long-term.

In France, Jean-Marc Borello is a well-known social entrepreneur and the founder of Groupe SOS, a conglomerate of social enterprises that employs 21,500 and is active in a spectrum of industries from health care to youth and employment to culture and food. Groupe SOS runs cafés throughout Paris, including one on the coveted Champs-Élysées, that are staffed by marginalized populations. The organization also operates an elderly-care facility, an incubator for cultural startups, hospitals in Paris, at-home care for disabled people and those with HIV/AIDS, cooperative farming projects, and even a finance platform for sustainable agriculture. It's a long roster of businesses, all of which serve society from a variety of angles.

In his 2017 book *Why We Need Common Good Capitalism*, Borello argues for a different model of capitalism, one that serves the common good. He writes on the opening page: "I'm not going to promise a new dawn or call for a revolution; that's not the best way to change societies and ways of thinking. This is about helping to bring about a profound change, by giving the economy and businesses new objectives and leaving behind the excess of finance capitalism."[3]

Borello wants to blend the two worlds that he's long operated in, the social and private sectors. Neither, he says, works well individually. "I now head up a group that functions like a business but has no shareholders. It's clear to me that we can't build tomorrow's world order if we remain in our silos," he writes.

To achieve this new order, he calls for the three sectors—the profit-driven, the nonprofit, and the common good sector—to work together. This three-pronged economic model "would be more attuned to social realities, to a world where growth is at 1 to 3 percent, rather than 5 to 10 percent."

A long-standing obsession with rapid growth has led us to this troublesome point: the world does not have limitless resources, and the growth of nations, companies, and individual wealth cannot be limitless, either. At some point it will have to slow down and level out.

That's why Borello proposes "common good capital"—a version of capitalism that creates a new path. It brings in the discipline of the for-profit model that needs to generate revenue, but it also works in industries that the public and social sector would be involved in. Eliminating the push for profit from shareholders, common good capital relies on capital from individuals to finance ventures—an equity crowdfunding model. But the investors do not control the business; the entrepreneurs do, to ensure that their mission is not diluted. There's even an incentive for long-term investing; short-term investments come with a tax that long-term investors don't pay.

Borello's financing model is based on years of experience keeping Groupe SOS away from investors. It relies on bank loans instead of venture capitalists: the company needs $110 million (€100 million) every eighteen months, he says, on which they pay a 2 percent interest. If Groupe SOS were getting this capital from citizen investors, they could instead provide a 2 percent return to individuals instead, he argues.

Borello's model of common good capital would assist everyday individuals in building wealth, even if they invest small sums, while enabling mission-driven companies to provide critical services in the economy that have fallen through the gaps.

A FINANCIAL SYSTEM FOR THE UNBANKED

Although his vision is not quite as egalitarian as Borello's, Bahniman Hazarika, director of investments at Gray Ghost Ventures, an Atlanta-based impact investor, says that his firm is working in a similar space. They back companies that take on issues and markets previously ignored by other sectors in society because there is little financial incentive involved. Plus, they do it sitting in Georgia, far from the glitz and glam of Silicon Valley. They're less likely to garner media attention and follow a nose-down attitude. For the past decade, they've had some success in the mobile money market, which has been booming in South Asia and East Africa. The path to profitability was precarious, Hazarika admits, but they were intrigued by the simple idea of making money cashless and streamlined for the millions of people who had never opened a bank account.

Beam, one of Gray Ghost's investments, is a mobile money company that offers financial services to low-income markets in India and is an example of impact investing that's willing to wait for years before seeing returns and growth, while addressing the part of society that still operates outside the traditional banking world. "It's a question of how patient is patient capital. It's taken us a decade to build this company. It might take twenty to twenty-five years to address the issue of financial inclusion for the base of the pyramid, because companies like Beam pick up where the public sector has failed in some sense," Hazarika says.

Less than 1 percent of Beam's customers have a bank account. These individuals live in a cash-based society—despite the surplus of digital apps, many Indians today still prefer cash. Even the "demonetization" period in 2017, when nearly 90 percent of the currency in circulation was devalued practically overnight by the Indian government, did not deter Indians from returning to cash shortly thereafter.

Beam is trying to serve a population that has no financial footprint: no bank account, no lines of formal credit, no insurance. These people rely on a wad of cash, which can be dangerous, unreliable, and difficult to transmit from point A to point B. When Beam started, seven hundred million Indians did not have a bank account. Since then, the government has introduced a variety of schemes to get more Indians into bank accounts. "But is a bank account always the answer? How many of these bank accounts are actively being used?" Hazarika asks.

In the side alleys of Delhi, a mobile money revolution started taking place in 2007. Instead of a person carrying around rolls of rupees, a basic cell phone could be used to transfer funds, pay for railway tickets, pay monthly bills, and help people cover small purchases. This was the beginning of a transformation from cash to digital transactions. And it didn't require opening a bank account.

Instead, the system relied on a network of agents with the authority to conduct financial transactions without the infrastructure of a brick-and-mortar bank. A hole-in-the-wall corner shop selling candies, soap, drinks, and biscuits can serve as a mobile money agent. Customers drop by with small amounts of cash, 100 to 1,000 rupees; this amount is then transferred to their phone. With this "mobile wallet," they could now make payments.

All of this sounds obvious because since then, the concept of mobile money has taken off. In the United States we use credit cards; in the rest of the world, mobile money companies have bypassed the credit card to serve much of the world's 1.7 billion unbanked population.[4] Yet two decades ago, in 2002, when Anand Shrivastav started Beam, he faced immense challenges: working through the tangled web of India's financial regulations, convincing customers that they could trust a non-bank entity, and figuring out how to reach the remote villages—thirty thousand of them—across India that didn't have banks or ATMs nearby.

Shrivastav started Beam after hearing his driver's story—it's common for upper- and middle-class families in Delhi to have a driver to shuttle them around the city. Shrivastav was heading to work when his driver told him that the driver's mother was gravely ill. He had sent money through the regular postal service for her to receive care. However, it arrived too late—two days after her funeral. "This is just obscene," Shrivastav says. "In today's day and age, why can we not send money more efficiently?"

Shrivastav, sixty-three, had a career in the corporate sector before diving into a startup. He was in his forties and financially secure when he started thinking about Beam. "I didn't need to start this company. But it just seemed like such an obvious need," he says.

In the last ten years, Beam has grown to a company that provides financial services for more than nineteen million Indians throughout the northern part of the country. But getting there has been a slog, even for this experienced entrepreneur and son of a cabinet secretary.

In 1973, Shrivastav won a scholarship to attend the New Jersey Institute of Technology; that was followed by a master's degree from Harvard's School of Engineering and Applied Sciences. After completing his education in the United States, he stayed for a couple years before returning to India. Before social media and internet advertising, Shrivastav was working with small shops, family-run operations, and *kirana* stores—shops that sell a bit of everything, much like a 7-Eleven. Here he saw that business was being conducted primarily in cash.

His next job was with Kerala State Drugs and Pharmaceuticals, selling neonatal care packages to mothers in rural India. This required an elaborate distribution network because the packages were designed for women living in villages. Shrivastav traveled extensively throughout India, visiting twenty of the twenty-eight states in the country. "I saw how life happened in rural markets," he says. After mastering marketing and rural distribution, he returned to Delhi, where he worked with his brother to install a network of 1,100 pay phones in Delhi and Mumbai, operated by franchisees who paid for the phone's ownership over an extended period of time. That led him to dabble more in technology. Now, his career had exposed him to all the elements he needed to establish Beam: an understanding of low-income and rural markets; how to scale up operations; and knowledge of the inner workings of the telecommunications and banking industries.

Inspired by Mahatma Gandhi's writings, Shrivastav speaks as enthusiastically about the beloved father of modern India as he does about telecommunications. He quotes the following statement from Gandhi: "Whenever you are in doubt, or when the self becomes too much with you, apply the following test. Recall the face of the poorest and the weakest man you may have seen and ask yourself if the step you contemplate is going to be of any use to him. Will he gain anything by it? Will it restore him, to a control over his own life and destiny? In other words, will it lead to *swaraj* [freedom] for the hungry and spiritually starving millions? Then you will find your doubts and self melt away."

Shrivastav had his doubts and critics when he started: Beam was neither a bank nor a telecommunications company. Instead, the company wanted to bring the two worlds together. But the Indian financial regulators had no name for this type of company; they urged Shrivastav to make Beam into a bank. But he didn't want that responsibility—he just wanted to facilitate transactions in a more efficient manner. For more than a decade, Shrivastav tried to build the infrastructure and frame the rulebook for mobile money.

In 2011, Dr. K. C. Chakrabarty, then deputy governor of the Reserve Bank of India, made a speech at St. Xavier's College in Mumbai outlining the need for financial inclusion: almost half the country was unbanked. Only 55 percent of the population had deposit accounts and 9 percent had credit accounts. India had the highest number of households excluded from banking in the world: 145 million. There was one bank branch per 14,000 people. "[The] exclusion is staggering whichever parameter one chooses to look at!" Chakrabarty proclaimed.

By that point, Shrivastav had been trying to address financial inclusion for nearly a decade. After five years of engaging with regulators, in 2007 he was granted permission to carry out pilot programs without converting to a bank because the government passed the Payment and Settlement Systems Act of 2007. It gave Beam legitimacy as a payment system. India had been one of the top recipients of international and domestic money transfers; now it would be possible to do them via mobile money.[5] By legalizing the payment structure, the act gave companies such as Beam a safety net and legitimacy.

"If it were unregulated, imagine if something were to fail at Beam, we would have created a shock to the system—fourteen million customers would be upset," he says. Instead, the new law gave the Reserve Bank of India responsibility for regulating nonbank entities such as Beam and ensuring that these companies were working in a responsible fashion.

Since then, Beam has overcome other hurdles: the rise of mobile money wallets by telecommunications operators such as Airtel; the emergence of other startups such as Paytm; and the constant ups and downs of Indian regulation. But Beam has managed to stay afloat and raise capital from US-based impact investors like Gray Ghost Ventures—who have been with the company since its early years.

The impact has been felt not just by the customers but by the agents as well. Shrivastav realized that Beam would work only if he had a massive network of agents and promoters of Beam. So, he created the role of a Beam agent, referred to as *sahayak*, a Hindi word meaning assistant or helper. The *sahayaks* include women and unemployed youth. In addition to working with *kirana* shops, Beam uses this network of agents to provide basic services such as adding more funds to a customer's account, issuing tickets for travel, making utility payments, and providing advance payment vouchers. The agents earn a commission based on their sales.

Beam is also encouraging more participation by women in the economy. "In our society, there is a stigma around women working," says Shrivastav. "They are not given as many opportunities, so they do not feel like they are contributing economically to society or to their families." To give women at home a supplementary income, Shrivastav came up with the *sahayak* network that enables women to earn from 1,000 to 10,000 rupees a month ($15 to $150).

More broadly, Beam has created a franchise business model. As of 2018, there were 24,000 franchises—both *sahayaks* and *kiranas*— that offer Beam services. The company now operates in twenty-seven Indian states and five Indian union territories. It's also adding some other vital services to the mix, such as remittances and credit. Though still in its early stages with the credit program, Gray Ghost's Hazarika says that Beam plans to offer very small loans, from 1,000 to 5,000 rupees ($15 to $75). Those may seem like minuscule amounts, but they are enough for an entrepreneur to buy some inventory or pay for an educational program.

"Everyone wants to be world-changers," Hazarika says. "But there are real business opportunities in some of these 'smaller' or niche markets. These are gaps, literally." And, "They're worth investing in." Gray Ghost Ventures, he adds, is not interested in selling companies for the sake of demonstrating a positive investment record, and they've gone through the ups and downs with Shrivastav since the beginning. Hazarika is very clear about Gray Ghost's long-term vision: the idea is to build companies, help them reach more customers, and solve difficult problems—not just get a financial return.

Atlanta-based Gray Ghost is unique in its own right: they hang on to their assets. Since 2008 they've sold only three companies in their portfolio and some shares of another company. The bulk of the firm's investments have continued to grow, and they've tried to nudge them in the right direction.

"We didn't get in this business to flip companies," says Hazarika. "The idea is to create sustainable and profitable businesses that solve hitherto unsolved problems, right? So why would I be fixated on exits?"

REWRITING TERM SHEETS

Triodos Bank has a similar perspective. Triodos was founded by social agitators, four individuals who were inspired by the student-motivated strikes and riots in Paris in the late 1960s and the overarching climate for social change. This Dutch institution has been bringing the impact investing community together to get more financiers to think beyond return on investment.

"It was a realization that money is powerful, a powerful tool for social change. If that is the case, then a bank, as a financial business, could drive change, not donations," says Marilou van Golstein Brouwers at the Triodos Bank offices, tucked away on the outskirts of Utrecht.

In 1968, Adriaan Deking Dura, an economist, Dieter Brüll, a professor in tax law, Lex Bos, a management consultant, and Rudolf Mees, a banker, met to figure out how money could be channeled toward environmental and social projects. Three years later they established a charitable foundation. But they became convinced that donations were not the answer; instead, they needed a bank. In

1980, with $597,000 (€540,000) in startup capital, they launched Triodos Bank.

"When the initiators of Triodos Bank first came together to discuss the role of money, there was a political crisis across Europe," van Golstein Brouwers says. "Many of the old institutions were failing to connect with the people they were there to serve. The founders discussed how a new economic reality could be created."

This was the 1960s, and these four were deeply studying the writings and philosophy of Dr. Rudolf Steiner, an Austrian philosopher who was the founder of the biodynamic movement in agriculture. Steiner argued that humans need to live in a more holistic manner, reflected in three overlapping spheres: the economic, the social, and the cultural. The four Triodos founders translated this concept into the idea for a bank, which now invests to create positive impact in these three spheres as well.

Steiner's thinking is "very much centered around the three ideas of the French Revolution: *fraternité*, *egalité*, and *liberté*," van Golstein Brouwers says. There are different interpretations of these, she clarifies, but the common thread is that they all look at the health of the human spirit and its place in nature.

Peter Blom, the CEO of Triodos, was one of the bank's first employees. He recalls that the bank started with humble roots, no computers, and an introspective look at what finance could bring to the human condition. Blom had also read Steiner in his youth. "Maybe some of the ideas are wrong," he says. "He's a human being after all. But it's about the development of mankind and there's a humility to that. It's about the gesture behind it."

Blom equates money to energy, saying, "Money is not just a commodity; it can enable things. It's always connected to people. It's the people that can make change." Profit, he says, is the sign of a healthy organization but not the ultimate goal. The first question that Triodos asks companies that come seeking funding is "How does this further sustainability?"

It's not just rhetoric. "Economy and ecology are very close together," Blom says, but "we have separated the two. We have to think about money more consciously. If we keep operating as we are, we will have more crashes."

The financial crash of 2008 didn't go far enough, he says—some banks resumed their old ways in the rebuilding after the global recession. Triodos, however, launched a responsible banking alliance in 2009, building a coalition of like-minded financiers around the world. Blom says he's less interested in preaching, and more interested in showing how it's done. People, he argues, respond better to action.

Van Golstein Brouwers had joined Triodos Bank early on, back in 1990. She had an education in agriculture and finance by the time she arrived at the bank. Her first job was as a commodity trader with the agricultural powerhouse Cargill; that led her to Minneapolis, then Geneva, and finally, Amsterdam. "In three years, I got an overview of how the food and agricultural system works. But the more I knew about it, the more I knew that I didn't want to be a part of it," she says.

She was concerned about Cargill's dominance in American farming: "It was like modern slavery, where farmers were being encouraged to only buy their inputs from Cargill and then sell to Cargill." After three years, she left and joined the banking system. "The same thing happened," she says. "I was working on the stock exchange and realized this has nothing to do with the economy actually."

But she had developed an understanding of both ends of the spectrum, which would become critical at Triodos Bank, in the Netherlands. "I was introduced to some folks at Triodos shortly after. This is a small country. If you're interested in these issues, you can find like-minded people and be plugged in," she says. That was in 1990. Van Golstein Brouwers has been with the institution ever since and now serves as the managing director of Triodos Investment Management. "I really wanted people to start thinking about how they can be more conscious with their money," she says. "Money is one of those things that people don't realize the power it holds."

She's referring to purchasing power, not just for consumers but for financial institutions. She points me to the bank's website, where consumers can find a detailed list of all the loans that Triodos has made. "Transparency, we feel, is essential," she says. That's evident in their nearly 250-page annual report, which seems to detail every activity of the bank.

Following the 2008 crash, Triodos Bank organized the creation of the Global Alliance for Banking on Values. Since 2012, the organization has been publishing data comparing the results of sustainable banking with traditional banking, making the argument that sustainable banking is not just about ethics and values but can provide some real results.[6] These banks support the real economy, not the financial economy. "The degree to which a banking institution finances the real economy is evident from the portion of assets on its balance sheet devoted to lending," she argues.

According to the 2017 report, sustainability-focused banks kept more deposits on hand to fund their loans than the big conventional banks: deposits to total assets for the sustainability-focused were 74 percent versus 55 percent for the conventional ones.[7] That means these banks are relying not on financial products on paper but on clients' deposits to finance their activities.

"Serving the real economy is what banks should do," van Golstein Brouwers says. "Focus on the real needs of individuals and enterprises. By offering opportunities to save money and by intermediating between clients with excess money and those in need of money for productive investments. This very much is the core of banking. All the projects and enterprises we finance can be found on our website, so depositors know exactly where their money is at work."

A big issue in the lead-up to the 2008 crash was that financial products had become so complex and multilayered that they were far removed from the everyday needs of Americans, and those financial products were manipulating the system.

For skeptics who still argue that a sustainability-led approach is a little too warm and fuzzy for them in the world of finance, Triodos has $15 billion (€14 billion) in assets under management, 800,000 accounts, and is seeing 10 to 20 percent growth annually. Much of this has to do with seeing trends and understanding the flaws of the system long before others do. For example, when van Golstein Brouwers joined in 1990, Triodos Bank started to invest in wind energy projects, looking at the renewables industry before the research on climate change had become mainstream.

"Our mandate was to look at how the bank could make a positive change. It wasn't simply what industries to avoid, but which ones to back as well," she notes. That has translated into investments in circular-economy businesses, organic agriculture brands, and fair supply chains. These include brands in the United States like Sprouts, a health food grocer that's headquartered in Arizona and has stores in nineteen states, and Hain Celestial, which markets numerous organic food and personal-care brands under its brand.

But the bank doesn't invest just in brands; it has also supported microfinance organizations and cooperatives in emerging markets that provide the raw materials to these brands. In 2017, they supported nearly 150,000 smallholder farmers in a dozen emerging markets. On the renewable energy front, Triodos has backed two hundred wind-power projects and two hundred solar projects, as well as a few biomass, heat, and cold storage projects.

Much of what they're trying to achieve through finance goes back to the UN's Sustainable Development Goals. That's why their annual reports include a review of how they stack up regarding each SDG.

In light of its long-term goals, the bank has no desire to be publicly traded on the stock exchange, Blom says. "We want to know who our shareholders are. We don't want anonymous shareholders. There are thirty-five thousand people who have invested in Triodos. We want to know them and what their priorities are."

That's why van Golstein Brouwers is a bit impatient with the banking industry. "Yes, there's progress. Yes, there's talk of impact investing. But vested interests are so huge in the financial industry. While bigger players like BlackRock seem to embrace impact investing, it's a tiny part of their portfolio. That's not where the change is coming from."

But the solution, she says, is not to make Triodos a global institution. They'd rather help cultivate similar institutions around the world.

Only about an hour from Triodos's headquarters is another creative financial institution, Oikocredit, a cooperative that lends to and has equity in two of the companies mentioned in this book—Divine Chocolate and Cafédirect.

Its headquarters sit in an unassuming building in Amersfoort, southeast of Amsterdam, where twenty different nationalities are represented by a staff of one hundred. Oikocredit has been impact investing and lending to microfinance organizations and agricultural cooperatives and pushing for financial inclusion since the late 1970s.

But beyond the Netherlands, jokes Ulrike Haug, Oikocredit's communications manager, it's more like, "Oiko-who?" Those within the social impact industry may know of them, but few beyond the sector recognize the name. With their focus on the developing world, Oikocredit doesn't actually invest in too many consumer-facing companies in Europe or the United States.

"We've always been about social and environmental impact," Managing Director Thos Gieskes says. "And we're not the best, perhaps, to judge the feasibility of a consumer-facing brand. Because these brands are competing with giants in the industry who have a lot of capital. And even if they succeed, the global companies end up acquiring them."

Oikocredit's roots are unlike those of any other impact investor. The cooperative dates back to 1968 and a conference of the World Council of Churches. In a meeting in Uppsala, Sweden, church leaders considered how to use their finances. "Facing some scrutiny from church members that their money was involved in politically driven wars and conflict and not having a positive impact on society, they decided to pull together their funds and instead put it toward the future of people," Gieskes says.

Looking for a base of operations that would be relatively neutral, they decided on the Netherlands, where the cooperative was legally established in 1975. That location worked in its favor, for today, most of Oikocredit's investors come from just over the border, in Germany. Set up as a cooperative, Oikocredit has more than five hundred member institutions, which represent over fifty-seven thousand members. Given regulatory hurdles, most of Oikocredit's funds come from investors in the European Union who can buy shares at $220 apiece. A few come from Canada as well.

Around 90 percent of their funding comes from individuals. If these investors ever choose to sell their share, the co-op will buy it from them and pay it off in five years. Dividends are provided, but they're "modest, very modest," Gieskes says. They've been 1 or 2 percent. "Compare that to industry standards, which were around 10 percent, if not higher," he says. "But the intention with Oikocredit is not that this is a money-making machine. The intention is different."

Instead, Oikocredit offers individuals a way to use their money for social and environmental benefit without reducing its real value. "That's really the key. In terms of real value, we give people a safe option to park their money, and we'll use it to create as much positive impact as possible."

The first projects financed in 1978 were in Ecuador and India. In Salinas, Ecuador, where salt fields were drying up, they encouraged salt harvesters to diversify their income: by making cheese and cured meats that could be sold in the cities, the harvesters would have a more stable income. As the activities of the farmers expanded, they needed working capital. Oikocredit provided a loan of $100,000, and today, Salinas is referred to as the "cheese capital" of the country.

In India, in the southern state of Tamil Nadu, they lent $200,000 to build affordable housing for low-income staff at a hospital: two hundred staff members received loans of $1,000 apiece to construct a dwelling. That loan was expanded to cover the needs of more than three hundred people. "The homes are still standing, and being used by the same families," Haug notes. "We visited them a few years ago and met some of the family members, now in the second or third generation of the family."

Though the beginnings of the organization were associated with Christian churches, Oikocredit was focused more on "human values," Gieskes says. "These are values that are underlining all religions, be it Christian or otherwise."

They've concentrated on three areas over the years: microfinance, agriculture, and renewable energy—the latest having been added in 2013. The microfinance loans are given largely to women—86 percent—and the organization focuses more on rural than urban issues. Oikocredit lends to organizations that have been around for at least three years and offers loans between $550,000 (€500,000) and $11 million (€10 million). Overall, Oikocredit has more than $1.4 billion in total assets, and the average loan size is $1.75 million.[8]

"We're careful not to overcredit institutions," Gieskes points out. "The traditional model or the Silicon Valley model is to give people more credit than they need. We don't want to do that." Too much money doesn't always solve the problem. "Traditional lending is not rocket science, really," says Gieskes. "It's about all the other things we can do as a lender to help these organizations for the long run."

The focus is on the long term—or as impact investors refer to it, "patient capital." But Gieskes notes that even triple bottom line (people, planet, and profit) investors have a spectrum on which they operate: at one end is an emphasis on social impact and at the other end, a keen interest in return on investment. Oikocredit is positioned toward the first end. "Again, we are not running after dividends, profits; we're just interested in repackaging existing capital so that it works for the client."

The clients are not a garage startup or a group of college grads; they're coffee farmers, cocoa farmers, tea pickers, female micro-entrepreneurs, mom-and-pop shops, motorcycle taxi drivers. These individuals are among the 1.7 billion people around the globe who are excluded from traditional finances: they have little or no collateral, they don't hold bank accounts, and many don't understand basic finances.[9]

Gieskes knows these markets because after graduate school, he lived and worked in Nicaragua, then ran Rabobank's business in Chile. Most recently, before coming to Oikocredit, he oversaw Rabobank's operations in Australia and New Zealand. He'd already worked in Central and South America, which gave him a firsthand understanding of what kinds of basic financial services could be helpful.

Gieskes clarifies that Oikocredit's model may not work for profit-driven individuals: "As an investor, you have to be clear about [your] intention," he says. "There are people who want to use money to make more money. Then there are those who want to use that money to make positive change. Just be clear where you stand. There are a lot of financial products in the market today. Not everyone has to use each one."

Outside the Netherlands, in an effort to be as close to their investments as possible, Oikocredit maintains overseas offices primarily in the countries where their borrowers live and work, places like Hyderabad, India; Manila, Philippines; Nairobi, Kenya; Abidjan, Ivory Coast; Lima, Peru; San José, Costa Rica; and Montevideo, Uruguay.

"A lot of the problem has been that these two worlds, the [Global] North and the [Global] South, live in very different societies. Can we as a financial institution bring them together and in a very real way, not just [by] transferring funds from one place to another?" he says. "That means the client has to be the driver, and the desire for change has to come from there, not here."

This is Oikocredit's bottom-up approach to development. Many impact investors sit in the North and speculate on what will work in the South, but they're too far removed from the reality to make accurate assessments about what's needed for success.

GETTING CLOSER TO INVESTMENTS

That's what Will Poole wants to fix as well. Based in Seattle, since 2015, Poole has been trying to build a network of funds that can provide locally sourced capital in Africa, South America, the Middle East, and Asia and which is led by regional talent, not Europeans or Americans.

In Nairobi's Kilimani neighborhood, I meet Mercy Mutua, the recently appointed regional director for Capria Ventures, the fund that Poole cofounded. She picks a coffee shop in a mall filled with people working on laptops. "These are all young people here, usually entrepreneurs, or working on social enterprises," she says.

Few, however, are Kenyan. That's been a problem in the region: an influx of well-intentioned entrepreneurs from the United States and Europe has descended on East Africa. Similarly, the capital they use to fund their startups is from foreigners. According to a survey conducted by the East Africa Venture Capital Association, 75 percent of the funds in the region had capital coming from abroad in 2017.[10]

Mutua's goal in her new position is to find local capital, finance African ventures, and help train a new generation of African fund managers. That, Poole says, is the long-term solution. He established Capria in 2015 with three partners in an effort to democratize impact investing.

"'Parachute' investing is a problem. If you're investing in early-stage companies from an airplane, you should consider philanthropy, not investing," he says. "Early-stage companies need help with everything, not just money. Flying in once a quarter is not going to cut it."

Poole is experienced in investing on international soil; his passion for Capria's network of funds, called the Capria Network, comes from time spent setting up one of the first impact investing early-stage funds, Unitus Ventures, which focused on South Asia, particularly the Indian market. Today, Unitus Ventures has $39 million of assets under management in companies in India that include health, education, and e-commerce.

When he launched in India, Poole didn't bring in all the capital from abroad; he wanted some of it to come from Indians themselves. "I was pretty adamant that we need to get at least one-third of the capital for that fund from Indian billionaires, and there are plenty of them. We had a lot of chai meetings to make it happen. But we did it. It's possible to unlock local capital. Not easy, but possible."

In spring 2018, Unitus did a second round of fundraising. Nearly half of the money came from Indians. That's the vision for Capria Network: galvanize local capital funds, help existing managers learn the fund-management trade and improve their skills, and create a network of fund managers in emerging markets that can invest in the next generation of startups.

Mutua notes that it's not as easy as it seems. In India, one was dealing with one country, one government, one system. For her, it's a bit more complicated. "Africa is not a country, though many people forget that. The regional differences, the government regulations, the literacy levels, everything is different as you move from East Africa to Nigeria to South Africa."

The first part of the challenge is that startups and entrepreneurship are relatively new to the region. "We [Kenyans] don't have that sophistication. We didn't go to school and specialize in private equity or entrepreneurship here in Kenya or on the continent," Mutua says. The data validates this: between 2007 and 2016, $4.8 trillion was raised for private equity funds globally, but only 0.6 percent, $28 billion, was allocated to Africa. East Africa got only a small slice of that 0.6 percent.[11]

But Mutua is keen to try to tackle the problem and reduce the funding gap. "We're at a significant point. In the next five to ten years, Africa will either make it big or bust," she says. That's why she signed on with Poole: to see if she could actually give rise to a new movement on the continent. The Capria Network aspired to have $1 billion in assets under management by the end of 2020; as of mid-2019, four years in, they were at $350 million.

Mutua notes that several of the African funds she'll be working with are not as far along: Alitheia IDF managers, an all-women team of private-equity investors from South Africa, Nigeria, and Zimbabwe, is one of the funds accepted into the Capria Network. Yet they're struggling to close their first fund and raise enough money, Mutua notes. "It's taken over a year, and we're still not there."

This is a missed opportunity since the women-led team wants to invest in businesses in the region that are run by women who have limited access to capital. Getting the fund off the ground will require time and a lot of trips back and forth between Nairobi and Lagos, Mutua says.

The second part of the challenge is simply understanding the different forms of financing available to African startups and companies. The answer is not always venture capital. It may be a loan, a grant, debt, or equity financing. In fact, Poole notes, some impact investing could be called "philanthropy on steroids."

But philanthropy is not the mission: "Impact investing is a strategy, an approach. In twenty years' time, it'll be mainstream and accepted. But as a whole, it still has to be profitable. It's not a charity, and we have to make that clear, particularly in markets such as Africa."

Mutua agrees that the culture of aid in Africa, and the dependence it creates, has to go. The solutions should come from within as much as possible, with support from people like Poole who want to connect the dots on the global map of finance. "Given that entrepreneurs and fund managers here need more than just money, the goal is definitely bigger—to see if we can improve the space as a whole, not just be another player," she concludes.

Anyone borrowing money, either here in the US or abroad, must reflect: What strings are attached, and do we have a true partnership here? Impact investing is not perfect yet, and not all self-described impact investors are deeply driven by impact. A simplistic approach of labeling all impact investors as positive forces in this regenerative framework, and regarding all conventional investors as money-minded, doesn't work. It's too black and white. And the world of money really does seem to reside in the middle gray zone. There has to be some probing process, a true scrutiny of the financial entity that you're thinking of marrying into. For investors, it's a difficult adjustment to forgo the short term for the long term and to assess whether one's firm can take on such a risk. This is why finance is perhaps one of the hardest aspects of this regenerative framework going forward. Money is a necessity. But how do we use it with dignity and respect?

ARE WE GETTING CLOSER?

Writing this book took more than three years, from interviewing all the subjects to writing the manuscript—and then addressing a pandemic. In that time, plastic straws became passé; grocery stores like Trader Joe's decided to cut down on their single-use plastics after being told to do so by nearly one hundred thousand customers; luxury fashion brands agreed not to burn their excess garments and instead to repurpose them; consumer brands like Häagen-Dazs, Unilever, and Proctor & Gamble partnered with New Jersey–based Terra-Cycle to build a new refill system for everyday products; Hollywood actresses started championing slow fashion in their public outings; and a slew of brands introduced carbon funds to offset their emissions.

One could say we're making progress.

But then amid all this "positive" news came reports from the United Nations stating that the world is on track to lose one million species, largely because of human activity and that much of the damage done by climate change is now irreversible with a small time window available to us to reverse it. This should come as no surprise, as reports by the Planetary Boundaries, a group of scientists at the Stockholm Resilience Centre delineating carrying-capacity-like limits, have been pointing out for years. The reports reminded readers that human life depends on the prosperity of these plant and animal species. If we keep wiping out more and more species, we too could face a bleak future. We rely on these ecosystems for food, medicine, and the health of the overall planet. As the human population is growing, earth's resources are not. And we better get moving if we don't want to see more irreversible damage in the future.

So, this book is merely a starting point for how business has to evolve. We have to understand a fundamental truth: human health depends on the health of where we live, the earth.

Konrad Brits, frustrated by this reality, despite his efforts as an entrepreneur in the coffee business, said to me, "Before enlightenment, chop wood, carry water. After enlightenment, chop wood, carry water." Translation: Keep life basic. Don't let it all go to your head.

If we as humans can respect that we are part of a mysterious world order—one which we do not completely understand—we can stay humble and grounded and recognize that our time on earth is meant to experience its wonders, not to accumulate its wealth. A desire to be at the forefront is what has gotten us in this mess—a desire to be in the limelight, a desire to build the biggest, most "successful" venture.

Yet, in the process, the intention gets lost. When Brits started his coffee company, it was to help humanity, the farmers growing coffee on small plots of land. When Galahad Clark, founder of Vivobarefoot, started his company, it was to help humanity connect back to the earth under our feet. When Sophi Tranchell took her post at Divine Chocolates, it was with the heart of an activist, in an effort to support women.

These businesses were started with the intent to respect humanity and to feel closer to what it means to be human. None of them has achieved a perfect solution, but each one has built a piece of the framework of a new world order, a new economy, and the era of restoration.

Capitalism has put us on a path where we have lost connection with humanity: working at a job that was designed to increase sales, improve productivity, and hoard wealth. Where is the dignity and respect for human life and the planet we live on?

That's why the stories of these companies are refreshing: their founders have rejected that paradigm and built an alternate ecosystem for themselves to operate in. As interest in these issues of waste, regenerative agriculture, wellness, and thoughtful finance continues to grow, and as the incoming generations ask for more purpose-driven lives and careers, the challenge now is to build on these foundations.

With that comes a hard, but essential, question: Are we ready to tame our lusts? To restrain ourselves?

This is the reality we now must face.

Veja founder Sébastien Kopp told me that some of his customers grew angry when the company ran out of a certain style of shoe; customers wrote to them asking when they would restock. When he told them the item was sold out, some were not happy. They turned to social media to vent their frustrations.

It's quite likely that another pair of shoes would suffice—either from Veja or another company. But as humans, we have a strange love for material objects. The answer to our challenges does not lie in having a closet stuffed full of slow-fashion pieces or a home crammed with ethical housewares and fair-trade food.

The answer is to cut back, simplify, and spend time immersed in life, not stuff.

Shopping, as banal as it may seem—or evil, as some cast it as—keeps the global economy ticking. It's not going to come to a halt anytime soon, but can business be tamed, and can the profits be channeled more equitably?

The earth has for too long been a forgotten stakeholder. Our ambitions have started to look outward—to the moon and Mars—while our home planet, and the species that reside on it, seem to be forgotten.

By themselves, the businesses profiled here cannot undo the pilfering and polluting of the last few decades. But they certainly can drive demand toward a new economy. More businesses like these—focused on taking action to realize their intentions, not just talking about them—are needed. It's not as simple as duplicating these companies and entrepreneurs but cultivating a new era of what it means to do business: to put the needs of humans and the planet at the heart of a business, not as an afterthought.

In conference after conference these days you can hear talk about "impact." Having impact does not mean making a donation, winning an award, writing an annual report, or spouting rhetoric. Impact is about actually putting those dollars to work to find solutions—which is what the entrepreneurs featured in this book have been trying to do.

You cannot take the riches with you—whether it's in the thousands, millions, or billions. But individuals and businesses can create a legacy of restoration, respect, and dignity for the people who worked in them and for the earth's environment, which enables it all.

ACKNOWLEDGMENTS

Special thanks to the Pulitzer Center on Crisis Reporting and the Ford Foundation for enabling me to go on this journey, meet these people firsthand, and devote two years to this project. An additional thanks to Karla Olson and John Dutton at Patagonia Books for their continued support in conceptualizing this project and putting it out there. A heartfelt thank-you to Jay Coen Gilbert of B Corp for his enthusiasm for this book. And, most important, to family and friends who endured this process with me patiently.

NOTES

INTRODUCTION

1. Kendall R. Jones et al., "The Location and Protection Status of Earth's Diminishing Marine Wilderness," *Current Biology* 28, no. 15 (August 6, 2018): 1 (Summary).
2. Robbie Gonzalez, "Your Poop Is Probably Full of Plastic," *Wired*, October 22, 2018, https://www.wired.com/story/your-poop-is-probably-full -of-plastic.

CHAPTER ONE: SOIL

1. UN Convention to Combat Desertification, *Global Land Outlook*, report (Bonn, Germany: Secretariat of the UN Convention to Combat Desertification, 2017), https://www.unccd.int/sites/default/files/documents/2017 -09/GLO_Full_Report_low_res.pdf, 52 (henceforth cited as UNCCD, *Global Land Outlook*).
2. UNCCD, *Global Land Outlook*, 11.
3. UNCCD, *Global Land Outlook*, 43.
4. UNCCD, *Global Land Outlook*, 45.
5. Leon Kolankiewicz, Roy Beck, and Anne Maneta, *Vanishing Open Spaces: Population Growth and Urban Sprawl in America*, report, presented at Earth Day Texas Eco Expo, April 26–27, 2014, https://www.numbersusa .com/sites/default/files/public/assets/resources/files/vanishing-open-spaces -study.pdf, iv.
6. US Environmental Protection Agency, "Nutrient Pollution: The Issue," September 2021, https://www.epa.gov/nutrientpollution/issue.
7. UNCCD, *Global Land Outlook*, 45.
8. Jenny Hopkinson, "Can American Soil Be Brought Back to Life?" *Politico*, September 13, 2017, https://www.politico.com/agenda/story/2017/09/13 /soil-health-agriculture-trend-usda-000513.
9. Marketwatch, "Athletic Footwear Market: Global Demand, Growth Analysis, & Opportunity Outlook 2023," press release, April 5, 2019.
10. US Department of Agriculture, Economic Research Service, "Organic Production, Documentation," September 30, 2019, https://www.ers.usda.gov /data-products/organic-production/documentation.

11. US Department of Agriculture, Economic Research Service, "Organic Production, Documentation."

12. Pramod Pandey et al., "A New Method of Converting Foodwaste into Pathogen Free Soil Amendment for Enhancing Agricultural Sustainability," *Journal of Cleaner Production* 112 (2016): 205–13, http://dx.doi.org /10.1016/j.jclepro.2015.09.045.

13. Bonnie Hawthorne, director, *Dreaming of a Vetter World*, film, produced by MightyCanoe, trailer (2019) at https://player.vimeo.com/video/165507512.

CHAPTER TWO: WASTE

1. Lydia McAllister, "Textile Waste by the Numbers," *Vox Magazine*, March 24, 2016, https://www.voxmagazine.com/news/textile-waste-by-the -numbers/article_9ea228ba-f13a-11e5-8c76-5b50180f85de.html.

2. Amy L. Brooks, Shunli Wang, and Jenna R. Jambeck, "The Chinese Import Ban and Its Impact on Global Plastic Waste Trade," *Journal of Science Advances* 4, no. 6 (June 2018), DOI: 10.1126/sciadv.aato131.

3. Laura Parker, "We Made Plastic. We Depend on It. Now We're Drowning in It," *National Geographic*, June 2018, https://www.nationalgeographic .com/magazine/2018/06/plastic-planet-waste-pollution-trash-crisis.

4. Ellen MacArthur Foundation and World Economic Forum, *The New Plastic Economy: Rethinking the Future of Plastics*, report, 2016, https://www .ellenmacarthurfoundation.org/publications/the-new-plastics-economy -rethinking-the-future-of-plastics.

5. Holly Elmore, "Plastics: A Double-Edged Sword," *Regeneration in Action*, October 13, 2019, https://zerowastezone.blogspot.com/2019/10/plastics -double-edged-sword.html.

6. Ellen MacArthur Foundation and Circular Fibers Initiative, *A New Textiles Economy: Redesigning Fashion's Future*, report, 2017, https://www. ellenmacarthurfoundation.org/assets/downloads/A-New-Textiles-Economy _Full-Report_Updated_1–12–17.pdf, 37.

7. Alden Wicker, "Fast Fashion Is Creating an Environmental Crisis," *Newsweek*, September 1, 2016, https://www.newsweek.com/2016/09/09/old -clothes-fashion-waste-crisis-494824.html.

8. Mark Walker, "Why Apparel Brands Should Work Together to Build a Sustainable Future," *Fashion Revolution* (blog), 2018, https://www .fashionrevolution.org/usa-blog/why-apparel-brands-should-work -together-to-build-a-sustainable-future.

9. Kimiko de Freytas-Tamura, "For Dignity and Development, East Africa Curbs Used Clothes Imports, *New York Times*, October 12, 2017, https://www.nytimes.com/2017/10/12/world/africa/east-africa-rwanda -used-clothing.html.

10. Elizabeth L. Cline, *Overdressed: The Shockingly High Cost of Cheap Fashion* (New York: Portfolio/Penguin, 2012).

11. Ellen MacArthur Foundation and Circular Fibers Initiative, *A New Textiles Economy*, 20.

12. Ellen MacArthur Foundation and Circular Fibers Initiative, *A New Textiles Economy*, 21.

13. Food and Agriculture Organization of the United Nations, "Food Loss and Waste Database," https://www.fao.org/food-loss-and-food-waste /flw-data, accessed November 2018; Zach Conrad et al., "Relationship Between Food Waste, Diet Quality, and Environmental Sustainability," *PLOS ONE* 13, no. 4 (April 18, 2018), https://journals.plos.org/plosone /article?id=10.1371/journal.pone.0195405.

14. Toast Ale website, www.toastale.com/about-us#homeBrewSection, accessed June 21, 2022.

CHAPTER THREE: SUPPLY CHAINS

1. Glenn-Marie Lange, Quentin Wodon, and Kevin Carey, eds., *The Changing Wealth of Nations 2018: Building a Sustainable Future* (Washington, DC: World Bank Group), https://openknowledge.worldbank.org/bitstream /handle/10986/29001/9781464810466.pdf, 5.

2. Laura Swanson Bowser, "Structural Inclusion: What It Means and Why It Matters," *B The Change* (blog), July 30, 2019, https://bthechange.com /structural-inclusion-what-it-means-and-why-it-matters-a4b85945cf71.

3. Sjoerd Panhuysen and Joost Pierrot, *Coffee Barometer 2018*, report (The Hague: Hivos, 2018), https://www.hivos.org/assets/2018/06/Coffee -Barometer-2018.pdf, 3.

4. Panhuysen and Pierrot, *Coffee Barometer*, 100.

5. Panhuysen and Pierrot, *Coffee Barometer*, 11.

6. Panhuysen and Pierrot, *Coffee Barometer*, 14.

7. Julia Lernoud et al., *The State of Sustainable Markets: Statistics and Emerging Trends 2017*, report (Geneva: International Trade Centre, 2017), https://orgprints.org/id/eprint/36881/1/State-of-Sustainable -Market-2017_web.pdf, 106, http://www.intracen.org/uploadedFiles /intracenorg/Content/Publications/State-of-Sustainable-Market-2017 _web.pdf.

8. Mujib Mashal, "Afghan Taliban Awash in Heroin Cash," *New York Times*, October 29, 2017, https://www.nytimes.com/2017/10/29/world /asia/opium-heroin-afghanistan-taliban.html.

9. UN Office on Drugs and Crime, *World Drug Report 2010*, report (Vienna: UN Office on Drugs and Crime, 2010), https://www.unodc.org /documents/wdr/WDR_2010/World_Drug_Report_2010_lo-res.pdf, 37.

10. UN Office on Drugs and Crime and Islamic Republic of Afghanistan Ministry of Counter Narcotics, *Afghanistan Opium Survey 2017: Cultivation and Production*, report (Vienna: UN Office on Drugs and Crime), https:// www.unodc.org/documents/crop-monitoring/Afghanistan/Afghan_opium _survey_2017_cult_prod_web.pdf, 5.

11. UN Office on Drugs and Crime and Islamic Republic of Afghanistan Ministry of Counter Narcotics, *Afghanistan Opium Survey 2017*, 13.

12. UN Office on Drugs and Crime and Islamic Republic of Afghanistan Ministry of Counter Narcotics, *Afghanistan Opium Survey 2017*, 13.

13. Minority Rights Group International, *World Directory of Minorities and Indigenous Peoples*, "Adivasis," https://minorityrights.org/minorities /adivasis-2, accessed November 2018.

CHAPTER FOUR: WORKFORCE

1. V. F. Corporation, "Schedule 14A – Proxy Statement Pursuant to Section 14(a) of the Securities Exchange Act of 1934 (Amendment No.)," https://www.sec.gov/Archives/edgar/data/103379/000119312518082379/d502014ddef14a.htm, 47; McDonald's Corp, "Schedule 14A – Proxy Statement Pursuant to Section 14(a) of the Securities Exchange Act of 1934 (Amendment No.)," https://www.sec.gov/Archives/edgar/data/63908/000120677419001299/mcd3477431-def14a.htm, 50.

2. US Bureau of Economic Analysis, "Gross Domestic Product, Fourth Quarter and Year 2021 (Second Estimate)," news release, February 24, 2022, https://www.bea.gov/news/2022/gross-domestic-product-fourth-quarter-and-year-2021-second-estimate.

3. Thomas B. Edsall, "Whatever Happened to 'Every Man a King'?," *New York Times*, February 11, 2014, https://www.nytimes.com/2014/02/12/opinion/edsall-whatever-happened-to-every-man-a-king.html; Ganesh Setty, "Democrats Bash Corporate Greed, but More Stocks for All Americans May Be a Better Wealth Redistribution Method," *The Bottom Line* (blog), CNBC, August 11, 2019, https://www.cnbc.com/2019/08/11/dems-slam-greed-but-more-stocks-for-all-can-address-wealth-inequality.html.

4. Jane Thier, "Executive Greed Is Driving the Labor Shortage, Says 93-Year-Old Leader Whose Workers Own 100% of the Company," *Fortune*, February 17, 2022, https://fortune.com/2022/02/17/bobs-red-mill-president-on-his-employee-owned-company.

5. Bureau of Labor Statistics, "Persons with a Disability: Labor Force Characteristics—2017," news release, June 21, 2018, https://www.bls.gov/news.release/archives/disabl_06212018.pdf.

6. Frank Viviano, "This Tiny Country Feeds the World," *National Geographic*, September 2017, https://www.nationalgeographic.com/magazine/2017/09/holland-agriculture-sustainable-farming.

CHAPTER FIVE: WOMEN

1. UN Women, "Learn the Facts: Rural Women and Girls," February 28, 2018, updated October 2021, https://www.unwomen.org/en/digital-library/multimedia/2018/2/infographic-rural-women.

2. UN Women, "Learn the Facts: Rural Women and Girls."

3. Bert D'Espallier et al., "Women and Repayment in Microfinance: A Global Analysis," *World Development* 39, no. 5 (2011): 758–72, accessed at https://www.researchgate.net/publication/222639246_Women_and_Repayment_in_Microfinance_A_Global_Analysis.

4. Jumia, *Kenya—Mobile Report 2019*, report, https://www.jumia.co.ke/mobile-report, accessed April 2019.

5. Aspen Institute, *The Alliance for Artisan Enterprise: Bringing Artisan Enterprise to Scale*, https://assets.aspeninstitute.org/content/uploads/files/content/images/Alliance%20for%20Artisan%20Enterprise%20Concept%20Note_0.pdf, accessed May 4, 2022.

6. USAID, "Kenya and East Africa: Gender Equality & Female Empowerment," September 2018, https://www.usaid.gov/east-africa-regional/gender

-equality-and-womens-empowerment-kenya, 2; USAID, "East Africa Gender
Fact Sheet," https://www.usaid.gov/documents/east-africa-gender-fact-sheet.
7. Coffee Quality Institute, *The Way Forward: Accelerating Gender Equity in
Coffee Value Chains,* report (Aliso Viejo, CA: 2015), https://www.coffee
institute.org/wp-content/uploads/2015/10/The-Way-Forward_Final-Full
-Length-Report_opt.pdf.

CHAPTER SIX: TRAVEL

1. Zephania Ubwani, "Serengeti National Park Overwhelmed by Visitors,"
The Citizen, December 24, 2017, https://www.thecitizen.co.tz/News
/1840340-4241162-3t6nwyz/index.html.
2. Felipe Villamor, "Idyllic Philippine Resort Island of Boracay Is Closed to
Tourists," *New York Times,* April 4, 2018, https://www.nytimes.com
/2018/04/04/world/asia/boracay-philippines-tourists-closed.html.
3. "Thailand: Tropical Bay from 'The Beach' to Close Until 2021," *BBC
News,* May 9, 2019, https://www.bbc.com/news/world-asia-48222627.
4. Manfred Lenzen et al., "The Carbon Footprint of Global Tourism," *Nature Climate Change* 8 (2018): 522–28.
5. UN World Tourism Organization, *UNWTO Tourism Highlights, 2018 Edi-
tion* (Madrid: UN World Tourism Organization, 2018), DOI: https://doi.
org/10.18111/9789284419876.
6. Naya Olmer and Dan Rutherford, *US Domestic Airline Fuel Efficiency
Ranking, 2015–2016,* report (Washington, DC: International Council on
Clean Transportation, December 2017), 1.
7. Purba Das, "Bring Jet Fuel Under GST: Indian Airlines Tell Govt," *Fortune
India,* August 10, 2018, https://www.fortuneindia.com/enterprise
/bring-jet-fuel-under-gst-indian-airlines-tell-govt/102272; "SpiceJet Operates
India's First Biojet Fuel Flight," *Times of India,* August 27, 2018, https://
timesofindia.indiatimes.com/business/india-business/spicejet-operates
-indias-first-biojet-fuel-flight/articleshow/65560164.cms.
8. eahern, "Could Algae Fuel Your Next Flight?" *Harvard Business School
Digital Initiative* (blog), November 3, 2016, https://digital.hbs.edu/platform
-rctom/submission/could-algae-fuel-your-next-flight-boeing-tests-biofuels
-potential.
9. Fulcrum Bioenergy, "Fulcrum Bioenergy Breaks Ground On Sierra Biofuels
Plant," news release, May 16, 2018, https://fulcrum-bioenergy.com/wp-content
/uploads/2018/05/2018-05-16-Sierra-Groundbreaking-FINAL-1.pdf.
10. Tracy Rucinski, "United Airlines Targets 50 Percent Cut in Greenhouse
Gas Emissions," Reuters, September 13, 2018, https://www.reuters.com
/article/us-ual-emissions/united-airlines-targets-50-percent-cut-in-greenhouse
-gas-emissions-idUSKCN1LT32A.
11. Matt McGrath, "Climate Change: IPCC Report Warns of 'Irreversible' Impacts of Global Warming," *BBC News,* February 28, 2022, https://www
.bbc.com/news/science-environment-60525591.
12. "Germany Launches World's First Hydrogen-Powered Train," *Guardian,*
September 17, 2018, https://www.theguardian.com/environment/2018/sep
/17/germany-launches-worlds-first-hydrogen-powered-train.

13. Petter Dybedal, Eivind Farstad, Per-Erik Winter, and Iratxe Landa-Mata, *Cruise Passenger Traffic to Norway—History and Forecasts Until 2060*, TØI report, prepared for Norwegian Coastal Administration (Oslo: Institute of Transport Economics, 2015), https://www.toi.no/getfile.php/1339880 /Publikasjoner/T%C3%98I%20rapporter/2015/1388–2015/1388 -summary.pdf, accessed April 2019.

CHAPTER SEVEN: HEALTH

1. Jennifer Tolbert and Kendal Orgera, "Key Facts About the Uninsured Population," issue brief, November 6, 2020, Kaiser Family Foundation, https://www.kff.org/uninsured/fact-sheet/key-facts-about-the-uninsured -population.
2. Cameo, *Freelancing in America: 2019*, report prepared for Upwork and Freelancers Union, 2019, https://cameonetwork.org/resource/freelancing -in-america-2019.
3. Irene Papanicolas, Liana R. Woskie, and Ashish K. Jha, "Health Care Spending in the United States and Other High-Income Countries," *Journal of the American Medical Association* 319, no. 10 (March 2018): 1024–39, DOI:10.1001/jama.2018.1150.
4. US Department of Justice, Office of the Attorney General, *The Accomplishments of the US Department of Justice, 2001–2009*, report (Washington, DC: Department of Justice, 2009), https://www.justice.gov/sites /default/files/opa/legacy/2010/03/08/doj-accomplishments.pdf, 12.
5. Kurt Eichenwald, "Tenet Healthcare Paying $54 Million in Fraud Settlement," *New York Times*, August 7, 2004.
6. Reed Abelson and Julie Creswell, "Hospital Chain Inquiry Cited Unnecessary Cardiac Work," *New York Times*, August 6, 2012, https://www .nytimes.com/2012/08/07/business/hospital-chain-internal-reports-found -dubious-cardiac-work.html.
7. Pavithra Mehta and Suchitra Shenoy, *Infinite Vision: How Aravind Became the World's Greatest Business Case for Compassion* (Oakland, CA: Berrett-Koehler, 2011), 285.
8. Lionel Beehner, "Iraq's Faltering Infrastructure," Council on Foreign Relations, June 22, 2006, https://www.cfr.org/backgrounder/iraqs-faltering -infrastructure.
9. Development Initiatives, *Global Nutrition Report 2017: Nourishing the SDGs*, Bristol, UK, 2017, file:///C:/Users/slumenello/Downloads/Global _Nutrition_Report_2017.pdf

CHAPTER EIGHT: ENERGY

1. UN Intergovernmental Panel on Climate Change, *Climate Change 2022: Impacts, Adaptation and Vulnerability*, report (Cambridge: Cambridge University Press, forthcoming), https://www.ipcc.ch/report/ar6/wg2/; Matt McGrath, "Climate Change: IPCC Report Warns of 'Irreversible' Impacts of Global Warming," *BBC News*, February 28, 2022, https://www.bbc .com/news/science-environment-60525591.

2. "Renewables Met 97% of Scotland's Electricity Demand in 2020," *BBC News*, March 25, 2021, https://www.bbc.com/news/uk-scotland -56530424.

3. Rhodium Group, "Preliminary US Emissions Estimates for 2018," January 8, 2019, https://rhg.com/research/preliminary-us-emissions-estimates -for-2018.

4. Eric Gimon, Mike O'Boyle, Christopher T. M. Clack, and Sarah Mckee, *The Coal Cost Crossover: Economic Viability of Existing Coal Compared to New Local Wind and Solar Resources*, report prepared for Energy Innovation and Vibrant Clean Energy (San Francisco: Energy Innovation, March 2019), https://energyinnovation.org/wp-content/uploads/2019/03 /Coal-Cost-Crossover_Energy-Innovation_VCE_FINAL.pdf.

5. Marlene Motyka, *2019 Renewable Energy Industry Outlook*, report prepared for Deloitte, https://www2.deloitte.com/us/en/pages/energy-and -resources/articles/renewable-energy-outlook.html.

6. Chimi Dema, "Zeroing In on Waste: Led by Bhutan's Prime Minister Dr. Lotay Tshering," *Daily Bhutan*, July 5, 2019, https://www.dailybhutan .com/article/zeroing-in-on-waste-led-by-bhutan-s-prime-minister-dr-lotay -tshering.

7. US Energy Information Administration, "Table 7.2 Coal Production, 1949–2011 (Million Short Tons)," *Annual Energy Review 2011* (Washington, DC: US Energy Information Administration, 2012), https://www .eia.gov/totalenergy/data/annual/pdf/aer.pdf; National Academies of Sciences, Engineering, and Medicine, *Monitoring and Sampling Approaches to Assess Underground Coal Mine Dust Exposures* (Washington, DC: National Academies Press, 2018), figure e-3, https://www.ncbi.nlm.nih.gov /books/NBK531861/figure/fig_E-3/?report=objectonly.

8. Christopher R. Bollinger, William H. Hoyt, David Blackwell, and Michael T. Childress, *Kentucky Annual Economic Report 2018* (Lexington: University of Kentucky, Center for Business and Economic Research, 2018), https://uknowledge.uky.edu/cber_kentuckyannualreports/23.

9. Lazard, "Levelized Cost of Energy 2017," November 2017, https://www .lazard.com/perspective/levelized-cost-of-energy-2017.

10. Ros Davidson, "US Wind Capacity Rises to 89GW," *Wind Power Monthly*, January 30, 2018, https://www.windpowermonthly.com/article /1455894/us-wind-capacity-rises-89gw.

11. Dan Hernandez, "Nevada Solar Industry Collapses After State Lets Power Company Raise Fees," *Guardian*, January 13, 2016, https://www.the guardian.com/environment/2016/jan/13/solar-panel-energy-power -company-nevada.

12. "French Nuclear Power Plants Pose a Grave Security Risk—Lawmakers," *DW*, July 5, 2018, https://www.dw.com/en/french-nuclear-power-plants -pose-a-grave-security-risk-lawmakers/a-44546734.

13. Bate Felix, "France to Revise Carbon Emissions Target After Missing 2016 Goal," Reuters, January 22, 2018, https://www.reuters.com/article /us-france-carbon-emissions-idUSKBN1FB2W0.

14. Julian Wettengel, "Citizens' Participation in the Energiewende," Clean Energy Wire, October 25, 2018, https://www.cleanenergywire.org/factsheets/citizens-participation-energiewende.

CHAPTER NINE: FINANCE

1. Erik Shilling, "Harvard, IKEA, and the Battle for Romania's Forests," *Atlas Obscura*, March 2, 2016, https://www.atlasobscura.com/articles/harvard-ikea-and-the-battle-for-romanias-forests.

2. Emily Flitter, "Think the Big Banks Have Abandoned Coal? Think Again," *New York Times*, May 28, 2018, https://www.nytimes.com/2018/05/28/business/banks-coal-loans.html and https://www.theguardian.com/environment/2019/oct/13/top-investment-banks-lending-billions-extract-fossil-fuels.

3. Jean-Marc Borello, *Why We Need Common Good Capitalism* (Paris: Débats publics, 2017).

4. Asli Demirguc-Kunt, Leora Klapper, et al., "The Unbanked," *The Global Findex Database 2017: Measuring Financial Inclusion and the Fintech Revolution* (Washington, DC: World Bank Group, 2018), https://globalfindex.worldbank.org/sites/globalfindex/files/chapters/2017%20Findex%20full%20report_chapter2.pdf, 35.

5. Dilip Ratha, "Remittance Flows to Developing Countries Are Estimated to Exceed $300 Million in 2008," *World Bank Blogs*, February 18, 2009, https://blogs.worldbank.org/peoplemove/remittance-flows-to-developing-countries.

6. Global Alliance for Banking on Values, *Research Report 2016*, https://www.gabv.org/resources-research/annual-research-2016

7. Global Alliance for Banking on Values, *Annual Report 2017*, https://www.gabv.org/resources-research/annual-research-2017 (link to report).

8. Oikocredit International, *Oikocredit Annual Report 2018*, https://www.oikocredit.coop/en/publications/annual-reports.

9. Demirguc-Kunt, Klapper, et al., "The Unbanked."

10. KPMG and East Africa Venture Capital Association, *KPMG and EAVCA: Private Equity Sector Survey of East Africa for the Period 2015 to 2016*, report (Nairobi: KPMG, June 2017), http://eavca.org/wp-content/uploads/2018/08/2017_KPMG_and_EAVCA_Private_Equity_in_East_Africa_Survey_Final.pdf.

11. KPMG and East Africa Venture Capital Association, *KPMG and EAVCA*, 6.

INDEX